Controversies in Feminism

Studies in Social, Political, and Legal Philosophy

Series Editor: James P. Sterba, University of Notre Dame

This series analyzes and evaluates critically the major political, social, and legal ideals, institutions, and practices of our time. The analysis may be historical or problem-centered; the evaluation may focus on theoretical underpinnings or practical implications. Among the recent titles in the series are:

Controversies in Feminism

Edited by
James P. Sterba

ROWMAN & LITTLEFIELD PUBLISHERS, INC.
Lanham • Boulder • New York • Oxford

ROWMAN & LITTLEFIELD PUBLISHERS, INC.

Published in the United States of America
by Rowman & Littlefield Publishers, Inc.
4720 Boston Way, Lanham, Maryland 20706
http://www.rowmanlittlefield.com

12 Hid's Copse Road
Cumnor Hill, Oxford OX2 9JJ, England

British Library Cataloguing in Publication Information Available

Library of Congress Cataloging-in-Publication Data

Controversies in feminism / edited by James P. Sterba
     p.   cm. — (Studies in social, political, and legal philosophy)
    Includes bibliographical references and index.
    ISBN 0-7425-0712-2 (alk. paper) — ISBN 0-7425-0713-0 (pbk. : alk. paper)
    1. Feminism.   I. Sterba, James P. II. Series.

HQ1206 .C696   2000
305.42—dc21   00-038271

Printed in the United States of America

♾™ The paper used in this publication meets the minimum requirements of
American National Standard for Information Sciences—Permanence of
Paper for Printed Library Materials, ANSI/NISO Z39.48-1992.

Contents

Introduction

Born in controversy, feminism continues to flourish in controversy. Some of these controversies are between self-identified feminists; others are between feminists and their nonfeminist opponents. The contributors to this volume provide opposing, or in some cases somewhat opposing, perspectives on some of the most important areas of dissension in feminism today. In section I, Martha Nussbaum and Jane Flax discuss the need for universal values. In section II, Claudia Card and Virginia Held debate the priority of justice and care along with the priority of evils and inequalities. In section III, Janet Kourany and Ellen Klein exchange views on the possibility of a feminist philosophy of science. And in section IV, Rosemarie Tong and Michael Levin discuss the significance of biology to social theory. Clearly the success of feminism depends on a defensible resolution of these opposing viewpoints, and the contributors to this volume hope to make an important contribution to that resolution. In this introduction, I provide an overview of each of the chapters that follow, noting some of the similarities and differences among the contributors, and then make a few remarks about how the issues covered in this volume might be further resolved.

FEMINISM AND UNIVERSAL VALUES

In "In Defense of Universal Values," Martha Nussbaum argues that legitimate concerns for diversity, pluralism, and personal freedom require that universal norms be recognized. She believes that these norms are best formulated as a set of capabilities for full human functioning. According to Nussbaum, this "capability approach" begins with a basic intuition—that in the political arena, human abilities exert a moral claim that they should be developed. In contrast, Jane Flax argues in "On Encountering Incommensurability: Martha Nussbaum's Aristotelian Practice" that rather than finding universal Aristotelian norms, postmodernists, like herself, can only find incommensurable differences. Nevertheless, Flax feels that abandoning the project of justifying universal norms does not logically entail or require automatic deference to local ones. Norms that are local in origin, she claims, can be translocal in application. We can criticize local ones in the name of our own local norms and offer a variety of arguments about why our norms are better. In Nussbaum's response to Flax's chapter, she argues that any project that does not defend a set of cross-cultural norms as goals of global political action owes us an account of how it will adequately respect pluralism and choice. Flax responds by claiming not to see how delineating universal human capabilities will enable oppressed women to locate the sources of their oppression or the mechanisms through which they are reproduced. Such mechanisms may resemble each other at the macro level, but their strongest force is likely to be found in their local particularities. Hence, Flax focuses on microanalyzing power as an indispensable requirement for political change.

JUSTICE, CARE, AND EVILS

In "Inequalities versus Evils," Claudia Card argues that an ethic of care without justice is ill-equipped to confront evil and that for a feminist, ethically opposing evils, especially oppression, should take priority over opposing inequalities. In "Caring Relations and Principles of Justice," Virginia Held argues that although justice might sometimes be shown to mesh with the requirements of care, it cannot always do so. Further, at least in some cases, where the two are in conflict, the care perspective can be seen to have priority over the justice perspective. Held offers an example of what she sees as just such a case.

A young child's father is also a teacher with a special talent for helping troubled young children succeed academically. If this father devotes more time to helping those troubled children (the justice perspective), and lets his wife and others care for his own child, he will accomplish much that is good. Even if the father accounts for the amount of good he can accomplish if he spends more time with his own child (the care perspective), the good he will accomplish by devoting more time to helping troubled young children succeed academically will be far greater. Nevertheless, Held believes that, in this case, the care perspective has priority over the justice perspective.

In her response, Claudia Card argues that even supposing Held were right about the particular moral requirements in her example, it is unclear that this is a case where care has priority over justice in this case. Card pointed out the possibility of viewing the father's requirement to spend more time with his child as a requirement of (particular) justice. Imagine that the child deserves more attention from his father, and that particular justice requires the father to give the child what he or she deserves. So construed, this would be a case where a requirement of (particular) justice has priority over a requirement of (universal) justice, namely the requirement to help others in need. In her response to Card's chapter, Held argues that evils cannot always take priority over inequalities because severe inequalities can also be evils, and that, in addition, major injustices can be wrong without causing harm.

FEMINISM AND PHILOSOPHY OF SCIENCE

"In What Does Feminism Contribute to Philosophy of Science?" Janet Kourany claims that, historically, women have been prevented from becoming scientists and that, even today, more subtle restrictions persist. She claims that in scientific research itself women have been left out or portrayed negatively. But along with drawing attention to the ways that the practice of science has been biased against women, Kourany argues that feminism can also contribute to making science itself more socially responsible—by developing a philosophy of science that, in order to be defensible, requires that feminist and other social and political values be included. In "Sorry Virginia, There is No Feminist Science," Ellen Klein critically discusses the work of major feminists such as Genevieve Lloyd, Evelyn Fox Keller, and Sandra Harding. She claims, among other things, that "feminists, in their hearts, are relativists at best, sexists at worst," and that "any commitment to objective criteria, including the hard facts provided by empirical investigations, is viewed by feminists . . . to be yet another male trick to oppress women." She also concludes that we should "throw feminism to the wind and reappropriate the classical tools of logic, reason and evidence."

In her response to Kourany's chapter, Klein denies that feminism has succeeded in drawing attention to ways in which science has been biased against women. She also does not see that feminism has contributed to making philosophy of science more socially responsible. According to Klein, feminism has made positive contributions neither to science nor to philosophy of science. In her reply, Janet Kourany argues that Klein has used shortcuts to reach her critical conclusions against feminism. For example, Kourany claims that Klein criticizes Genevieve Lloyd without setting out her views or the historical evidence to which she appeals in support of them. According to Kourany, Klein also provides only a single quotation from Darwin, about a "wonderfully-intelligent" and loyal female terrier, to counter Keller's claim that women and the feminine are portrayed negatively within science. In addition, Kourany says, Klein leaves out Keller's and other feminists' numerous examples documenting that Darwin and other scientists have portrayed women as inferior to men in intelligence, as well as in moral, sexual, and social development.

FEMINISM AND SOCIAL THEORY

In her "A Millennial Feminist Vision," Rosemarie Tong traces the history of feminism in the United States. According to Tong, there have been three waves of feminism in the United States: the first wave from the mid-nineteenth century to about

1920, the second from the 1960s to the early 1990s, and the third, which began later in the 1990s. She notes the similarities and differences between the Seneca Falls Declaration of Sentiments in 1848 at the beginning of the first wave, the Bill of Rights of the National Organization of Women (NOW) issued in 1967 at the beginning of the second wave, and the Beijing Declaration (which emerged from the World Congress on Women's Rights sponsored by the United Nations in 1995) at the beginning of the third wave. In "Maritime Policy for a Flat Earth," Michael Levin argues that feminism's continuing denial of biological reality puts it on the wrong side of every issue. He reviews the empirical data supporting biological differences between men and women, arguing that these biological differences are the best explanation of the social differences we currently observe between men and women. But, of course, the social differences between men and women do change over time, and some of them disappear. For example, in the United States, women will soon represent 50 percent of the paid labor force. So while we do need an explanation of why these social differences change over time and disappear in some cases, it is not clear how the biological differences between men and women can, all by themselves, constitute that explanation.

In his response, Levin claims that Tong's account of the three waves of feminism shows that none of these feminist proponents paid the least attention to biology. Tong responds by challenging Levin's biological determinism. She admits that biology does play a role, but she argues that economic and cultural factors can explain many of the social differences that we still observe between men and women. She further argues that as these economic and cultural factors change, many of the social differences between men and women we observe will change or disappear as well.

Reflecting on the four controversies in feminism discussed in this volume, it is clear that the differences between Nussbaum and Flax (on universal values), between Kourany and Klein (about the possibility of a feminist philosophy of science), and between Tong and Levin (regarding the significance of biology to social theory) are quite severe, unlike the differences between Claudia Card and Virginia Held over the priority of justice and care and the priority of evils and inequalities, which appear minor by comparison. Yet even considering the significant differences, there may be more common ground than initially seems apparent. For example, with respect to the differences between Nussbaum and Flax, the universal values that Flax criticizes may not be the same as those Nussbaum defends. For example, Nussbaum can allow that the universal values she defends are still "local in origin" in that their recognition and implementation depends on favorable conditions not uniformly present in societies. Nor is it clear that the local values or norms that Flax thinks are better for a variety of reasons are all that different from what Nussbaum would regard as universal norms applied to those local contexts. Moreover, Nussbaum can also agree with Flax that focusing on the microanalysis of power is an indispensable requirement for political change.

When we look at the differences between Janet Kourany and Ellen Klein about the possibility of a feminist philosophy of science, common ground may be more difficult to find. Of course, the resolution of many of their disagreements will depend on a detailed evaluation of the work of particular feminist thinkers such as Genevieve Lloyd, Evelyn Fox Keller, and Sandra Harding. Nevertheless, if these thinkers can clearly be shown not to be relativists, it would seem that much of the grounds for Klein's objections to their views would be eliminated.

Probably most difficult to overcome are the differences between Rosemarie Tong and Michael Levin in respect to the significance of biology to social theory. Both agree that biology does play a role in explaining the observed social differences between men and women, but they clearly disagree as to whether, or to what extent, economic and cultural factors can explain those social differences. Here, however, it does seem that we can conceive of an experiment that might decide the issue. We could arrange for a group of boys and girls to be brought up under conditions of economic and cultural equality and then see whether their biological differences lead them to reinstate the same social inequalities between men and women that are present in existing societies. While this experiment would clearly decide the issue between Tong and Levin, it would be difficult to practically carry out. Even so, we should try our best to approximate it.

Although the controversies in feminism discussed in this volume will persist for some time to come, the work done by the contributors to this volume will surely help to bring about their eventual resolution.

Section I

Feminism and Universal Values

1

In Defense of Universal Values

Martha C. Nussbaum

I found myself beautiful as a free human mind.
—Mrinal, in Rabindranath Tagore's "Letter from a Wife"

It is obvious that the *human* eye gratifies itself in a way different from the crude, non-human eye; the human *ear* different from the crude ear, etc. . . . The *sense* caught up in crude practical need has only a *restricted* sense. For the starving man, it is not the human form of food that exists, but only its abstract being as food; it could just as well be there in its crudest form, and it would be impossible to say wherein this feeding activity differs from that of *animals*.
—Marx, *Economic and Philosophical Manuscripts of 1844*

Ahmedabad, in Gujarat, is the textile-mill city where Mahatma Gandhi organized labor in accordance with his principles of nonviolent resistance. Tourists visit it for its textile museum and its Gandhi ashram. But today it attracts attention, too, as the home of another resistance movement: the Self-Employed Women's Association (SEWA). With more than 50,000 members, SEWA has been helping female work ers to improve their living conditions through credit, education, and a labor union for more than twenty years. On one side of the polluted river that bisects the city is the shabby old building where SEWA was first established, now used as offices for staff. On the other side are the education offices and the SEWA bank, newly housed in a marble office building. All the customers and all the employees are women.

Vasanti sits on the floor in the meeting room of the old office building, where SEWA members meet to consult with staff. A tiny, dark woman in her early thirties, she wears an attractive electric-blue sari, and her long hair is wound neatly into a bun on the top of her head. Soft and round, she seems more comfortable sitting than walking. Her teeth are uneven and discolored, but otherwise she looks to be in reasonable health. Marty tells me later she is a Rajput, that is, of good caste; I've never figured out how one would know that. She has come with her older (and lower caste) friend Kokila, maker of clay pots and a janitor at the local conference hall, a tall fiery community organizer who helps the police identify cases of domestic violence. Vasanti speaks quietly, looking down often as she speaks, but there is animation in her eyes.

Vasanti's husband was a gambler and an alcoholic. He used the household money to get drunk, and when he ran out of that money he got a vasectomy to take advantage of the cash incentive offered by the local government. So Vasanti has no children to help her. Eventually, as her husband became more abusive, she could live with him no longer and returned to her own family. Her father, who used to make Singer sewing machine parts, has died, but her brothers run an auto parts business in what used to be his shop. Using a machine that used to be her father's, and living in the shop itself, she earned a small income making eyeholes for the hooks on sari tops. Her brothers got her a lawyer to take her husband to court for maintenance—quite an unusual step in her economic class—but the case has dragged on for years with no conclusion in sight. Meanwhile, her brothers also gave her a loan to get the machine that rolls the edges of the sari; but she didn't like being dependent on them, since they are married and have children, and may not want to support her much longer.

With the help of SEWA, she got a bank loan of her own to pay back the brothers, and by now she has paid back almost the entire SEWA loan. Usually, she says, women lack unity, and rich women take advantage of poor women. In SEWA, by contrast, she has found a sense of community. She clearly finds pleasure in the company of Kokila, a woman of very different social class and temperament.

By now, Vasanti is animated; she is looking us straight in the eye, and her voice is strong and clear. "Women in India have a lot of pain," she says. "And I, I have had quite a lot of sorrow in my life. But from the pain, our strength is born. Now that we are doing better ourselves, we want to do some good for other women, to feel that we are good human beings."

Jayamma stands outside her hut in the wilting heat of a late March day in Trivandrum.[1] The first thing you notice about her is the straightness of her back, and the muscular strength of her movements. Her teeth are falling out, her eyesight seems clouded, and her hair is thin—but she could be a captain of the regiment, ordering her troops into battle. It doesn't surprise me that her history speaks of fierce quarrels with her children and her neighbors. Her jaw juts out as she chews tobacco. An Ezhava—a lower but not "scheduled" caste—Jayamma loses out in two ways: she lacks good social standing but is ineligible for the affirmative action programs established by the government for the lowest castes. She still lives in a squatter's colony on some government land on the outskirts of Trivandrum.

For approximately forty-five years, until her recent retirement, Jayamma went every day to the brick kiln and spent eight hours a day carrying bricks on her head, five hundred to seven hundred bricks per day. She never earned more than five rupees a day, and employment depends on the weather. Jayamma balanced a plank on her head, stacked twenty bricks at a time on the plank, and then walked rapidly, balancing the bricks by the strength of her neck, to the kiln, where she then had to unload the bricks without twisting her neck, handing them two by two to the man who loads the kiln. Men in the brick industry typically do this sort of heavy labor for a while, and then graduate to the skilled (but less arduous) tasks of brick molding and kiln loading, which they can continue into middle and advanced ages. Those jobs pay up to twice as much, though they are less dangerous and lighter. Women are never considered for these promotions and are never permitted to learn the skills involved. Like most small businesses in India, the brick kiln is defined as a cottage industry, and thus its workers are not protected by any union. All workers are badly paid, but women suffer special disabilities. Jayamma felt she had a bad deal, but she didn't see any way of changing it.

Now in her middle sixties, unable to perform the physically taxing job of brick carrying, Jayamma has no employment to fall back on. She refuses to become a domestic servant, because in her community such work is considered shameful and degrading. Jayamma adds a political explanation: "As a servant, your alliance is with a class that is your enemy." Although she is a widow, she is unable to collect a widow's pension from the government: the village office told her that she was ineligible because she has able-bodied sons, even though in fact her sons refuse to support her. Despite all these reversals (and others), Jayamma is tough, defiant, and healthy. She doesn't seem interested in talking, but she shows her visitors around and makes sure that they are offered lime juice and water.

Jayamma and Vasanti have been raised in a nation in which women are formally the equals of men, with equal political rights and nominally equal social and employment opportunities. (Discrimination on the basis of sex is outlawed by the Indian Constitution itself.) Both women, however, have suffered from deprivations that do arise from sex: problems of discrimination in education and employment, and problems of male nonsupport—indolence in Jayamma's case, domestic abuse and alcoholism in Vasanti's case. The problems they face are particular to the social situation of women in particular caste and regional circumstances in India. One can't understand Jayamma's choices and constraints without understanding, at many different levels of specificity and generality, how she is socially placed: what it means to be an Ezhava rather than a Pulaya, what it means to live in Kerala rather than some other state, what it means to be in the city rather than in a rural area. One can't understand Vasanti without understanding the double bind of being both upper caste—with lots of rules limiting what is proper to do—and very poor, with few opportunities to do nice proper things that bring in a living. One also can't understand her story without knowing about family-planning programs in Gujarat, the progress of the SEWA movement, the background Gandhian tradition of self-sufficiency on which the Gujarat women's movement draws. No doubt all this particularity shapes the inner life of each, in ways that it's hard for an outsider to begin to understand.

On the other hand, their problems are not altogether and unrecognizably different from problems of many women (and many poor people generally) in many parts of the world. In the intense desire of both women for independence and economic self-sufficiency, the desire of both to have some money and property in their own names—these are wishes common to women in many parts of the world. The body that labors is the same body all over the world, and its needs for food, nutrition, and health care are the same—so it's not too surprising that the female manual laborer in Trivandrum is, in some ways, comparable to a female manual laborer in Beijing or even in Chicago. She doesn't seem to have an utterly alien consciousness or an identity that is unrecognizably strange, strange though the circumstances are in which her consciousness takes root. Similarly, the body that gets beaten is, in a sense, the same all over the world, concrete though the circumstances of domestic violence are in each society.

Even what is most apparently strange in the circumstances of each is also, at another level, not so unfamiliar. We find it odd that the brick kiln makes women do all the heavy jobs and then pays them less—but many forms of sex discrimination in employment exhibit similar forms of irrationality. Again, the fact that a woman as strong and resourceful as Vasanti doesn't want to go to school seems odd—but of course it isn't so surprising, given that she doesn't see any signs of a better way of life that she could get by becoming educated. How to think well about what is similar and what is different in these lives: that is the task I'll begin to undertake in today's lecture.

An international feminism that is going to have any critical bite quickly gets involved in making normative recommendations that cross boundaries of culture, nation, religion, race, and class. It will therefore need to find descriptive and normative concepts adequate to that task.[2] This enterprise is fraught with peril, both intellectual and political. Where do these categories come from, it will be asked? And how can they be justified as appropriate ones for lives in which those categories themselves are not explicitly recognized? The suspicion uneasily grows that the theorist is imposing something on people who surely have their own ideas of what is right and proper. And this suspicion grates all the more unpleasantly when we remind ourselves that theorists often come from nations that have been oppressors, or from classes in poorer nations that are themselves unusually privileged. Isn't all this philosophizing, then, simply one more exercise in colonial or class domination?

Of course, no normative political theory uses terms that are straightforwardly those of ordinary daily life. If it did, it probably could not perform its special task as theory, which involves the systematization and critical scrutiny of intuitions that in daily life are often unexamined. Theory gives people a set of terms with which to criticize abuses that otherwise might lurk nameless in the background. Jayamma's use of the Marxian language of class struggle is just one obvious example of this point.

But even if one defends theoretical abstractions as valuable for practice, it may still be problematic to use concepts that originated in a culture that has colonized and oppressed the culture being described. Attempts by international feminists today to use a universal language of justice and human rights frequently encounter charges of "westernizing" and colonizing—even when the universal categories are used by feminists who live and work within the nation in question itself. In one way, the charge of westernizing is obviously a cheap political trick, of the sort involved when Lee Kuan Yew says that "the East" doesn't value freedom: a way of discrediting opponents who are pressing for change. Applied to India, such a claim about women's rights and liberties is not only cheap, but also unconvincing. It ignores tremendous chunks of reality, including indigenous movements for women's education, for the end of purdah, and for women's political participation, which gained strength straight through the nineteenth and early twentieth centuries in both Hindu and Muslim traditions, in some ways running ahead of British and U.S. feminist movements.[3] And it ignores the founding of the Indian nation itself, where sex equality was adopted by overwhelming consensus in 1951, as among the Fundamental Rights— something the United States, of course, has been unable to do. We need to remind ourselves that sex equality is an Indian constitutional idea, and it is not an American constitutional idea. How condescending to suggest that in striving for it, Nehru and Ambedkar were dupes of Western colonial thinking.

On the other hand, when we propose a universal framework to assess the quality of life for women, we face three more respectable arguments that deserve to be seriously answered.

First is an *argument from culture.* A more subtle and sincere version of the anti-westernizing argument, it says that Indian culture contains powerful norms of female modesty, deference, obedience, and self-sacrifice that have defined women's lives for centuries, in both Hindu and Muslim tradition. Feminists should not assume without argument that those are bad norms, incapable of constructing good and flourishing lives for women. Western women are not so happy, with their high divorce rate and their exhausting careerism. They condescend to Third-World women when they assume that only lives like their own can be fruitful.

My full answer to this point will emerge from the proposal I shall make, which certainly does not preclude any woman's choice to lead a traditional life, so long as she does so with certain economic and political opportunities firmly in place. But the objection, once again, oversimplifies tradition. It ignores the countertraditions of female defiance and strength; it ignores women's protests against harmful traditions; and in general it forgets to ask women themselves what they think of these norms, which are traditionally purveyed through male texts and the authority of male religious and cultural leaders, against a background of almost total economic disempowerment for women. Neither Vasanti nor Jayamma comes close to defending such traditions. Philosopher Uma Narayan had a middle-class upbringing that did endorse traditions of female submissiveness, silence, and purity; yet, she records that she heard from her mother, all the while, a constant stream of highly articulate protest against the misery such confining traditions had caused. "The shape your 'silence' took," she addresses her mother, "is in part what has incited me to speech." It would be mistaken to describe only the official teaching as Indian tradition, ignoring the protest.

The argument from culture shows us, then, that we should be ready to learn from what we see and to treat seriously any cultural proposal that has serious support. It does not, and could not, show that there is a single norm of modesty and subservience that is "the Indian tradition." Cultures are scenes of debate, so appealing to culture gives us questions rather than answers. It certainly doesn't show that universal norms are a bad answer to those questions.

Let us now consider the argument that I'll call the *argument from the good of diversity*. This argument reminds us that our world is rich in part because we don't all agree on a single set of practices and norms. We think the world's different languages have worth and beauty, and that it's a bad thing that diminishes the expressive resources of human life in general, if any language ceases to exist. So too, each cultural system has a distinctive beauty, and it would be an impoverished world if everyone took on America's value system.

Here we should distinguish two claims the objector might be making. She might be claiming that diversity is good as such; or she might simply be saying that there are problems with the value system of America, and that it would be too bad if the rest of the world emulated our materialism and aggressiveness. This second claim, of course, doesn't yet say anything against universal values, it just suggests that their content should be critical of some American values. So the real challenge to our enterprise lies in the first claim. To meet it, we must ask how much cultural diversity really is like linguistic diversity, or the diversity of species. The trouble with the analogy is that languages don't harm people, and cultural practices frequently do. We could think that Cornish or Breton should be preserved, without thinking the same about domestic violence. In the end, then, the objection doesn't undermine the search for universal values. It requires it, for it invites us to ask whether the cultural values in question are among the ones worth preserving; and this entails at least a very general universal framework of assessment, one that will tell us what is and is not beyond the pale.

I will be offering just such a very general framework, one that allows a great deal of latitude for diversity, but one that also sets up some general benchmarks that will tell us when we are better off letting a practice die out. Traditional practices like the division of labor in Jayamma's brick kiln site, or Vasanti's husband's highly traditional practice of wife beating are not worth preserving simply because they are there, or because they are old. To make a case for preserving them, we have to assess the contribution they make and the harm they do. This requires a set of values that gives us a critical purchase on cultural particulars. The argument gives us reasons to preserve types of diversity that are compatible with human dignity and other basic values; but it does not undermine and even supports our search for a general universal framework of critical assessment.

Finally, we have the *argument from paternalism*. This argument says that when we use a set of universal norms as benchmarks for the world's varied societies, we show too little respect for people's freedom as agents (and, in a related way, their role as democratic citizens). People are the best judges of what is good for them, and if we say that their own choices are not good for them, we treat them like children. This is an important point and one that any viable cross-cultural proposal should bear firmly in mind. But it hardly seems incompatible with the endorsement of universal values. Indeed, it appears to endorse explicitly at least some universal values, such as the value of the political liberties and other opportunities for choice. Thinking about paternalism gives us a strong reason to respect the variety of ways citizens actually choose to lead their lives in a pluralistic society, and therefore to prefer a form of universalism that is compatible with freedom and choice of the most significant sort. But such respect naturally leads us to value religious toleration, associative freedom, and the other major liberties. These liberties are themselves universal values, and they are not compatible with views that many real people and societies hold.

We can make a further claim: that many existing value systems are themselves highly paternalistic, particularly toward women. They treat women as unequal under the law; as lacking full civil capacity; as not having the property rights, associative liberties, and employment rights of males. If we encounter a system like this, it is in one sense paternalistic to say, sorry, that is unacceptable under the universal norms of equality and liberty that we would like to defend. In that way, any bill of rights is "paternalistic" vis-à-vis families, or groups, or practices, or even pieces of legislation, that treats people with insufficient or unequal respect. The Indian Constitution is, in that sense, paternalistic when it tells people that it is, from now on, illegal to use caste or sex as grounds of discrimination. But that is hardly a good argument against fundamental constitutional rights or, more generally, against opposing the attempts of some people to tyrannize over others. We dislike paternalism because there is something else that we like, namely liberty of choice in fundamental matters. It is fully consistent to reject some forms of paternalism while supporting those that underwrite these basic values.

Nor does the protection of choice require only a formal defense of basic liberties. The various liberties of choice have material preconditions, in whose absence there is merely a simulacrum of choice. In a sense, Jayamma had the choice to go to school, but the economic circumstances of her life made this impossible. Nothing told Vasanti that she couldn't have economic independence from her brothers, but in the absence of the SEWA bank, the independence she now enjoys would not have been available to her. Children in the desert areas of Andhra Pradesh have the right to go to school—but there aren't any schools or teachers, since nobody has decided to spend money on creating them. All women in India have equal rights under the constitution; but in the absence of effective enforcement and programs targeted at increasing female literacy, economic empowerment, and employment opportunities, those rights are not real to them.

In short, liberty is not just a matter of having rights on paper; it requires being in a position to exercise those rights. And this requires material resources. The state that is going to effectively guarantee the rights of its people must recognize universal norms beyond the small menu of basic rights: it will have to take a stand on the redistribution of wealth and income, on employment, land rights, health, and education. That requires yet more universalism and, in a sense, paternalism, but we could hardly say that the children of rural Andhra Pradesh, living in a state of virtual anarchy, with no water, no buses, and no teachers, are especially free to do as they wish.

The argument from paternalism indicates, then, that we should prefer a universal normative account that allows people plenty of liberty to pursue their own conceptions of value, within limits set by the protection of the equal worth of the liberties of others. It does not give us any good reason not to endorse any universal account, and some strong reasons why we should do so, including in our account not only the liberties themselves, but also forms of economic empowerment that are crucial in making the liberties truly available to people. And the argument suggests one thing more—that the account we search for should preserve liberties and opportunities for each and every person, taken one by one, respecting each of them as an end, rather than simply as the agent or supporter of the ends of others. Women are too often treated as members of an organic unit such as the family or the community, and their interests subordinated to the larger goals of that unit, which means, typically, those of its male members. However, Gujarat's impressive economic growth meant nothing to Vasanti so long as her husband deprived her of control over resources. We need to consider not just the aggregate, whether in a region or in a family; we need to consider the distribution of resources and opportunities *to each individual*, thinking of each as an end.

Veena Das has claimed that Indian women lack this intuitive idea—that each person has her own dignity and well being, distinct from that of the family. If this claim simply means that Indian women frequently judge sacrifice for the family to be a good thing, and frequently subordinate their own well-being to the well-being of others, it is plausible enough. But it is hardly an objection to the concern for the individual that I recommend; there is no incompatibility between the idea that politics should treat each person as an end and the idea that some people choose to make sacrifices for others. If, however, Das really means to say that Indian women can't tell their own hunger apart from the hunger of a child or a husband, can't really distinguish their own body and its health from someone else's body and its health, then what she says just seems false. Certainly, in some ways Jayamma puts others first and herself second. She puts sugar in her tea, for example, while she allows her husband and her children to take the more expensive milk. But even in that act she is distinguishing her own well-being from that of others; in general, she budgets the family account with intense awareness of the separateness of its various people, asking how much shall be spent on each one. Indeed, we might say that the poorer people are, the more likely they are to be keenly aware of the separateness of their well-being—for hunger and hard physical labor are great reminders that one is oneself and not someone else. Bengali author Manik Bandyopadhyay put it this way, in his story "A Female Problem at a Low Level":

A slum girl and daughter of a laborer cannot mentally depend on her father or brother, like the daughters of the babu families who even as grown women see individual disaster in any family mishap. She is used to fending for herself, relying on her own wits.[4]

In other words, forgetting about distinctions of well-being in the family is an upper middle class privilege, alien to those who are really struggling to survive.

Let me recapitulate. The argument from culture reminded us that we should leave space for women who may wish to choose a traditional hierarchical way of life. But it said nothing against using a universal account to criticize unjust cultural practices; indeed, we were reminded that the activity of criticism is deeply internal to Indian culture itself. The argument from the good of diversity told us something important about any proposal we should endorse—that it ought to provide spaces in which valuably different forms of human activity can flourish. We should not stamp out diversity, or even put it at risk, without a very strong reason. But in light of the fact that some traditional practices are harmful and evil, and some are actively hostile to other elements of a diverse culture, our interest in diversity itself forces us to develop a set of criteria against which to assess the practices we find, asking which are acceptable and worth preserving, and which are not. As for the argument from paternalism, it nudges us strongly in the direction of what might be called *political* rather than *comprehensive liberalism*, in the sense that it urges us to respect the many different conceptions of good that citizens may have and to foster a political climate in which each will be able to pursue the good (whether religious or ethical) according to their own lights. In other words, we want universals that are facilitative rather than tyrannical,[5] that create spaces for choice rather than dragooning people into a desired total mode of functioning. But understood at its best, the paternalism argument is not an argument against cross-cultural universals. For it is all about respect for the dignity of persons as choosers. This respect requires us to defend universally a wide range of liberties, plus their material conditions, and to defend them for each and every person.

Another way of seeing why universal norms are badly needed in the international policy arena is to consider what the alternative has typically been. The most prevalent approach to measuring quality of life in a nation used to be simply to ask about the gross national product (GNP) per capita. This approach tries to weasel out of making any universal claims about what has value—although note that it does assume the universal value of opulence. What it omits, however, is much more significant. We are not even told about the distribution of wealth and income, and countries with similar aggregate figures can exhibit great distributional variations. Circus girl Sissy Jupe, in Dickens's *Hard Times*, already saw the problem with this absence of normative concern for the individual—she says that the economic approach doesn't tell her "who has got the money and whether any of it is mine." So too with Jayamma and Vasanti: the fact that Gujarat is in general a much more prosperous state than Kerala is only a part of the story; it doesn't tell us what government has done for each of them, or how they are doing. To know that, we'd need to look at their lives; but then we need to specify, beyond distribution of wealth and income itself, what parts of their lives we ought to look at—such as life expectancy, infant mortality, educational opportunities, health care, employment opportunities, land rights, and political liberties. Seeing what is absent from the GNP account nudges us sharply in the direction of mapping out these and other basic goods in a universal way, so that we can use the list of basic goods to compare quality of life across societies.

A further problem with all resource-based approaches, even those that are sensitive to distribution, is that individuals vary in their capacity for converting resources into the ability to function. Some of these differences are straightforwardly physical. Nutritional needs vary with age, occupation, and sex. A pregnant or lactating woman needs more nutrients than a woman who isn't pregnant. A child needs more protein than an adult. A person whose limbs work well needs few resources to be mobile, whereas a person with paralyzed limbs needs many more resources to achieve the same level of mobility. Many such variations can escape our notice if we live in a prosperous nation that can afford to bring all individuals to a high level of physical attainment; in the developing world, we must be highly alert to these variations in need. Again, some of the pertinent variations are social, connected with traditional hierarchies. If we wish to bring all citizens of a nation to the same level of educational attainment, we will need to devote more resources to those who encounter obstacles from traditional hierarchy or prejudice. Thus, women's literacy will prove more expensive than men's literacy in many parts of the world. If we operate only with an index of resources, we will frequently reinforce inequalities that are highly relevant to well-being.

I will now argue that a reasonable answer to all these concerns—an answer capable of giving good guidance to governments establishing basic constitutional principles and to international agencies assessing the quality of life—is given by a version of the *capabilities approach*—an approach to the quality of life assessment pioneered within economics by Amartya Sen,[6] and by now highly influential through the *Human Development Reports* of the United Nations Development Programme (UNDP).[7] My own version of this approach differs in several ways from Sen's; I will simply lay out my view as I would currently defend it.

The central question asked by the capabilities approach is not, "How satisfied is Vasanti?" or even "How much in the way of resources is she able to command?" It is, instead, "What is Vasanti actually able to do and to be?" Taking a stand for political purposes on a working list of functions that would appear to be of central importance in human life, users of this approach ask, "Is the person capable of this, or not?" They ask not only about the person's satisfaction with what she does, but about what she does, and what she is in a position to do (what her opportunities and liberties are). They ask not just about the resources that are present, but also about how those do or do not go to work, enabling Vasanti to function.

The intuitive idea behind the approach is twofold: first, that there are certain functions that are particularly central in human life, in the sense that their presence or absence is typically understood to be a mark of the presence or absence of human life. Second, and this is what Marx found in Aristotle, that there is something that it is to do these functions in a truly human way, not a merely animal way. We judge, frequently enough, that a life has been so impoverished that it is not worthy of the dignity of the human being; that it is a life in which one goes on living, but does so more or less like an animal, not being able to develop and exercise one's human powers. In Marx's example, a starving person doesn't use food in a fully human way—by which I think he means a way that is infused with practical reasoning and sociability. He or she just grabs at the food in order to survive, and the many social and rational ingredients of human feeding can't make their appearance. Similarly, the senses of a human being can operate at a merely animal level—if they are not cultivated by appropriate education, by leisure for play and self-expression, by valuable associations with others. We should add to the list some items that Marx probably would not endorse, such as expressive and associational liberty, and the freedom of worship. The core idea seems to be that of the human being as a dignified free being who shapes his or her own life, rather than being passively shaped or pushed around by the world as if a member of a "flock" or "herd."[8]

At one extreme, we may judge that the absence of capability for a central function is so acute that the person isn't really a human being at all, or is no longer human—as in the case of certain very severe forms of mental disability or senile dementia. But I am less interested in that boundary (important though it is for medical ethics) than in a higher one, the level at which a person's capability is "truly human," that is, *worthy* of a human being. Note that this idea contains a reference to an idea of human worth or dignity. Marx was departing from Kant in some important respects by stressing (along with Aristotle) that the major powers of a human being need material support and cannot be what they are without it. But he also learned from Kant, and his way of expressing his Aristotelian heritage is distinctively shaped by the Kantian notion of the inviolability and the dignity of the person.

Note that the approach makes each person a bearer of value and an end. Marx, like his bourgeois forebears, holds that it is profoundly wrong to subordinate the ends of some individuals to those of others. That is at the core of what exploitation is, to treat a person as a mere object for the use of others. This approach is after a society in which individuals are treated as beings worthy of regard, and in which each has been put in a position to live really humanly.

I think we can produce an account of these necessary elements of truly human functioning that commands a broad cross-cultural consensus. Although this list of basic capabilities is somewhat different in both structure and substance from Rawls's list of primary goods, it is offered in a similar, political liberal spirit—as a list that can be endorsed for political purposes by people who otherwise have very different views of what a complete good life for a human being would be. (In part, as we will see, this is because the list enumerates capabilities or opportunities for functioning, rather than actual functions. In part, it is because the list leaves spaces for people to pursue other functions that they value.) The list is supposed to provide a focus for the quality of life assessment and for political planning, and it aims to select capabilities that are of central importance in any human life, whatever else the person pursues or chooses. Therefore, they have a special claim to be supported for political purposes in a pluralistic society.[9]

The list represents the result of years of cross-cultural discussion, and comparisons between earlier and later versions will show that the input of other voices has shaped its content in many ways. Thus it represents a type of *overlapping consensus* on the part of people with otherwise very different views of human life. It remains open-ended and humble; it can always be contested and remade. Nor does it deny that the items on the list are to some extent differently constructed by different societies. Indeed part of the idea of the list is that its members can be more concretely specified in accordance with local beliefs and circumstances. Here is the current version of the list:[10]

CENTRAL HUMAN FUNCTIONAL CAPABILITIES

1. *Life*. Being able to live to the end of a human life of normal length, not dying prematurely, or before one's life is so reduced as to be not worth living.
2. *Bodily Health*. Being able to have good health, including reproductive health,[11] to be adequately nourished, to have adequate shelter.
3. *Bodily Integrity*. Being able to move freely from place to place; to be secure against violent assault, including sexual assault and domestic violence; having opportunities for sexual satisfaction and for choice in matters of reproduction.
4. *Senses, Imagination, and Thought*. Being able to use the senses, to imagine, think, and reason—and to do these things in a truly human way, a way informed and cultivated by an adequate education, including, but by no means limited to, literacy and basic mathematical and scientific training. Being able to use imagination and thought in connection with experiencing and producing works and events of one's own choice, religious, literary, musical, and so forth. Being able to use one's mind in ways protected by guarantees of freedom of expression with respect to both political and artistic speech, and freedom of religious exercise. Being able to have pleasurable experiences, and to avoid non-necessary pain.
5. *Emotions*. Being able to have attachments to things and people outside ourselves; to love those who love and care for us, to grieve at their absence; in general, to love, to grieve, to experience longing, gratitude, and justified anger. Not having one's emotional development blighted by fear and anxiety. (Supporting this capability means supporting forms of human association that can be shown to be crucial in their development.)
6. *Practical Reason*. Being able to form a conception of the good and to engage

in critical reflection about the planning of one's life. (This entails protection for the liberty of conscience.)

7. *Affiliation.* (A) Being able to live with and toward others, to recognize and show concern for other human beings, to engage in various forms of social interaction, to be able to imagine the situation of another and to have compassion for that situation, to have the capability for both justice and friendship. Protecting this capability means protecting institutions that constitute and nourish such forms of affiliation, and also protecting the freedom of assembly and political speech. (B) Having the social bases of self-respect and nonhumiliation, being able to be treated as a dignified being whose worth is equal to that of others. This entails protections against discrimination on the basis of race, sex, sexual orientation, religion, caste, ethnicity, or national origin.[12]

8. *Other Species.* Being able to live with concern for and in relation to animals, plants, and the world of nature.[13]

9. *Play.* Being able to laugh, to play, to enjoy recreational activities.

10. *Control Over One's Environment.* (A) *Political.* Being able to participate effectively in political choices that govern one's life; having the right of political participation, protections of free speech and association. (B) *Material.* Being able to hold property (both land and movable goods), having the right to seek employment on an equal basis with others, having the freedom from unwarranted search and seizure.[14]

The list is, emphatically, a list of separate components. We cannot satisfy the need for one element by giving a larger amount of another one. All are of central importance, and all are distinct in quality. The irreducible plurality of the list limits the trade-offs that will be reasonable to make, and thus limits the applicability of a quantitative cost-benefit analysis. At the same time, the items on the list are related to one another in many complex ways. One of the most effective ways of promoting women's control over their environment, and their effective right of political participation, is to promote women's literacy. Women who can seek employment outside the home have more resources in protecting their bodily integrity from assaults within it. Such facts give us still more reason not to promote one capability at the expense of the others.

Among the capabilities, two—practical reason and affiliation—stand out as of special importance, since they both organize and suffuse all the others, making their pursuit truly human. To use one's senses in a way not infused by the characteristically human use of thought and planning is to use them in a merely animal manner.[15] Tagore's heroine describes herself as "a free human mind"—and this idea of oneself infuses all one's other functions. At the same time, to reason for oneself without considering the circumstances and needs of others at all is, again, to behave in a way that is not fully human.

In the political arena, the basic intuition from which the capability approach begins is that human abilities exert a moral claim that they should be developed. Human beings are creatures that, provided with the right educational and material support, can become fully capable of these human functions. That is, they are creatures with certain lower level capabilities (which I call *basic capabilities*[16]) to perform the functions in question. When these capabilities are deprived of the nourishment that would transform them into the high-level capabilities that figure on my list, they are fruitless, cut off in some way, but a mere shadow of themselves. If a turtle were given a life that afforded a merely animal level of functioning, we would have no indignation, no sense of waste and tragedy. When a human being is given a life that blights powers of human action and expression, that does give us a sense of waste and tragedy—the tragedy expressed, for example, in Mrinal's statement to her husband, in Tagore's story, when she says, "I am not one to die easily." In her view, a life without dignity and choice, a life in which she could be no more than an appendage, was a type of death.

We begin, then, with a sense of the worth and dignity of basic human powers, thinking of them as claims to a chance for functioning, claims that give rise to correlated social and political duties. And in fact there are three different types of capabilities that play a role in the analysis.[17] First, there are the basic capabilities: the innate equipment of individuals that is the necessary basis for developing the more advanced capability, and a ground of moral concern. Second, there are *internal capabilities*: that is, states of the person herself that are, so far as the person herself is concerned, sufficient conditions for the exercise of the requisite functions. A woman who has not suffered genital mutilation has the internal capability for sexual pleasure; most adult human beings everywhere have the internal capability for religious freedom and the freedom of speech. Finally, there are *combined capabilities*,[18] which may be defined as internal capabilities combined with suitable external conditions for the exercise of the function. A woman who is not mutilated, but who has been widowed as a child and is forbidden to make another marriage, has the internal but not the combined capability for sexual expression (and, in most such cases, for employment, and political participation).[19] Citizens of repressive nondemocratic regimes have the internal but not the combined capability to exercise thought and speech in accordance with their conscience. The list, then, is a list of combined capabilities. To realize one of the items on the list entails not only promoting the appropriate development of people's internal powers, but also preparing the environment so that it is favorable for the exercise of practical reason and the other major functions. In other words, its liberties and opportunities correspond to Rawls's ideas of "the equal worth of liberty" and "truly fair equality of opportunity," rather than to his thinner notions of "formally equal liberty" and "formal equality of opportunity."

A focus on capabilities as social goals is closely related to a focus on human equality, in the sense that discrimination on the basis of race, religion, sex, national origin, caste, or ethnicity is taken to be itself a failure of associational capability, a type of indignity or humiliation. And making capabilities the goals entails promoting a greater measure of material equality for all citizens than exists in most societies, since we are unlikely to get all citizens above a minimum threshold of capability for truly human functioning without some redistributive policies. On the other hand, it is possible for supporters of the general capability goal to differ about the amount of material equality a society focused on capability should seek. Complete egalitarianism,[20] a Rawlsian difference principle, and a weaker focus on a (rather ample) social minimum would all be compatible with the proposal as so far advanced. Where women are concerned, almost all world societies are very far from providing even the basic minimum of truly human functioning.

I have spoken both of functioning and of capability. How are they related? Getting clear about this is crucial in defining the relation of the capabilities approach both to Rawlsian liberalism and to our concerns about paternalism and pluralism. For if we were to take functioning itself as the goal of public policy, the liberal pluralist would rightly judge that we were precluding many choices that citizens may make in accordance with their own conceptions of the good, and perhaps violating their rights. A deeply religious person may prefer not to be well nourished, but to engage in strenuous fasting. Whether for religious or for other reasons, a person may prefer a celibate life to one containing sexual expression. A person may prefer to work with an intense dedication that precludes recreation and play. Am I declaring, by my very use of the list, that these are not fully human or flourishing lives? And am I instructing government to nudge or push people into functioning of the requisite sort, no matter what they prefer?

It is important that the answer to these questions is no. Capability, not functioning, is the political goal. This is so because of the very great importance the approach attaches to practical reason, as a good that both suffuses all the other functions, making them human rather than animal,[21] and figures, itself, as a central function on the list. It is perfectly true that functioning, not simply capability, is what renders a life fully human. If there were no functioning of any kind in a life, we could hardly applaud it, no matter what opportunities it contained. Nonetheless, for political purposes, it is appropriate for us to shoot for capabilities, and those alone. After that, citizens must be left free to determine their courses. The person with plenty of food may always choose to fast, but there is a great difference between fasting and starving, and it is this difference that we wish to capture. Again, the person who has normal opportunities for sexual satisfaction can always choose a life of celibacy, and we say nothing against this. What we do speak against (for example) is the practice of female genital mutilation, which deprives individuals of the opportunity to choose sexual functioning (and indeed, the opportunity to choose celibacy as well).[22] A person who has opportunities for play can always choose a workaholic life; again, there is a great difference between that chosen life and a life constrained by insufficient maximum-hour protections and/or the "double day" that makes women unable to play in many parts of the world. The approach does not rest content with internal capabilities, indifferent to the struggles of individuals who have to try to exercise these in a hostile environment. In that sense, it is highly attentive to the goal of functioning, and instructs governments to keep it always in view. On the other hand, it does not push individuals into functioning—once the stage is fully set, the choice is up to them. Another way in which the list respects choice is in the prominent place it gives to the political liberties and the liberty of conscience, and the personal capability for practical reasoning and life planning.

I have argued that legitimate concerns for diversity, pluralism, and personal freedom are not incompatible with the recognition of universal norms, and indeed that universal norms are actually required if we are to protect diversity, pluralism, and freedom, treating each human being as an agent and an end. The best way to hold all these concerns together, I have argued, is to formulate the universal norms as a set of capabilities for fully human functioning, emphasizing the fact that capabilities protect, and do not close off, spheres of human freedom.

Let us now return to Vasanti and Jayamma. The script of Vasanti's life has been largely written by men, on whom she has been dependent: her father, her husband, and the brothers who helped her when her marriage collapsed. This dependency put her at risk with respect to life and health, denied her the education that would have developed her powers of thought, and prevented her from thinking of herself as a person who has a plan of life to shape and choices to make. In the marriage itself, she fared worst of all, losing her bodily integrity to domestic violence, sacrificing her emotional equanimity to fear, and being cut off from meaningful forms of affiliation—familial, friendly, and civic. For these reasons, she did not really conceive of herself as a free and dignified being whose worth is equal to that of others. We should note that mundane matters of property, employment, and credit play a large role here. The fact that she held no property in her own name, had no literacy and no employment-related skills, and no access to a loan except from male relatives, all these cemented her dependent status and kept her in an abusive relationship far longer than she would otherwise have chosen. We see here how closely all the capabilities are linked to one another, how the absence of one, bad in itself, also erodes others.

Vasanti also had some good luck: she had no abusive in-laws to put up with, and she had brothers who were more than usually solicitous of her well-being. Thus she could and did leave the marriage without turning to any physically dangerous or degrading occupation. But this good luck created new forms of dependency; Vasanti thus remained highly vulnerable and lacking in confidence.

The SEWA loan changed this picture. Vasanti now had not only an income, but also independent control over her livelihood. Even when she still owed a lot of money, it was better to owe it to SEWA than to her brothers. Being part of a mutually supportive community of women was crucially different, in respect to both practical reason and affiliation, from being a poor relation being given a handout. Her sense of her own dignity increased as she paid off the loan and began saving. By the time I saw her, she had achieved considerable self-confidence and a sense of worth, and her affiliations with other women, in both groups and personal friendships, were a new source of both pleasure and pride to her. Her participation in political life had also gone way up, as she joined in Kokila's project to prod the police to investigate more cases of domestic violence. Interestingly, she now felt that she had the capacity to be a good person by giving to others, something that the narrow focus on survival had not permitted her to do.

Reflecting on her situation, we notice how little the public sector did for her, and how lucky she was that one of the best women's nongovernmental organizations (NGOs) in the world was right in her backyard. Government failed to ensure her an education; it failed to prosecute her husband for abuse, or to offer her shelter from that abuse[23]; it failed to secure her equal property rights in her own family; and it failed to offer her access to credit. Indeed, the only strong role government played in Vasanti's life was negative—the cash payment for her husband's vasectomy, which made her vulnerable position even more so.

Jayamma's situation provides an interesting contrast. On the one hand, she had a much worse start in life than Vasanti and has done worse throughout her life on some of the measures of capability. She has had to worry constantly about hunger, and she has at times suffered from malnutrition; she has engaged in extremely dangerous and taxing physical labor. She has had no supportive male relatives, and, although she has had children, as Vasanti has not, they have been more of a liability than an asset. She has no savings, and has never had a loan; her property rights to the land on which she squats are not clearly established. She has suffered from discrimination in employment, with no chance of rectification. And she has had to do what countless women in developing countries routinely do (but Vasanti did not)—to shoulder all the burden of running a household with children, after working a full day at a demanding job.

On the other hand, Jayamma has in some ways done better than Vasanti. Her health has been good, no doubt because of her impressive physical strength and fitness, and she has never suffered physical abuse from her husband, who seems to have been a lot weaker than she was. She doesn't seem to be intimidated by anyone, and she has a consciousness of political issues that Vasanti developed only recently. Unlike Vasanti, she has never been encouraged to be submissive, and she certainly isn't. Through the years, she has fought effectively to keep her family together and to improve its standing.

Government has done much more for Jayamma than for Vasanti. The squatters on government land now have been given property rights in the land, although they will need to go to court to clearly establish their claim. Services provided by the government are invaluable aids in Jayamma's taxing day. Water now comes into the squat itself, and a government program built her an indoor toilet. Government medical services are nearby, good, and available free of charge. Even though Jayamma did not take advantage of educational opportunities for her own children, her grandchildren have profited from the government's aggressiveness against traditions of non-education. The government certainly failed to eradicate sex discrimination in her place of employment. But in many respects, the government of Kerala can be given good marks for promoting human capabilities.

Used to evaluate these lives, the capabilities framework does not look like an alien importation—it squares pretty well with the things these women are already thinking about, or start thinking about at some time in their lives. Insofar as it entails criticism of traditional culture, these women are already full of criticism; indeed, any framework that didn't suggest criticism wouldn't be adequate to capture what they want and aim for. In particular, the ideas of practical reason, control over environment, and freedom from humiliation seem especially salient in their thoughts, alongside more obvious considerations of nutrition, health, and freedom from violence. Even where the list doesn't exactly echo their thoughts—as, for example, in the value it ascribes to education—it still seems to capture well, for normative political purposes, aspects of life that stand between these women and the general goals of independence, dignity, and mastery for which they are both intensely striving.

Vasanti and Jayamma, like many women in India and in the rest of the world, have lacked support for central human functions, and that lack of support is, to some extent, caused by their being women. But women, unlike rocks and trees, have the potential to become capable of these human functions, given sufficient nutrition, education, and other support. That is why their unequal failure in capability is a problem of justice. It is up to all human beings to solve this problem. I claim that a universal conception of human functioning gives us good guidance as we pursue this difficult task.

NOTES

1. Unlike Vasanti, Jayamma has already been studied in the development economics literature. See Leela Gulati, "Jayamma, the Brick Worker," in *Profiles in Female Poverty: A Study of Five Poor Working Women in Kerala* (Delhi: Hindustan Publishing Company, 1981). See also Leela Gulati and Mitu Gulati, "Female Labour in the Unorganised Sector: The Brick Worker Revisited," *Economic and Political Weekly* (May 3, 1997): 968–71, also scheduled for publication in *Widows and Social Responsibility,* ed. Martha Chen, (Delhi: Sage). I am very grateful to Leela Gulati for introducing me to Jayamma and her family and for translating.

2. For earlier articulations of my views on matters contained in this lecture, see "Nature, Function, and Capability: Aristotle on Political Distribution," in *Oxford Studies in Ancient Philosophy,* Supplementary Volume I: 1988, 145–84, abbreviated hereafter as NFC; "Aristotelian Social Democracy," in *Liberalism and the Good,* ed. R. B. Douglass et al. (New York: Routledge, 1990), 203–52, abbreviated hereafter as ASD; "Non-Relative Virtues: An Aristotelian Approach," in *The Quality of Life,* ed. M. Nussbaum and A. Sen (Oxford: Clarendon Press, 1993), abbreviated hereafter as NRV; "Aristotle on Human Nature and the Foundations of Ethics," in *World, Mind and Ethics: Essays on the Ethical Philosophy of Bernard Williams,* ed. J. E. J. Altham and Ross Harrison (Cambridge: Cambridge University Press, 1995), 86–131, hereafter abbreviated as HN; "Human Functioning and Social Justice: In Defense of Aristotelian Essentialism," *Political Theory* 20 (1992): 202–46, abbreviated hereafter as HF; "Human Capabilities, Female Human Beings," in *Women, Culture,*

and Development, ed. M. Nussbaum and J. Glover (Oxford: Clarendon Press, 1995), 61–104, abbreviated hereafter as HC; "Capabilities and Human Rights," *Fordham Law Review* 1997; and in two forthcoming papers: "The Good as Discipline, the Good as Freedom," in *The Ethics of Consumption and Global Stewardship*, ed. D. Crocker and T. Linden (Lanham: Rowman and Littlefield, forthcoming 1998), abbreviated hereafter as GDGF; and "Women and Cultural Universals," chapter 1 in Nussbaum, *Sex and Social Justice*, (New York: Oxford University Press, 1999).

3. For two good overviews, see Barbara Metcalf, "Reading and Writing about Muslim Women in British India," and Faisal Fatehali Devji, "Gender and the Politics of Space: The Movement for Women's Reform, 1857–1900," both in *Forging Identities: Gender, Communities and the State in India*, ed. Zoya Hasan, (Delhi: Kali for Women, and Boulder, Colo.: Westview Press, 1994), 1–21 and 22–37; also in *Modernization and Social Change Among Muslims in India*, ed. Imtiaz Ahmad (Delhi: Manohar, 1983). For the special situation of Bengal, which in some ways developed progressive educational ideas earlier than other regions, under the influence of the reforms of Rammohun Roy and the Brahmo movement, see Kalpana Bardhan, "Introduction" in *Women, Outcastes, Peasants and Rebels* (an anthology of Bengali fiction about political change from the nineteenth and twentieth centuries; Berkeley: University of California Press, 1990), 42; and Susobhan Sarkar, *On the Bengal Renaissance* (Calcutta: Papyrus, 1979). Both in East and West Bengal, schools for girls were well established by 1850, and Bethune College, which opened in 1849, in 1888 became the first college in India to teach women through the MA level.

4. Bardhan, *Women, Outcastes, Peasants, and Rebels*, 155.

5. For the charge that international human rights norms are tyrannical, see Wendy Brown, *States of Injury* (Princeton: Princeton University Press), 19.

6. The initial statement is in Sen, "Equality of What?" in *Tanner Lectures on Human Values* 1, ed. S. McMurrin (Cambridge: Cambridge University Press, 1980), reprinted in Sen, *Choice, Welfare, and Measurement* (Oxford and Cambridge, Mass.: Basil Blackwell and MIT Press, 1982). See also various essays in *Resources, Values, and Development* (Oxford and Cambridge, Mass.: Basil Blackwell and MIT Press, 1984); *Commodities and Capabilities* (Amsterdam: North-Holland, 1985); "Well-Being, Agency, and Freedom: The Dewey Lectures 1984," *The Journal of Philosophy* 82 (1985); "Capability and Well-Being," in *The Quality of Life* ed. Nussbaum and Sen (Oxford: Clarendon Press, 1993), 30–53; "Gender Inequality and Theories of Justice," in *Women, Culture, and Development*, ed. J. Glover and M. Nussbaum (Oxford: Clarendon Press, 1995), 153–98, abbreviated hereafter as WCD; *Inequality Reexamined* (Oxford and Cambridge, Mass.: Clarendon Press and Harvard University Press, 1992).

7. *Human Development Reports: 1993, 1994, 1995, 1996* (New York: United Nations Development Programme).

8. Compare Amartya Sen, "Freedoms and Needs," *The New Republic* (January 10/17, 1994): 38. "The importance of political rights for the understanding of economic needs turns ultimately on seeing human beings as people with rights to exercise, not as parts of a "stock" or a "population" that passively exists and must be looked after."

9. Obviously, I am thinking of the political more broadly than does Rawls, for whom the nation state remains the basic unit. I am envisaging not only domestic deliberations but also cross-cultural quality of life assessments and other forms of international deliberation and planning.

10. The current version of the list reflects changes made as a result of my discussions with residents of India. The primary changes are a greater emphasis on bodily integrity and control over one's environment, and a new emphasis on dignity and nonhumiliation. Oddly, these features of human "self-sufficiency" and the dignity of the person are the ones most often criticized by Western feminists as "male" and "Western," one reason for their more muted role in earlier versions of the list. See my "The Feminist Critique of Liberalism," in *Sea and Social Justice*, ch. 2.

11. The 1994 International Conference on Population and Development (ICPD) adopted a definition of reproductive health that fits well with the intuitive idea of truly human functioning that guides this list: "Reproductive health is a state of complete physical, mental and social well-being and not merely the absence of disease or infirmity, in all matters relating to the reproductive system and its processes. Reproductive health therefore implies that people are able to have a satisfying and safe sex life and that they have the capability to reproduce and the freedom to decide if, when, and how often to do so." The definition goes on say that it also implies information and access to family planning methods of their choice. A brief summary of the ICPD's recommendations, adopted by the Panel on Reproductive Health of the Committee on Population established by the National Research Council, specifies three requirements of reproductive health: "1. Every sex act should be free of coercion and infection. 2. Every pregnancy should be intended. 3. Every birth should be healthy." See Amy O. Tsui, Judith N. Wasserheit, and John G. Haaga, eds., *Reproductive Health in Developing Countries* (Washington: National Academy Press, 1997), 14.

12. This provision is based on the Indian Constitution Article 15, which adds (as I would) that this should not be taken to prevent government from enacting measures to correct the history of discrimination against women and against the scheduled tribes and castes.

13. In terms of cross-cultural development, this has been the most controversial item on the list. It also properly raises the question of whether the list ought to be anthropocentric at all, or whether we should seek to promote appropriate capabilities for all living things. I leave these important questions for another occasion.

14. ASD argues that property rights are distinct from, for example, speech rights, in the sense that property is a tool of human functioning and not an end in itself. See also "Capabilities and Human Rights."

15. See HN, ASD.

16. See NFC, with reference to Aristotle's ways of characterizing levels of *dunamis*.

17. See NFC, referring to Aristotle's similar distinctions; and, on the basic capabilities, HC. Sen does not use these three levels explicitly, although in practice many of his statements assume related distinctions.

18. Earlier papers called these "external capabilities" (see NFC), but David Crocker persuaded me that this misleadingly suggested a focus on external conditions rather than internal fitness.

19. See Martha A. Chen, *The Lives of Widows in Rural India*, forthcoming; and "A Matter of Survival: Women's Right to Employment in India and Bangladesh," in WCD, 37–57.

20. Notice, however, that capability equality wouldn't necessarily entail equality of resources—that all depends on how resources affect capabilities once we get well above the threshold. Aristotle thought that we reach a point of negative returns: after a certain "limit," wealth becomes counterproductive, a distraction from the things that matter.

21. See HN, with discussion of Marx.

22. See my "Double Moral Standards?" (a reply to Yael Tamir's "Hands Off Clitoridectomy") *The Boston Review* (October–November 1996) and "Religion and Women's Human Rights," *Religion and Contemporary Liberalism*, ed. Paul J. Weithman (Notre Dame, Ind.: Notre Dame University Press, 1997), 1–37, reprinted in revised form in *Sex and Social Justice*, chapters 3 and 4.

23. The number of women's shelters in India is extremely small, indeed close to zero.

2

On Encountering Incommensurability: Martha Nussbaum's Aristotelian Practice

Jane Flax

So, if the person does not speak, he ceases to be one of us, and we are not required to take account of him. If he does speak, we can urge him to take a close look at his linguistic practices and what they rest on. In doing this we are giving him the *paideia* he lacks, a kind of initiation into the way we do things. Sometimes the opponent will not listen. 'Some need persuasion, others need violence,' Aristotle remarks somewhat grimly. Philosophy, at the level of basic principles, seems to be a matter of bringing the isolated person into line, of dispelling illusions that cause the breakdown of communication. Sometimes this can be done gently, sometimes only with violence; and sometimes not at all.[1]

We are all along talking about content, and the actual living of lives—though at a very general level. This inquiry is, in fact, continuous with a more general inquiry into the quality of life, or what the ancient Greeks (who did much to develop this approach) would have called the question of human flourishing, or the good life for a human being. It provides some parameters for such an inquiry, by showing us which lives fall altogether beyond the pale of humanness.[2]

ARISTOTELIAN PRACTICE[3]

I puzzled for a long time about how to write about Martha Nussbaum's extensive and multifaceted work. Since her explicit intent is to inform human practice, I decided to try to adopt her "Aristotelian" approach and apply it to my immediate context: her texts. This thought experiment could test its efficacy as a method to generate productive conversation. I could also explore the plausibility of its substantive propositions on the existence of commonly shared "deep" experiences and their intrinsically correlated ethical commitments. This puzzlement also set me to thinking about issues of style. As Nussbaum rightly emphasizes, style, including voice and genre, is an important but often overlooked aspect of philosophizing. Neither of us finds the dominant style in academic philosophy—that abstract, authoritative, detached voice from nowhere—particularly congenial or generative.[4] So I decided to imagine her *paideia*. I would try to initiate myself into her "grounding experiences." In trying to sustain communication, I would notice when I found these difficult to adopt. Trying to entertain the possibility of being deluded, I would struggle to adopt her views as my own. To make the engagement as intimate as possible, I decided to focus on a single essay, "Non-Relative Virtues: An Aristotelian Approach."[5] No single essay could possibly represent the complex reach of Nussbaum's work. However, this one expresses central concerns and specifies her recommended approach for ethical inquiry.

However, my experiment failed. I soon found myself in a world so unlike my own that encountering it generated a renewed appreciation for the stubborn incommensurabilities of thought. Agreement on some propositions conceals underlying differences. The basis of agreement and our underlying commitments differ radically. Repeated effort only increases my perplexity. Perhaps this reflects a deficient ability to comprehend her views. However, I would rather think that this is a cautionary tale. Engagement can intensify awareness of differences. It can disclose incommensurability of thinking about reason, ethics, and subjective and social worlds.

I discovered that an attempt to understand unfamiliar practices need not signify a tacit acceptance of the priority of practical reason or its centrality in a good life. Struggling to adopt another's approach can reflect commitments to courtesy and respect, as one would honor the customs in a foreign land. It can also be an aesthetic experiment, as one might take up writing haiku to explore its possibilities. Imaginative exploration does not require a belief that its object is the best intellectual practice, the privileged mode of ethical investigations, or the basis for a good life. It does not imply consent that an inquiry into living well is the only or best path for a good life. Nor, as will become apparent, do I share the belief that the search for the good life, as Nussbaum conceives it, is the superordinate good. I remain unpersuaded that there is any such good for all humans, or that this search for the good, however conceived, is the definitional or even a particularly accurate way to characterize human experience. I do not mean to suggest that ethical inquiry is impossible or unimportant; there are, however, many ways to practice it.[6]

Nussbaum and I do share many objections to certain philosophic views. Our shared terrain includes a rejection of the claim that it is possible for an abstract reason to generate transcendental standards for adjudicating conflict. Even if such standards could be posited, they would be of little use in clarifying or resolving problems that subjects face in specific cultural and historical contexts. The unavailability of transcendental algorithms, however, does not imply that only purely local criteria remain. Nor does it follow that one can criticize social practices only from within the stated commitments of the practicing culture.[7]

Both of us reject simple notions of the emotions, whether described as "raw feels" or as impediments to wise decisions about social or philosophic problems. We harbor common concerns about the frequent narrowness of academic philosophy. The restrictions of this philosophy on the material considered germane to its inquiries reproduce this confined scope. I sense in Nussbaum my own aversion to the unnecessary indignities, constrictions, and cruelties inflicted on the less powerful. Our work is shaped by a strong desire to contribute to the lessening of such injustice.

Despite this shared terrain, our paths soon diverge. For me a disturbing disjunction emerged between Nussbaum's political commitments and the effects of her Aristotelian approach. Reading her work leaves me with contradictory feelings: admiration for her passion for justice and resistance to a system of philosophic force whose coherence requires denial of many aspects of the human lives it seeks to enhance. Her practice illustrates the discomforting overlap between dispelling "illusions" that obscure acceptance of objectively true statements and bringing others into line. The shared experience she finds is a consequence of her mode of inquiry rather than an objective grasp of the "deep structures" of the phenomena it analyzes.

Nussbaum might dismiss my concerns as a consequence of a philosophic lack, a mis-educated relativist position. However, her characterization of alternative approaches is too simple. She divides current philosophizing into the Aristotelian, the Kantian, and the postmodernist or relativist. The Kantian (or Platonist) believes that general algorithms or rules exist (or can exist) to resolve ethical problems. She collapses the relativist and the postmodernist. Both can only endorse local evaluative standards. Inevitably, these favor the strong over the weak. The Aristotelian approach represents the philosophic golden mean; it shares the strengths of both while lacking their deficiencies.

None of these positions corresponds to my own. Nussbaum's construction of postmodernist approaches permits an avoidance of the full force of their implications for her assumptions. In her view, postmodernists claim that knowledge and power are identical. Therefore, no knowledge is available to criticize power relations. Because power is everywhere, making discriminations among forms of its exercise is impossible. However, the project of many postmodernists is to track the complex relationships between knowledge and power, not to assert their identity.[8] Postmodernism does not render making ethical or political claims on behalf of the less powerful impossible. Postmodernists often favor those whose marginalization is generated by contemporary circuits of power.[9]

What the postmodernist does have to rule out is the possibility of legitimizing such claims by stipulating an objective single standard of goodness or truth. No standpoint totally unmarked by existing social relations, including those through which power circulates, is available. Hence, what it resists partially constitutes any standard, as does the desire of subjects who construct it. Aspects of such constitution are so embedded in a way of life that they are unknowable to anyone who shares it. Juxtaposing differing commitments can sometimes expose some of these background assumptions. Therefore, assuming incommensurable differences is an ethical commitment. The existence of a single standard can signal coercion, not truth.

I prefer to focus on the process of discovering what makes it possible to believe we have the answers and what motivates our desire for transcultural ones.[10] Often a condition of possibility for certainty is an inattention to another aspect of conversation (and ethics)—listening. Learning how to listen and how to sustain attention is difficult. It requires the willed suspension of belief in one's own position and an imaginative attempt to enter into other worlds. Listening reminds us that communication is interactive and relational; it often changes its participants. It involves a commitment to avoid determining in advance what is right. Listening, like speaking or writing, is necessarily imperfect and inaccurate. There are so many gaps between intention, conscious and unconscious motive, and speech. What we say and hear is shaped by the only partially knowable operations of language.

The purposes of conversation include making space for a multiplicity of voices and developing the skills to hear them. Successful conversation would generate polyphony, not consensus. Fostering polyphony is itself an ethical commitment, for it assumes human fallibility and the temptations of passionate attachment to our own goods. For me, a more salient feature of human practice than seeking the good is the repeated and often lethal efforts to impose such visions on others. Learning to evaluate and often resist such temptations is a central aspect of my understanding of ethics. Lacking the assurance of rightness and transparency to ourselves and others, we must act anyway. This fosters both the freedom and tragedy of action in political and social contexts.

Nussbaum asserts that this stance necessarily restricts the postmodernist to "a reliance . . . on norms that are local both in origin and in application" (p. 243). However, to abandon the project of justifying a single norm does not logically entail or require automatic deference to local ones. Norms that are local in origin can be translocal in application. One can criticize local ones in the name of one's own local one. We can offer a variety of arguments about why ours is better. It might more fully achieve another culture's stated purposes. We might think it is better in terms of its organizing values or the variety of ways of life it makes possible. Furthermore, even within one context, multiple standards and commitments exist. The "received" is not homogeneous. Part of my practice is to identify the gaps, contradictions, and lack of homogeneity within "received" ways of thought. Critical leverage is gained, not by positing universally shared deep experience, but by locating the marginal within the received. The received is dislodged by reconstructing it as a position or a set of positions enabled through power, not truth.

As Nussbaum replies to the Kantian, only if we think some transcultural objective truth exists is its absence a problem for ethical discourse. If all evaluative standards are context-dependent, no one can dismiss them solely on that basis. If social construction is all there is, we cannot refuse ideas simply because they arise from it. We can only require an objective standard if we think it is possible to generate one—

a circular argument. If we do not think it is possible, we will not feel its lack. Nussbaum herself admits that we can critique existing social arrangements by stressing cultural differences (p. 263). What would a social critic gain by engaging in a "critical debate in search of the human good" (p. 262)? In a thoroughly constructed social world, why would one assume such a standard is available or necessary?

Evidently, Nussbaum believes that the claim of objectivity provides additional force to ethical norms. In her quest for objectivity, however, Nussbaum counters the idealized abstractions of Kantian approaches with a concrete abstraction, the good. She universalizes her approach, positing a search for a single good as a general human practice. She thinks that she can ground this claim in actual experience and thereby avoid the criticisms lodged against pure abstraction. I do not think this works. As I will argue below, "experience" cannot ground objective, transhistorical claims about human capabilities or the good. Her concept of objectivity is dependent on claims about practical reason that are highly problematic. Practical reason can locate a single objective standard only if it denies its contextual dependence and complex constitution.

Nussbaum's approach precludes an inquiry into the desire for such a good. The absence of such inquiry undercuts the plausibility of her argument. In Nussbaum's approach, participants in conversation are not equal, for one party a priori has something the other does not (truth on one's side). Nussbaum does not convince this reader of the objectivity, plausibility, payoff, or desirability of such a trump. Nor does she adequately weigh the costs for ethics and political practice of such a belief and its enactment. The effects of these prior commitments often exceed or undermine the analyst's intent. For example, consideration of Nussbaum's spheres of experience reveals that, despite her political commitments, her approach excludes much for which she claims sympathy. This includes many aspects of the imagination and the emotions and important effects of gendered and raced social relations.

PRACTICING ARISTOTELIAN

In pondering Nussbaum's ideas, I identified some of my own. I do not doubt that my beliefs affect my capacity to imagine Nussbaum's approach. To imagine her world, I contemplated this statement: "Providing a powerful account of rational ethical argument seems to me to be one of the central challenges for a practical philosophy, a philosophy that will really help people to make progress on troublesome human problems" (p. 233). I can empathize with a desire for a practical philosophy, defined as one that will help people. (What constitutes "progress" is more problematic.) But why does such a philosophy require a powerful account of rational ethical argument? I tried to identify some assumptions that would render this claim intelligible and persuasive: the capacity for practical reason is universally shared.

Humans want to submit their practices to the scrutiny of practical reason. Living well requires bringing our practices into accordance with practical reason. All humans want to live well; therefore, if one can identify their rational commitments, one can appeal to their reason and persuade them to change their practices. All humans share a process of reasoning; we can count on something reliable and stable for appeal and response. Therefore, engaging in rational ethical argument is a powerful means to make practical progress. It enables us to achieve consensus both on when something is a problem and what should be done about it. As Nussbaum puts it:

> Both Aristotle and Socrates believe that the best articulation of each individual's internal system of beliefs will also be an account shared by all individuals who are capable of seriously pursuing the search for truth. This is so because they believe that the outstanding obstacles to communal agreement are deficiencies in judgment and reflection; if we are each led singly through the best procedures of practical choice, we will turn out to agree on the most important matters, in ethics as in science. I believe that this position is substantially correct.[11]

These assumptions require other ones. We must posit that rational ethical argument has a singular, intrinsic method. Nussbaum believes she has correctly identified it: "an approach based on the concept of human functioning and an idea of the human being" (p. 326). This entails two stages of inquiry: the "initial demarcation of sphere of choice, of the 'grounding experiences' that fix the reference of the virtue term" and the "ensuing more concrete inquiry into what the appropriate choice in that sphere is" (p. 249). The Aristotelian process identifies several spheres "of life with which all human beings regularly, and more or less necessarily, have dealings" and then asks, "what it is to choose and respond well within that sphere? And what is it to choose defectively?" (p. 245). The Aristotelian can confidently enumerate this corresponding set of human virtues. "The 'thin account' of each virtue is that it is whatever being stably disposed to act appropriately in that sphere consists in" (p. 245). These virtues are universal. It does not seem

> an open question, in the case of a particular agent, whether a certain virtue should or should not be included in his or her life—except in the sense that she can always choose to pursue the corresponding deficiency instead. The point is that everyone makes some choices and acts somehow or other in these spheres: if not properly, then improperly. . . . No matter where one lives one cannot escape these questions, so long as one is living a human life" (p. 247).

This approach ensures the possibility of real progress in ethics. "And we can understand progress in ethics, like progress in scientific understanding, to be progress in finding the correct fuller specification of a virtue, isolated by its thin or nominal definition" (p. 248).

POINTS OF DEPARTURE

Nussbaum thoughtfully provides some objections to her own approach. She agrees there is no language-neutral bedrock experience on which an account of virtue can be based (p. 261). However, she claims that such a bedrock is not necessary to make objective claims about grounding experiences and their correlative virtue. This claim is not argued for; she shifts the burden of proof to the relativist: "But the relativist has so far shown no reason why we could not, at the end of the day, say that certain ways of conceptualizing death are more in keeping with the totality of our evidence and the totality of our wishes for flourishing than others . . ." (p. 261). This simply begs the question. The burden of proof rests on her. To say that an idea more approximates the present totality of evidence does not support a claim that an objective standard is possible. It avoids consideration of an important issue: who is the "our" in "our evidence" or our wishes? Unless we presuppose a universal epistemic position for this "we," the correspondence of concept and wish is not evidence of general truth.

To shore up her position, Nussbaum claims, "we do recognize the experiences of people in other cultures as similar to our own. We do converse with them about matters of deep importance, understand them, allow ourselves to be moved by them"(p. 261). What accounts for these feelings, however, is not self-evident. Alternate explanations that do not posit the existence of deep commonalities are equally plausible. We might look at other cultures, imagine we find parallels to our own, translate these phenomena into our own language and then say, "oh, there is another x." I might look at an ancient African statue, admire its formal planes, and conclude that artists everywhere address universal problems. The maker of the statue may not even have thought of himself or herself as an artist. The artist might have been preoccupied with matters utterly foreign to me, such as generating the most powerful totem or creating a tool for certain sacred practices. The statue would have functioned very differently in her or his own context.

The romantic or aesthetically minded among "us" might say that others move us because they are not us. Imagination reworks existing material. The objects we observe, since they are works of imagination, exceed their authors' purposes and cultural contexts, as well as our reading of them. Humans are not transcendent, but works of art are. The Gothic stonemason may have labored on a cathedral's flying buttress to lead our spirit to his God; I, lacking such a belief, admire its architecture. Moderns might focus on the domestic psychodramas of Shakespeare's plays, while his contemporaries may have been amused by his political commentary. Our sense of recognition arises from imaginative transfiguration, not a commonly shared deep structure of already present experience.

The "family relatedness" Nussbaum affirms in support of her position may reflect the effects of categories as they generate and shape observation. We find what our concepts direct and enable us to seek. Nussbaum looks at a variety of human activities practiced over time in many cultures and finds a multitude of Aristotelian philosophers. She assumes that all humans approach life by evaluating alternatives and looking for the best. Everyone is motivated by a "search for the good;" all are "prepared to defend their decisions as good or right" (p. 259). No competing ways of life exist. Evidently people are not driven by a desire for the beautiful, the efficient, the pleasurable, or by spiritual fulfillment. Humans are not simultaneously engaged in multiple searches with different value commitments for each sphere of experience. Her subjects do what she does. Like Nussbaum, "the parties do in fact search for the good, not the way of their ancestors." Not surprisingly, her "inhabitants of different conceptual schemes do tend to view their interaction in the Aristotelian and not relativist way" (p. 262).

Only by excluding other ways societies act can this claim serve as proof of the universality of the Aristotelian approach. Theocracies may evaluate innovations by consulting religious figures about their acceptability according to the appropriate sacred texts. Others, while rejecting the value schemes of their originating culture, may treat technical innovations as potential solutions to their own problems. Bill Gates may celebrate the liberating effects of global communication. Others may welcome computers as devices to better control their population. Innovations are woven into nationalist claims about the need to preserve existing cultures from Western pollution. They are read as evidence of difference and threat, not shared problems.

BACKTRACK

At this point, I will try to bracket my skepticism regarding Nussbaum's claims about grounding experiences. I will consider the question: if there are deep spheres of experience, what might they be? What are these areas of greater universality, family resemblances, and overlap (p. 263)? Is Nussbaum's list reasonably inclusive and accurately described? Are there substantial exclusions or redescriptions that would impel changes in her concepts of human capacities, human life, and human functioning? In considering each of her spheres, I found that alternate constructions are possible, and that important kinds of human practice are missing. This throws into doubt the particular sorts of claims she makes regarding the constitution of human life as lived and its correlated notions of human flourishing and virtue. In the next section I will raise more general questions about her approach.

Nussbaum enumerates the following grounding spheres:

(1) Mortality: knowledge of mortality "shapes every aspect of more or less every human life" (p. 263). As stated, this is so formal as to be empty of content. What cultures do with such knowledge is equally important. There are cultures in which death is salvation and deliverance, not damage. In these cultures, faith might be a correlated virtue, not courage. The agent might not see the exercise of faith as a choice. Furthermore, in cultures where belief in

reincarnation or resurrection is widely shared, mortality may function quite differently than in those lacking it.

Nussbaum simply dismisses such ways of life by asserting that the centrality of human mortality renders belief in immortality irrelevant to "our" lives. She emphasizes our dependence as mortal beings on the world outside us, including food, drink, and the help of others. Why, then does she exclude production from her spheres of experience? It is also odd that while Nussbaum treats death as a grounding experience, she does not consider birth to be one as well. This exclusion is surprising, since a great deal of feminist literature has speculated about the effects on subjects and societies of the (current) fact that we are all "of woman born."[12]

(2) The body:

> We are born with human bodies, whose possibilities and vulnerabilities do not belong to any culture rather than any other. Any given human being might have belonged to any culture. The experience of the body is culturally influenced; but the body itself, prior to such experience, provides limits and parameters that ensure a great deal of overlap in what is going to be experienced, where hunger, desire, and the five senses are concerned" (p. 263).

This suggests a curious, almost Cartesian, body/mind split. How can there be a body prior to cultural experience? The subject's body begins life within another's body; its own body is shaped by what its host eats; its health, diseases, and drug habits; and probably its affective condition. The claim that any given human being might have belonged to any culture does not make sense. Contemporary, middle-class Western bodies are quite different in size, health, and strength from those of many poorer ones today or even from our own not-so-distant ancestors. Many currently existing bodies would be dead if not for socially constructed practices such as inoculation, clean water, and safer birth. Furthermore, this statement excludes the effects of race/gender in marking bodies and determining their fates. Human beings with female bodies could not belong within the culture of the polis. In the United States, white and black bodies have been segregated through force, violence, social custom, and law. Our history of slavery shows that cultures can read bodies so differently that some are not even considered fully human. Nussbaum describes how having a female body in many cultures today will determine a great deal about whether that body's hunger is satisfied or whether its senses are assaulted by rape or other forms of abuse. The coding and experiencing of bodies within race/gender are social, not biological, facts.

(3) Pleasure and pain: Nussbaum believes that every culture displays overlapping conceptions of pain; "these conceptions . . . can plausibly be seen as grounded in universal and pre-cultural experience . . . negative response to bodily pain is surely primitive and universal, rather than learned and optional" (p. 264). The plausibility of this claim again requires us to exclude many human prac-

tices, such as masochism, or the equation of suffering and holiness. Dancers and athletes distinguish between good and bad pain. Excellent performance requires the active undertaking of painful practices.

(4) Cognitive capability: Nussbaum cites Aristotle as the authority here, quoting his claim that "all human beings by nature reach out for understanding" (p. 264). Again, this obliterates quite a few human practices. It excludes the vast number of cultures that reach out for faith or who see human understanding as a mirage. It eliminates, for example, mystical or Zen approaches that seek to quiet or empty the mind.

(5) Practical reason: Nussbaum asserts that "all human beings, whatever their culture, participate (or try to) in the planning and managing of their lives, asking and answering questions about how one should live and act" (p. 264). Nussbaum assumes that everyone is a rational deliberator. Each person approaches life problems with an assumption that there is a rational choice to be made. The way to goodness or a good life is to find the appropriate virtue. Through a process of rationally assessing alternatives, one will figure out what that is. This categorical assertion, too, seems to require the exclusion of many modes of human being; for example, those structured through tradition or faith. Facing a problem, one might ask the rabbi, consult a sacred text or oracle, or talk with a wise man. A religious person may decide to leave such questions in God's hands. Others may strive for detachment or to open themselves up to chance operations. Some humans may hope for redemption to another world or relief from returning through another cycle of reincarnation. Their goal is less enmeshment, including planning and managing, in the material world.

(6) Early infant development: According to Nussbaum, "prior to the greater part of specific cultural shaping, though perhaps not free from all shaping, are certain areas of human experience and development that are broadly shared and of great importance for the Aristotelian virtues: experiences of desire, pleasure, loss, one's own finitude, perhaps also envy, grief, and gratitude" (p. 264). Oddly, though Nussbaum cites Freud and Klein as authorities on human development, she excludes what is for them a central infantile (and innate/human) drive: aggression.[13] Perhaps this exclusion can be explained by the difficulty of imagining a correlative virtue. However, if we list potential candidates for spheres of human experience, surely aggression, violence, war, and killing are widely shared. Furthermore, it is hard to know how to make sense of the claim that emotions like envy, grief, pleasure, loss, or finitude are prior to most cultural shaping. These are profoundly relational emotions, hence subject to pervasive cultural shaping. They are evoked by and experienced in relation to specific human objects. Each emerges within preexisting cultural contexts that determine, for example, how often a baby is fed, how it is talked to or stimulated, who is available to gratify its desires, how

many siblings it has to compete with, and how frequently it is touched or held. The interactive learning of how to get and hold attention and the kinds of caretaking, including attentiveness and responsiveness to desire, shape pleasure and other emotions such as finitude and loss.

Although we may all begin as "hungry babies," concepts of the nature of babies are themselves cultural artifacts. Nussbaum's own characterization of babies as "perceiving their own helplessness, their alternating closeness to and distance from those on whom they depend" reflects a particular, dominant modern Western sensibility (p. 264). An important dilemma for such subjects—separation and individuation—is posited as universally problematic.[14] Furthermore, feeding these hungry babies is not necessarily a universally shared practice. Some female babies are left to die, and the feeders of babies tend to be women. This social division of labor may shape envy, loss, grief, and the experiencing subject.[15]

(7) Affiliation: Humans are social animals. Nussbaum insists that despite variation in conceptions of friendship and love, "there is great point" in seeing them as instances of "shared human needs and desires" (p. 264). However, this point is not clear. As her own consideration of Foucault's work on desire illustrates, needs and desires change. Forms of desire available in other cultures may not be present in ours. Furthermore, how people interpret needs and desires is variable, and their interpretation affects their experience. If neither emotion nor experience are "raw feels," then, in particular cultural contexts, all emotive statements such as "I love you" will be experienced differently by both speaker and listener. Such statements function more like performatives than labels, and their meaning necessarily depends on being embedded in a specific way of life.

It is also curious that Nussbaum excludes an alternative to affiliation—solitude—which many humans crave equally (if not more than) affiliation. Human practices such as imagination and creativity appear to require solitude. Think, for example, of Winnicott's moving accounts of children, lost in play, as a basis for creativity.[16] Since Nussbaum emphasizes sociability and "our" sensitivity to the needs of and our pleasure in the company of beings similar to ourselves, it is equally striking that adult practices of child-rearing are absent from her account of spheres of experience.

(8) Humor: citing Aristotle, Nussbaum calls humans "the laughing animal" (p. 265). Under humor, she includes a need for space for play. Mention of this "need" highlights another surprising gap in her work: a lack of sensitivity to the complexities and compulsions of creativity and imagination. This gap is especially puzzling considering her passionate defense of literature, imagination, and the emotions.[17] Perhaps it is partially a consequence of the "architectonic role" she attributes to affiliation and practical reason. She believes that these two capacities suffuse and organize all others; "all others count as

truly human functions only insofar as they are done with some degree of guidance from both of these" (p. 265). This structuring of capacities necessarily does violence to modes of life in which other qualities such as visual or kinesthetic imagination play an architectonic role. Think, for example, of George Balanchine's famous injunction to his dancers, "don't think; just do," or Edward Weston's orienting his travels through his desire for certain sorts of light.[18] She confidently cites Aristotle's claim that there is no virtue involving the regulation of seeing pleasing sights (p. 248). Humans in some cultures would disagree with Aristotle's claim, evincing instead an intense moral interest in these matters. Consider, for example, the importance of the prohibition of graven images in Orthodox Judaism. This dictum apparently rules out philosophies of visual aesthetics and their related intellectual practices.

Only by excluding such alternate modes of life can Nussbaum make her truth claims. She states, for example, that sensitivity to context is always a virtue. It is never "right only relative to or inside, a limited context." On the contrary, she asserts, "it is right absolutely, objectively, anywhere in the human world, to attend to the particular features of one's context" (p. 257). This, however, is not self-evidently true. Nussbaum assumes detachment or transcendence is wrong; contextual responsiveness is an intrinsic part of getting it right. This injunction may apply to some contexts and some practices, but not others. Writing, painting, choreographing, rebelling politically, or engaging in certain spiritual practices (meditation) often require ignoring particular features of one's own context. Furthermore, subjects often find themselves in multiple contexts with competing contradictory demands regarding sensitivity to them. To satisfy my vision as a writer, I may have to suspend responsiveness to the demands of my parenting context and to the literary conventions of my milieu. I may feel compelled to rigorously attend to the particular features of my spiritual discipline that require me to discard all others.

ADDITIONAL OBJECTIONS

I will make three additional objections to Nussbaum's approach. First, I do not think that concepts of human functioning or capabilities can do the work that Nussbaum wishes. Nussbaum claims that her approach allows one to simultaneously hold onto a general (and open-ended) picture of human life, while at every stage immersing ourselves in the concrete circumstances of history and culture (p. 259). These two facets are far more exclusionary and mutually undermining than she would like. Examining Nussbaum's account of human life as lived demonstrates that the effects of generalization are not neutral. Coherent generalization rests on and requires the exclusion of many other equally plausible narratives. Second, her approach to ethics is not very useful for contemporary political theorizing and practice. She conflates problems of individual and political virtue and choice and obscures their crucial differences. Nussbaum is insufficiently critical of the genealogy of "norms" of flourishing and inattentive to their regulatory effects. Finally, I disagree with her about the purposes of ethical inquiry. The need for political ethics arises because there is no single or objective human good. The possibility of good lives depends on a capacity to forge connections through multiplicity, not on locating common grounding.

Nussbaum claims that Aristotle believes there is "no incompatibility between basing an ethical theory on the virtues and defending the singleness and objectivity of the human good. Indeed, he seems to have believed that these two aims are mutually supportive" (p. 244). However, the basis for Aristotle's confidence is important. These hang together because the ultimate ground of the "single objective account of the human good" is natural law. Natural law is knowable, but not created, by human reason. Intrinsic to being rational is the obligation and capability to discover this law and adjust our souls and social arrangements accordingly. Natural law endows each thing, person, human association, or practice with a particular *telos. Telos* connotes purpose, end, and good. This objectively existing natural order guarantees the identity of the purpose, end, and good of each thing. In realizing its purpose, the thing also attains its natural completion and its good.[19]

Rather than employing the vocabulary of natural law, Nussbaum deploys "human nature." However, human nature provides the same grounding for her as natural law does for Aristotle. In substituting human nature, Nussbaum makes a move that is common in modern political thought.[20] Its purpose is to deduce incontestable claims about the good or the state from objective statements about human nature. However, this move is deeply problematic. It requires an assumption that human nature is a stable object, fixed rather than evolving. This excludes the possibility that entire ways of being might die out or be exterminated. Some ways of being are so context-specific as to be incomprehensible outside it. Furthermore, the meanings and uses of the term human nature are notoriously slippery and contested. Annas, for example, distinguishes three notions of human nature:

> an empirical notion: what we find out about ourselves and refine in an ongoing way as we learn more about various forms of social life . . . a conceptual notion: what is shared and obvious and can be appealed to in a distinctively human form of life . . . a moral notion: a normative idea playing a determinate role in an ethical theory."[21]

Nussbaum conflates these three (the empirical, the conceptual, and the moral). She confuses human capacities with human nature. She moves too readily from listing (empirical) capacities to a normative narrative of human nature. Since this is predicated on the view that such capabilities reflect "deep structures," identifying such capacities cannot provide evidence for the accuracy of her belief. Even assuming that such deep structures could exist, it is not evident that they could ground ethics.

Nussbaum's own list of "human capacities" is very restricted and predetermines the successful outcome she finds. Recurrent features of human practices such as aggression, hate, rationalization, or cruelty are absent. Without such selectivity, it is evident that identifying and building moral theory on "what is deepest" is problematic. What if what is deepest is not the basis for virtue? For Freud, what is deepest is that "man is wolf to man."[22] What is the corresponding virtue to Freud's death instinct or Hobbes' war of all against all?

Nussbaum assumes that human capacities bring with them a moral weight and an obligation for fulfillment within a good life. Identifying what is shared or enumerating our deepest commitments will necessarily lead to a normative idea of human functioning/nature. However, without prior supporting assumptions about its innate qualities, human nature cannot itself be a moral notion. What moral conclusions can we draw, if as Machiavelli says, "what we are and what we would like to be are so different?[23] If human nature means "the way we are"—but this is not already moralized—it might provide a basis for moral judgments. To be plausible, this requires an implicit teleology in which nature, purpose, end, and good are intertwined. Understanding the nature of a thing tells us its purpose and its good. However, Nussbaum does not provide a convincing argument for this teleology. Without it, the moral force of constructing a narrative of a general notion of a human life is lost.

It is equally plausible that the practices she surveys are not instances of a common x. The commonality she sees could be a function of definition. The ordered patterns could reflect the effects of social expectations, chance, shared language games, convention, or force. If the background world is random and chaotic, order might be a function of control, not rightness. Furthermore, we have to make some problematic assumptions to connect the ideas of an "objective human morality based on the idea of virtuous action" and "appropriate functioning in each human sphere" (p. 250). We have to assume that appropriate functioning in each sphere requires virtuous action, a virtue that is good in some cross-sphere sense. We then have to presuppose what is in question, that people do in fact seek the good and that there is a single, generalizable good available. This excludes the possibility that to do it well, each sphere requires a variety of functioning. Some required capabilities might not even be called good in that sphere, much less in another one. Conversely, function in a sphere, say waging war, may have correlated standards that are not generalizable to other ones.

Despite her eloquent writings on the complexity of emotions, Nussbaum's argument depends on a split between reason and emotion. It rests on three background assumptions: that we can grasp some things about experience separate from our interpretations of it, that reason has the capacity to recognize these deep structures, and that submitting human activity to the categorization of reason has no intrinsic effects on the resulting analysis. As Nussbaum acknowledges, each of these postulates is highly contested and problematic. However, she underestimates how her own work illustrates the force of contrary positions. It must preclude in advance the existence and effects of something like an unconscious. According to Nussbaum, emotion can be "highly discriminating evaluative responses, very closely connected to beliefs about what is valuable and what is not." Reasoned argument can change the heart or "powerfully influences a person's passions and motivations" (p. 239). Her argument, however, would be in trouble if passion, desire, and irrationality were intrinsic, not simply complementary to, reason. The blurring together of reason and rationalization is not considered. Somehow rational deliberation is self-correcting. It is not shaped by desires that remain inaccessible to the conscious mind. She also does not do justice to the positive possibilities of the resistance of imagination to reason or to the importance of fantasy as a human capacity. This rationalism diminishes the usefulness of her approach, especially in understanding or ameliorating political problems.

A central postmodernist claim about language is that it affects the construction of experience and thinking about it. Nussbaum acknowledges that this postulate has some validity. However, her way of connecting spheres of experience and virtue employs a surprisingly nominalist view of language. She quotes Wittgenstein, but evidently disregards his linguistic philosophy. As she describes it, we "begin with some experiences—not necessarily our own, but those of members of our linguistic community, broadly construed. On the basis of these experiences, a word enters the language of the group (referring to) whatever it is that is the content of those experiences" (p. 247). This is not a plausible account of the relationship between word and experience.

As Nussbaum admits, experience is already linguistically organized. Words are saturated with social meanings. They incorporate accounts of experience and ways of recognizing it as a case of x as opposed to y. It is not possible to have social experience outside language. Nussbaum says "experiences fix the reference of the corresponding virtue word" (p. 248). However, the word does not exist outside the reference of the corresponding experience—which is socially constructed.

Despite her intent, thinking about naming opens up investigation into the relationship between naming and power. Nussbaum's value commitments lead her to overestimate the role of rational inquiry in generating ethical "progress." Naming, whether of virtues or any other human practice, both generates and reflects power. Often thought is after the fact; for example, what some now call marital rape was once called marital rights. This change of vocabulary is a consequence of the changed views of women as a result of social movements, not a rational search for more accurate descriptions of things. Through action, the object itself has changed. These new circumstances can affect the definition of virtue, or change virtue altogether. In naming, as Hobbes recognizes, we are not doing something outside culture.[24] It is a social practice, not a matter of putting neutral labels on things. This would especially seem to apply to complex terms such as virtues. Virtues function more like performatives than nominals. What creates the sense of appropriateness is the internal logic of the practice, which takes on meaning from and is internal to the culture.[25] Intrinsic to such practices is establishing which subjects' sense of appropriateness must be satisfied in generating and applying a particular norm.

Nussbaum has a very limited view of ethics. Despite her intentions, her approach is of little use in politics—unless we make the Platonic assumption that the state is simply the soul writ large. According to her, the task of government is to "make available to each and every member of the community the basic necessary conditions of the capability to choose and live a fully good human life, with respect to each of the major human functions included in that fully good life" (p. 265). For an Aristotelian, this is a surprisingly individualist view of the nature of politics. Nussbaum's account entails a collapse of individual ethical inquiry and collective levels of politics. According to her, ethics concerns "living well as a human being" (p. 333). This definition can be generalized only if one assumes, as Aristotle does, that the best polis and the best person can coincide or possess and require the same virtues. However, it is not clear that this is the case, especially in modern states with their centralized bureaucracies and their technologies of mass violence. As Machiavelli recognized, the virtues required for ruling or being a good citizen are not necessarily the same as those required for individual goodness. The good ruler or citizen and the good person may not coincide. This is not just a problem of a "plurality of components" (p. 333), which may conflict, but a plurality of lives, each with their own good(s) and purposes.

Following Nussbaum's own maxim, in politics, it is frequently a mistake to ignore specific contexts. Inquiry at a structural level is different, because politics involves problems such as the collective use of violence and the distribution of public goods. The requirements of individual virtue or rational choice do not necessarily tell us what is needed at structural levels to produce the flourishing of public spheres. Sometimes these requirements may be irreconcilable.[26] Asking the question, "what it is to live the life of a *human being*, and not some other life?" (p. 266) may not be the most salient starting point in the making of public policy.

Furthermore, Nussbaum does not place this question into its context or pursue its political costs. She seems to assume that for twentieth-century citizens, it can have the same genealogy, meanings, and effects as it did for the classic Greeks. However, this simply ignores a major transformation in the organization of modern states and the contemporary circulation of power: the emergence of biopower. Modernity is saturated with new mechanisms of power. These claim the body and human life as their rightful domain. Power is expressed through the creation of norms and the regulation of the population. As Foucault puts it, "what was demanded and what served as an objective was life, understood as the basic needs, man's concrete essence, the realization of his potential, a plenitude of the possible."[27]

The state's concern for the proliferation of the population and its standard of living is not an unalloyed good. Concepts of "flourishing" are deeply shaped by processes of normalization. In making demands on the state for the necessary conditions to live a fully good human life, we are also ratifying the legitimacy of its interest in and control over bodies and populations. Connecting the state to human flourishing entails generating and participating in ever-widening circuits of power, regulation, and normalization. To meet these expectations, new regulatory mechanisms with their administrative apparatus, norms, appropriate knowledge, and experts arise. Demands must be translated into bureaucratic form, conforming to the standards of the appropriate agency. In formulating political theories and practices, it is important to recognize the costs of locating ethical demands within circuits of biopower. It is as likely that assigning to the state the care of the population's flourishing will lead to increased regulatory control as greater human well-being. For example, in the area of public health, policies of forced sterilization result as frequently as good medical care. This is not to say that no such demands should be made, but any chance of minimizing the costs requires recognition of our context's intrinsic dangers.

My basic disagreements with Nussbaum do not arise from a belief that an inclusive or even more accurate account of experience and virtue is possible. Rather, I worry about the plausibility and costs of her project. Nussbaum's narrative shows the slippery character of "experience" and its inability to ground anything, including claims about human nature or functioning.[28] One necessarily begins with a concept of human capacities; the diversity of human practices is organized into spheres of experience (and contradictory practices are excluded). Analysis of these spheres then confirms the concept. Any accounting of spheres already presupposes ideas about what a flourishing life entails, what virtues count, and where excellence can exist. This is evident in Nussbaum's treatment of faith and spiritual world views and imaginative/creative ones—both spheres in which practical reason is not the most appropriate or useful faculty. It presupposes a hierarchy of excellence, capacities, and virtues, and describes life accordingly.

Nussbaum underestimates the difficulties and the potential dangers of looking for what is shared. The coherence of Nussbaum's narrative incurs high costs. The plausibility of her claims requires subordinating or translating many modes of life into hers: the realization of a particular idea of living well. However, her approach reveals more about the power of conceptual schemes than human practices. The specificity of her commitments cannot be obviated by her claim that lives lived according to other ones are simply not fully human lives. This argument presupposes what is in question: that Nussbaum has objective knowledge that other subjects have yet to attain about true human flourishing.

Even if we localize her claim to the contemporary West, Nussbaum's notion of what humans seek is too homogeneous. For her, living well incorporates the Aristotelian processes of balancing, moderation, rational choice, etc. However, this vision cannot do justice to alternate, equally compelling ones. Not all humans seek lives in which reason and affiliation play architectonic roles. Some humans seek modes of life that favor the romantic, unbalanced, and obsessed; as Neil Young sings, they find it is better to burn out than to rust.[29]

Finally, I want to return to the double-edged quality of Nussbaum's approach. A desire for a single standard has consequences that exceed our intents. Although we may search for a singular, binding standard in an effort to hold dictators or torturers accountable, deciding that some "lives fall altogether beyond the pale of humanness" is a dangerous enterprise. Paradoxically, given Nussbaum's commitments, I think hers is a fundamentally Platonic wager. It requires a belief in the purifying power of reason and the goodness of the inquirer that is beyond my range of capabilities. I am too skeptical to put my faith in the objectivity of any such standard and too suspicious of my own will to power to believe in the neutrality of such an inquiry. Lacking such a faith, it is too easy for me to recall recent, much less benign, uses of such phrases as lives that fall "beyond the pale of humanness." A reduction of domination and injustice is more likely to follow from the assumption that many of us, in different ways, suffer from a lack of *paideia*. Sometimes the distribution of power permits only a singular voice, sometimes the structure of discourse we have created silences subjects. The content of speech and the social locations of speakers cannot be utterly separate. Breakdowns in communication have many causes; they cannot all be attributed to the lacks of the listener. What appears to be communication is already broken down, fragmented, within and between speakers and listeners.

If philosophy, at "the level of basic principles" is a matter of bringing isolated people into line, then ethics ought to include an inquiry into the desire of the philosopher. Here Aristotle cannot help us. Instead we could turn to Freud, Nietzsche, Foucault, and others who suggest that ethics require a persistent interrogation of the subjects of authoritative speech. Many important ethical dilemmas are neither generated nor resolved by what is held in common. The need for ethics is highest when incommensurable differences arise, and, as this encounter evinces, such differences pervade human life as it is lived now.

NOTES

1. Martha C. Nussbaum, *The Fragility of Goodness: Luck and Ethics in Greek Tragedy and Philosophy* (Cambridge, Mass.: University of Cambridge Press, 1986), 252–53. Nussbaum also cites this statement by Aristotle in "Sophistry About Conventions," in her *Love's Knowledge: Essays on Philosophy and Literature* (New York: Oxford University Press, 1990), 223. Here she characterizes the statement as "wry" rather than somewhat grim.

2. Martha C. Nussbaum, "Non-Relative Virtues: An Aristotelian Approach," in *The Quality of Life*, ed. Martha C. Nussbaum and Amartya Sen (Oxford: Clarendon Press, 1993), 327. Subsequent references to this essay in this chapter are cited with the page number in parentheses; several references to the same page in a single paragraph are cited at the end of the paragraph.

3. Many of the ideas in this paper emerged through conversation with Joan Retallack. I am grateful for our continued banquets of food, wine, and thought.

4. See, for example, Nussbaum, "Introduction: Form and Content, Philosophy and Literature," in *Love's Knowledge*, 3–53; Jane Flax, *Thinking Fragments: Psychoanalysis, Feminism & Postmodernism in the Contemporary West* (Berkeley, Calif.: University of California Press,

1990), chapter 1; and Jane Flax, "Minerva's Owl: Fragments of a Thinking Life," in *Disputed Subjects: Essays on Psychoanalysis, Politics and Philosophy* (New York: Routledge, 1993), 3–33.

5. Nussbaum, *The Quality of Life*, 242–76.

6. Quite the contrary, I have written extensively on such topics. See, for example, my "The Play of Justice," in *Disputed Subjects*, 111–28; and Jane Flax, *The American Dream in Black and White: The Clarence Thomas Hearings* (Ithaca, N.Y.: Cornell University Press, 1998), especially chapter 8.

7. I have written before on these topics and will not rehash my arguments here. See Jane Flax, "Responsibility without Grounds," in *Rethinking Knowledge: Reflections Across the Disciplines*, ed. Robert F. Goodman and Walter F. Fisher (Albany: SUNY Press, 1995), 147–67; and Jane Flax, "Displacing Woman: Towards an Ethics of Multiplicity," in *Daring to Be Good: Essays in Feminist Ethico-Politics*, ed. Bat-Ami Bar On and Ann Ferguson (New York: Routledge, 1998), 143–55.

8. Michel Foucault, for one, emphasizes this point frequently. See his "Truth and Power," in *Power/Knowledge: Selected Interviews & Other Writings, 1972–1977*, ed. Colin Gordon (New York: Pantheon, 1980), 109–33; and his "On Power," in *Michel Foucault: Politics, Philosophy and Culture, Interviews and Other Writings, 1977–1984*, ed. Lawrence D. Kritzman (New York: Routledge, 1990), 96–109.

9. Contemporary writers/activists concerned with issues of race/gender and sexuality, for example, acknowledge their indebtedness to postmodernists such as Foucault. See, for example, *Representing Black Men*, ed. Marcellus Blount and George P. Cunningham (New York: Routledge, 1996); Naomi Zack, *Race/Sex: Their Sameness, Difference and Interplay* (New York: Routledge, 1997); and *Feminist Genealogies, Colonial Legacies, Democratic Futures*, ed. M. Jacqui Alexander and Chandra Talpe Mohanty (New York: Routledge, 1997).

10. I argue this in more detail in *Thinking Fragments*, "Responsibility without Grounds," and "Race/Gender and the Ethics of Difference: A Reply to Okin's Gender Equality and Cultural Differences," *Political Theory* 23, no. 3 (August 1995): 500–510.

11. Nussbaum, *The Fragility of Goodness*, 11.

12. This phrase is Adrienne Rich's. See her *Of Woman Born: Motherhood as Experience and Institution* (New York: W. W. Norton, 1976), and also Dorothy Dinnerstein, *The Mermaid and the Minotaur: Sexual Arrangements and Human Malaise* (New York: Harper & Row, 1976).

13. See Sigmund Freud, *The Ego and the Id* (New York: W. W. Norton, 1960); and Melanie Klein, "On the Development of Mental Functioning," in her *Envy and Gratitude and Other Works 1946–1963* (New York: Dell, 1975), 236–46.

14. On this point, see Jessica Benjamin, *The Bonds of Love: Psychoanalysis, Feminism, and the Problem of Domination* (New York: Pantheon, 1988), especially chapter 5; Alan Roland, *In Search of Self in India and Japan: Toward a Cross-Cultural Psychology* (Princeton, N. J.: Princeton University Press, 1988); Anne Parsons, *Belief, Magic, and Anomie: Essays in Psychosocial Anthropology* (New York: The Free Press, 1969), especially chapters 13 and 14; and Jane Flax, "Taking Multiplicity Seriously: Some Implications for Psychoanalytic Theorizing and Practice," *Contemporary Psychoanalysis* 32, no. 4: 1996, 577–93.

15. In *The Mermaid and the Minotaur*, Dinnerstein opens up many, still underexplored, ways to think about these relationships.

16. D. W. Winnicott, *Playing and Reality* (New York: Basic Books, 1971); and "The

Capacity to Be Alone," in *The Maturational Processes and the Facilitating Environment* (New York: International Universities Press, 1965), 29–36.

17. However, it fits with the rather narrow ways she analyzes literature. Literature's importance for her seems to be didactic. It offers a source of moral lessons and evidence for commonly shared values. She rarely discusses other aspects of literature such as experimentation (with forms and language), the pleasure of writing and reading, or the desire of the writer to generate imaginative recreations of or alternatives to currently available experience. See for example, Nussbaum, *Love's Knowledge*, especially chapters 4, 6, and 9.

18. On Balanchine, see Francis Mason, *I Remember Balanchine: Recollections of the Dance Master by Those Who Knew Him* (New York: Doubleday, 1991). According to his dancers, while its requirements are neither derived from nor organized through practical reason, Balanchine taught them that ballet is a profoundly ethical practice. See Robert Tracy with Sharon DeLano, *Balanchine's Ballerinas: Conversations with the Muses* (New York: Simon & Schuster, 1983). On Edward Weston, see Charis Wilson and Wendy Madar, *Through Another Lens: My Years with Edward Weston* (New York: North Point Press, 1998), 49. Perhaps if Nussbaum put philosophizing into conversation with other arts, especially ones not dependent on writing, her approach might be somewhat altered.

19. Aristotle, *The Politics* (London: Penguin, 1981), 59.

> Therefore every state exists by nature, as the earlier associations too were natural. The association is the end of those others, and nature is itself an end; for whatever is the end product of the coming into existence of any object, that is what we call its nature—of a man, for instance, or a horse or a household. Moreover the aim and the end is perfection; and self-sufficiency is both end and perfection.

On Aristotle's teleology and its centrality to his political and ethical thought, see Ernest Baker, *The Political Thought of Plato and Aristotle* (New York: Dover, 1959), especially chapters 6 and 8.

20. Hobbes, of course, develops his claims in direct opposition to the "schoolmasters"—proponents of natural law. Thomas Hobbes, *The Leviathan*, ed. C. B. Macpherson (Baltimore: Penguin, 1968), especially chapter 3, part I. Niccolo Machiavelli, *The Prince*, ed. Quentin Skinner and Russell Price (Cambridge, Mass.: Cambridge University Press, 1988), especially chapter XVII, claims that humans by nature are selfish and greedy. Hobbes and Rousseau believe virtues are conventional; humans by nature are not sociable. Jean Jacques Rousseau, *Discourse on the Origin and Foundations of Inequality*, ed. Roger D. Masters (New York: St. Martins, 1964), especially First Part. Sigmund Freud, *Civilization and Its Discontents* (New York: W. W. Norton, 1961), especially chapter III, claims that the deepest structure of human life is the unconscious drives, especially *eros* and *thanatos*. The immense variation in claims about human nature, all offered with great confidence and conviction by their authors, is an additional reason for my skepticism about the usefulness of this approach.

21. Julia Annas, "Women and the Quality of Life: Two Norms or One," in *The Quality of Life*, 291.

22. Freud, *Civilization*, 58.

23. Machiavelli, *The Prince*, 54.

24. Hobbes, *The Leviathan*, chapter 18, part II.

25. On performatives, language, and politics, see Hanna Fenichel Pitkin, *Wittgenstein and Justice: On the Significance of Ludwig Wittgenstein for Social and Political Thought* (Berkeley, Calif.: University of California Press, 1972).

26. Machiavelli, *The Prince*, especially chapters XV to XX; Max Weber, "Politics as a Vocation," in *From Max Weber: Essays in Sociology*, ed. H. H. Gerth and C. Wright Mills (New York: Oxford University Press, 1985), 77–128. On constructing specifically political ethics, see Anna Yeatman, *Postmodern Revisioning of the Political* (New York: Routledge, 1994); *Deconstruction and the Possibility of Justice*, ed. Drucilla Cornell, Michel Rosenfeld, and David Gray Carlson (New York: Routledge, 1992); Wendy Brown, *States of Injury: Power and Freedom in Late Modernity* (Princeton, N.J.: Princeton University Press, 1995); Bonnie Honig, *Political Theory and the Displacement of Politics* (Ithaca, N.Y.: Cornell University Press, 1993); Melissa A. Orlie, *Living Ethically: Acting Politically* (Ithaca, N.Y.: Cornell University Press, 1997); and Flax, *The American Dream*, chapter 8.

27. Michel Foucault, "Right of Death and Power Over Life," in *The Foucault Reader*, ed. Paul Rabinow (New York: Pantheon, 1984), 266–67. See also Brown, *States of Injury*; and *The Foucault Effect: Studies in Governmentality*, eds. Graham Burchell, Colin Gordon, and Peter Miller (Chicago: University of Chicago Press, 1991).

28. On this point, see Joan Scott's classic article, "Experience," in *Feminists Theorize the Political*, eds. Judith Butler and Joan Scott (New York: Routledge, 1993), 22–40.

29. It is not even clear how representative Aristotle's idea of living well is of his local context. Evidently many competing life worlds existed even in classic Greece. How classical Athenians imagined their worlds is unknowable. Their worlds are reimagined through subsequent cultures. Western writers seem particularly prone to use "the Greeks" or "the classical world" as a screen onto which their own dilemmas are projected and worked through. Famous reconstructions include Friedrich Nietzsche, *The Birth of Tragedy* (New York: Random House, 1967); E. R. Dodds, *The Greeks and the Irrational* (Berkeley, Calif.: University of California Press, 1973); and Michel Foucault, *The History of Sexuality*, 3 vols. (New York: Vintage, 1990). Each of these authors' narratives differs radically from Nussbaum's Aristotelian one.

3

A Constructionist Despite Herself?
On Capacities and Their Discontents

Jane Flax

Martha Nussbaum's "In Defense of Universal Values" (chapter 1) provides an eloquent rebuttal to her own central claims. She does not and cannot provide universal norms that serve as preemptive standards for evaluative judgment. Rather than persuade her readers that universal norms are possible, she elegantly demonstrates that the appearance of universality is an effect of particular contexts. Her norms cannot do the work she hopes—to provide universally binding principles that will underpin political constitutions or guarantee their goodness. Nor can these norms serve as universal standards by which to judge actually existing states. She disproves her claim that universals are required to protect her preferred values. Formulating the norms as a set of capabilities for fully human functioning starkly reveals their social and historical determination. The narratives from her fieldwork call into question the political efficacy of her capabilities approach. Instead, they suggest that protecting human freedom requires a radical questioning of Nussbaum's own "political-liberal" commitments. Nussbaum does show that if a society is committed to a way of life that incorporates freedom of choice, diversity, pluralism, and the dignity of the individual, it ought to take her policy recommendations seriously. Even for pragmatic purposes, however, Nussbaum's approach is problematic. She fails to persuade her readers that her preferred way of life and its correlative norms and political strategies will reduce gender domination or promote human flourishing.

My disagreement with Nussbaum's approach does not arise from its context dependence. I do not believe any approach could be otherwise. Basic ethical commitments are matters of belief, not rational argument or empirical evidence. They are striations in what Wittgenstein calls an "ungrounded ground," background sets of practices and beliefs comprising particular ways of life.[1] Mine are not the objections—culture, diversity, and paternalism—she addresses. I agree that asserting it is a priori disrespectful to evaluate other cultures by "extrinsic" standards is mistaken. However, my basis for this claim differs. My belief in the social construction of human practices makes me highly suspicious of arguments stemming from cultural integrity or "tradition." Cultures and traditions are not independently existing homogeneous facts residing in the world, nor are claims to their authority or interpretation unmarked by the will to power.

I agree that to assert the impossibility of ethical and multicultural discourse based on the situatedness of its participants is equally mistaken.[2] Distributions of power often do create advantaged and disadvantaged positions. However, no one operates outside social relations. Contexts both enable and constrain the generation of claims, including normative ones. Without them no intelligible practice is possible. Therefore, the sheer presence of necessarily partial and determined subjects and practices does not undermine the possibility of ethical discourse or justice. Partiality of a claim per se neither invalidates it nor renders it oppressive.

However, as I will discuss in this chapter, unlike Nussbaum, I do not think any norm can be universal in the sense that it does not favor some goods over others. I would argue, for example, that her particular, interwoven constellation of norms and practices could only be intelligible in certain historical contexts. While they are not Western, they are probably modern. They are generated by and reflect ways of life that did not exist before the eighteenth century. I doubt that any devout tenth-century peasant would find them appealing. Their historical specificity does not invalidate them, but it ought to induce caution about what gives her claims force.

My most serious problems with her approach, however, reside elsewhere than in the particularities of its "capacities" contents. They concern Nussbaum's denial of the context-dependent nature of her claims, her positing of them as universals, and her assertion that normative discourse requires universal values. Not only are these claims untenable, but they are self-defeating. Much of the richness of her work lies in its attention to context. This conflict between theory and content creates many tensions in the text. The effort to preserve her universalizing project despite its contradictory material results in theoretical incoherence. The meaning of "universal" is increasingly elusive and confusing. She still provides no persuasive argument for why the mere existence of capacities compels any moral duty. Why these generate political obligations for the nation-state is even less clear. Tying her account of these capacities to the protection of political-liberal values further undermines her claim of metaphysical neutrality. I am more skeptical than she of the utility of state intervention (at least most currently existing states) for such purposes. Partially this is because I focus more on the enormous power of modern states and their capacities for harm (many examples of which Nussbaum herself provides). Although Nussbaum provides wonderful narratives of gender relations, placing politics within the framework of universal norms is counterproductive. Redistribution of power is the solution her material suggests. Even if it were possible, I do not see how articulating universal norms will achieve this end. I will develop each of these points further below.

NUSSBAUM'S ONTOLOGY

Nussbaum's profession of "metaphysical agnosticism" is unpersuasive. Her position requires the auxiliary support of highly contested metaphysical and ontological beliefs. Despite enlisting Rawls for support, she is not a deontological moral philosopher.[3] The coherence of her argument requires the belief that there is a good and that this good should have priority. This grounding generates and gives coherence and weight to her claims that definitive human capacities exist and that their existence intrinsically compels a moral duty of fulfillment.

Her "core idea seems to be that of the human being as a dignified free being who shapes his or her own life."[4] Allegiance to this core idea enables Nussbaum to delineate what appear to her to be universalizable dimensions of a life worth living. This commitment produces her preference for "a universal normative account that allows people plenty of liberty to pursue their own conceptions of value, within limits set by the protection of the equal worth of the liberties of others" (p. 10). Why else would she require an account that preserves "liberties and opportunities for each and every person, taken one by one, respecting each of them as an end, rather than simply as the agent or supporter of ends of others" (p. 10)?

However, her standards exist and are binding only within a particular way of life and its correlative values. Nussbaum's favored way of life is a "political-liberal" one. Like any way of life, this one is predicated on and upholds certain core goods. It requires and cannot be free of metaphysical commitments. As she tells us, she prefers:

> a form of universalism that is compatible with freedom and choice of the most significant sorts. But such respect naturally leads us to value religious toleration, associative freedom, and the other major liberties. These liberties are themselves universal values, and they are not compatible with views that many real people and societies hold (p. 9).

However, the identity of this "us" is not clear. Nor is it obvious how respect for each human life "naturally" leads to the values she lists or in what sense they are universal. "Universal" cannot mean empirically universal, since many people do not share such values. Perhaps universal means right or true, but recognizing their beliefs as errors would require that many real people and societies change their ways of life. Universal, then, cannot mean neutral in the sense that commitment to these values does not favor any way of life.

Nussbaum hopes to avoid these problems by formulating her norms as a "universal" set of human capabilities. She claims to select "capabilities that are of central importance in any human life, whatever else the person pursues or chooses" (p. 14). However, what is central in human life, the value of particular capabilities, and the concept of capacity itself are derivative of her commitments to a way of life. Nussbaum's values dictate the organization of diverse human practices into her conceptual scheme (the "capabilities," for example). The concept of capability pre-supposes the priority of purposive individual action and actualization. Her scheme and its capacities make sense within a liberal world view. As she says, "we are forced by our interest in diversity itself to develop a set of criteria against which to assess the practices we find" (p. 11). This interest:

> nudges us strongly in the direction of what might be called *political* rather than *comprehensive liberalism* . . . it urges us to respect the many different conceptions of the good citizens may have . . . we want universals . . . that create spaces for choice. . . . For it is all about respect for the dignity of persons as choosers. This respect requires us to defend universally a wide range of liberties, plus their material conditions, and to defend them for each and every person (p. 11).

Her capacities do "have a special claim to be supported for political purposes in a pluralist society" (p. 14). This context dependence, however, means that a notion of "human life" conceived in terms of capabilities cannot justify or underpin the way of life it presupposes. Its organizing categories cannot serve as universal or deontological norms. The value of these capacities is derivative and not probative of the goodness of her preferred way of life. These commitments necessarily exclude ways of life that reject the idea that all persons are of equal moral worth or that liberty means maximal individual freedom of choice. Advocates of alternatives are not all tyrants or anti-universalists. A Platonist, for example, would reject most of Nussbaum's premises. Subjects situated within cultures lacking a moral notion of *individual* agency or preferring contemplation to action might find the organization of human practice into "capacities" quite puzzling.

Developing some of the capacities Nussbaum lists would be offensive to and destructive of ways of life that incorporate alternative ideas of the fully human. Such societies do not violate "universal norms" when they fail to create environments that nurture certain capacities. They do contradict the (perfectly defensible) demands of justice congruent with other ways of life. Their acts are unjust only for those with a certain vision of the good and its correlated ideas about what constitutes a fully human life. Nussbaum's argument would be stronger if she acknowledged her ontological premise and defended it as such. Her preferred way of life is well worth defending, but the strategy here is self-defeating.

HUMAN CAPABILITIES AND MORAL CLAIMS

Nussbaum yokes together three very different ideas: (1) we can identify activities characteristically performed by humans; (2) some of these are so central that they seem definitive of a life that is truly human; and (3) the very existence of such activities logically and necessarily entails a universal obligation to protect the functions without which (meaning the availability of which) we would regard a life as not, or not fully, human (pp. 12–13).

In support of these claims, she offers only an ill-supported intuition. This

> basic intuition from which the capability approach begins in the political arena is that human abilities exert a moral claim that they should be developed. Human beings are creatures such that, provided with the right educational and material support, they can become fully capable of these human functions (p. 16).

A cursory survey of contemporary moral philosophy suggests that Nussbaum's intuition regarding capacities and moral claims is neither basic nor a necessary condition for moral discourse.[5] Even if humans engage in certain activities across cultures, it does not follow that these constitute moral capabilities or that ways of doing them can function as universal norms. We may be capable of these functions, but this tells us nothing about why the environment, much less the state, should provide support for them. It also does not tell us why such capabilities have moral force.

What transforms a recurrent human practice into a normative capacity? Violence and cruelty are common human practices. We also share a capacity for illness and death. Yet Nussbaum clearly states that the mere existence over time or cultures of an ability does not transform it into a moral claim. She does not insist that all such human practices, for example, the unprovoked killing of other humans, demand development. On the contrary, as she indicates in the manuscript from which this essay is derived, capacities such as cruelty lack moral force. However, she only offers a circular argument for why this is so—such qualities lack moral standing. She says, "not all actual human abilities exert a moral claim, only the ones that have been evaluated as valuable from an ethical viewpoint."[6]

A standard extrinsic to the capabilities must, therefore, exist that enables us to determine which capacities exert normative force. This background standard, not human capacities per se, would be the ground of their normativity. It would also generate the correlative political duties. Nussbaum's ungrounded ground generates her intuitions. As she says, she "begin(s), then, with a sense of the worth and dignity of basic human powers" (p. 16). These basic human powers exist independently of their empirical exercise. They are metaphysical in the sense that they are innate positive human potentials awaiting actualization; the term *capabilities* is appropriate within her scheme. Without this assumption and its implicit teleology, we cannot arrive at her second premise: that these powers generate "claims to a chance for functioning, claims that give rise to correlated social and political duties" (p. 16).

Even if we could agree that a universalist typology of "human capabilities" is possible, what follows? We might grant that these capacities are worth developing, either for their instrumentality to a way of life or as ends in themselves. The mere belief that human capabilities exist does not compel the conclusion that, therefore, the state is obligated to ensure their functioning. The premise regarding the state requires an additional set of beliefs and arguments. These concern the nature of the modern nation state and the basis of its legitimacy. In addition to the problems of obligation, the belief that the state is a desirable locus of demand or provision is also not self-evident. One does not have to accept Foucaultian critiques of law or bureaucratic regulation and normalization to be alert to the ambiguities of the relationships between modern states and human well-being. One might as readily cite Isaiah Berlin's or John Stuart Mill's ideas to support a wary approach.

ON THE NECESSITY OF UNIVERSAL NORMS

While she has refined her description of central human capacities, Nussbaum's basic claim is unchanging and unequivocal. Justice cannot exist without a binding consensus on a universalist account of human functioning and its regulative force. Those most deprived of support for the essential human capacities (often women outside the West) have the most urgent need for such norms. Denying their existence casts such persons into a permanent abyss of hopelessness and oppression. However, despite her attractive, passionate commitment to justice and the considerable rhetorical force of her arguments, Nussbaum is not persuasive.

The meaning of "universal" remains elusive. Does it mean applicable to all, a general right in the sense that all are entitled to it, or absolutely true and binding independent of cultural beliefs and practices? Now that these norms take the form of capabilities, its meaning is even murkier. Nussbaum delineates three kinds of capabilities: innate, internal, and combined (p. 16). She is clear that her list enumerates combined capacities. The term "combined" applies because, while humans may have an innate ability to exercise such capacities, the ability to do so requires environmental support. As expressed, then, any capacity is a product of interaction between the individual and her social world. If this is the case, the capacity as exercised and observable is heavily shaped by its production within a particular culture. What we are pointing to as a capacity may be so intrinsic to a particular way of life that we mistake one of its products for a universal. Furthermore, since thought itself is a combined capacity (p. 14), it is also shaped by its environment. What we conceive as a capacity shared across time and space may be quite heterogeneous behavior. We organize observed activity into our categories so it will be intelligible to us. However, the coherence lies in our categories, not human nature. How can such an overdetermined capacity function as a universal norm? If Nussbaum wants to claim Marx for her project, does not his view of humans as socially produced cut across her construction of capacities as universal norms?

Furthermore, all this is quite unnecessary. Universalist standards are not the only possible grounds for criticizing human practices. The search for them rests on several confused ideas. The first is that the justification and criticism of states require the existence of grounds that are universally good, therefore neutral (in the sense of good for all). This assumes that there is a necessary and determining relationship between the origin of something and its current condition or moral status. However, there is no reason to believe this. Products of human activity arise from complex and often conflicting practices. The relationship of current practices to antecedent ones is often paradoxical, unintended, or contradictory. Thus, even if we could track "origins" or prior grounds of a practice, these would only be contingent, and probably heterogeneous, not determining or unidirectional. Since, as Nussbaum says, cultures are not homogeneous, the constructionist can often find points where a practice violates the culture's own stated commitments. One does not have to be an Aristotelian to observe that what is presented as sacred tradition often merely rationalizes existing relations of domination. One can analyze who truth claims serve and whose interests they reflect. A Foucaultian suspicion of the relationships between truth claims and power enables one to track where domination is masked behind appeals to authoritative forms of grounding.

What follows from the heterogeneous and contingent grounds of politics is simply that such practices are contestable. The lack of purity or unadulterated goodness of antecedent activities does not mean that normative evaluation of human practices (including states) is impossible.[7] Practices differ in the possibilities they generate or prohibit. These can be evaluated according to standards generated by specific moral commitments. In such normative disputes, local beliefs have no more "privilege" than any others. Only if one conceives local practices as functioning as embedded universals would one have to abstain from such critical activity. Here, one would accord such local practices the status of absolute truths within a particular context. This is exactly what a thoroughgoing social constructionist rejects.

The absence of guaranteed grounds invites debate, not ethical indifference or silence. No principle limits a social constructionist to negative or critical arguments. While she cannot claim the trump of universal truth, nothing prohibits her from making arguments for the worth of her practices and commitments. She can give rich accounts of her views of justice or of the beauty or goodness of certain practices. She can try to persuade others that adopting such practices would better or enrich their own. Like Nussbaum, she can construct narratives to enlist appeals to the imagination in making her case.

Furthermore, a constructionist attitude is more likely to produce Nussbaum's desired effect—critical discourse—than her own approach. A function of universalist claims is to end conversation rather than to impel it. Once we posit universal claims, discourse can only concern descriptive details or application. Questioning their truth, the potential will to power of their advocates, or the social relations in which they are embedded is ruled out in advance.

Even from a pragmatic point of view, it is not clear what added purchase claiming such a label allows. The efficacy of universal norms assumes what is in question—that they exist. Although Nussbaum uses the language of overlapping consensus, her diversity does not go all the way down. The logic of her argument requires the existence of some prior space that is neutral regarding people's basic practical and ethical ways of life. If it does not, if there is not a universally shared good, then there cannot be neutral norms to settle basic normative disputes. The most fundamental differences are likely to lie outside the overlap of consensus. To get our opponent to agree to our norm, we must persuade her of the validity of our grounds for such a claim. Since this would entail convincing her of the validity of our way of life, the problem of diversity is moot. Alternatively, the admissible range of diversity must be limited, so that the norm will not violate the basic commitments of those to whom it applies. This is what Nussbaum does; certain ways of life, such as those that would eradicate liberty of conscience, must be excluded.

THE POLITICS OF GENDER

Rejection of Nussbaum's approach is not equivalent to denying injustice or undercutting the urgent need to attack it. As Nussbaum's own narratives illustrate, communities of solidarity do emerge within overlapping commitments that for "political purposes" we will agree to focus on certain goals. These communities require no agreement on universal standards or human functioning for their political efficacy or emotional power.[8] In many ways, Nussbaum's approach is not very political. It is not likely to offer much practical payoff and may be counterproductive. A puzzle of her approach is how quickly a crucial element of legal-political arrangements—power relations—disappears. This is one unfortunate effect of subsuming politics under the search for universal norms. It obscures many distinctive and salient aspects of political life, including the pervasiveness of conflict and multiple forms of power. Specific power arrangements within particular societies sustain gender domination. Those with power will legitimate it through a variety of means, including appeals to tradition or universal truth. Dismantling such power relationships requires close attention to particular, local ways in which they are reinstated and to their specific points of weakness, leverage, and resistance. I do not see how delineating universal human capabilities enables an oppressed person to locate the sources of her oppression or the mechanisms through which they are replicated. Such mechanisms may resemble each other at the macro level, but they are likely to have the strongest force in their local particularities. Focusing on the microanalysis of power is an indispensable element of political change, not a denial of its possibility.

Among the forms of power are those requiring violence, expressed or implied. Oppression and resistance to it may equally require their use. Asymmetric power relationships are notoriously unmoved by "moral stand-taking." Those with the most power in oppressive societies are not anti-universalist thinkers. I cannot remember a single oppressive ruler who presented himself or herself as a contingently positioned holder of an infinitely contestable set of claims to truth and power. Many of those who are engaged in systematic violence against women (for example, the Taliban in Afghanistan) believe they are engaged in universalist moral stand-taking. Insisting on the need for universals cannot mask the problem Nussbaum elides: why ought the grounding of her moral stand-taking—a combination of Kantian ethics and Aristotelian natural law—be any less open to question than theirs (a particular interpretation of the Koran)?

Furthermore, as she notes, constitutional principles, with or without universalist underpinnings, provide no guarantee of justice. She observes, "All women in India have equal rights under the Constitution . . . liberty is not just a matter of having rights on paper, it requires being in a position to exercise those rights. And this requires material resources." Her explanation for the inefficacy of principles is an absence of effective enforcement and programs; "those rights are not real to them." Her remedy, however, is more norms and state action: "The state that is going to guarantee people rights effectively is going to have to recognize universal norms beyond the small menu of basic rights; it will have to take a stand about the redistribution of wealth and income, about employment, land rights, health, education" (pp. 9–10).

The material in her text suggests another conclusion. What seems to make a difference is not universal norms or a state's commitment to them, but the political activities of the state's subjects. The focus on norms has a depoliticizing effect and is more likely to generate disempowerment than to reduce domination. The patterns of dominance, privilege, resistance, and subordination she describes require and reproduce entrenched and unjust relations of power. Only persistent action generates any positive state action. This is part of why I think putting the emphasis on norms is dangerous: because rather than protect or promote agency, it undercuts it. It shifts the locus of efficacy from power to belief. It supports an illusion that efficacy and the protection of freedom lies within discovery of principles, not in the struggle and conflict that proceeds and will follow it.[9] Even if we arrive at what seems like stable moral ground, this too will crack.

In this way, talk of norms reminds me of another one of Marx's concepts—fetishism.[10] Fetishism, as in commodity fetishism, is a process by which humans produce something but then the thing takes on the power of its producers. Their generative efforts disappear, and they become subjected to their own (congealed) activity. I would say this is what has happened in Nussbaum's text: heterogeneous kinds of human activity, practical and interpretative, have been organized into abstract categories called capacities. These capacities, which are then abstracted from particular social contexts and patterns of subject-making and acting (and because they are so abstracted), take on the thing-like appearance of a universal norm. These norms are given power that only situated subjects, acting within and for particular ways of life, can exercise. Luckily Nussbaum's sensibilities resist her principles. Her text undermines its author's intentions and thereby greatly edifies her reader.

NOTES

1. I am thinking particularly of Wittgenstein's discussions of what generates the conviction of certainty and the work that this conviction then does. See Ludwig Wittgenstein, *On Certainty*, ed. G. E. M. Anscombe and G. H. von Wright (New York: Harper & Row, 1972).

2. For detailed argument, see my recent essay, "Displacing Woman: Toward an Ethics of Multiplicity," in *Daring to be Good: Essays in Feminist Ethico-Politics*, ed. Bat-Ami Bar On and Ann Ferguson (New York: Routledge, 1998), 143–55.

3. Rawls's insistence on the cultural specificity of his project could be usefully taken up by Nussbaum. See John Rawls, *Political Liberalism* (New York: Columbia University Press, 1993), 174–75 where Rawls insists on the

> distinction . . . basic for my discussion: namely the distinction between a political conception of justice and a comprehensive religious, philosophical, or moral doctrine. I said there that the features of a political conception of justice are, first, that it is a moral conception worked out for a specific subject, namely, the basic structure of a constitutional democratic regime; second, that accepting the political conception does not presuppose accepting any particular comprehensive religious, philosophical, or moral doctrine; rather the political conception presents itself as a reasonable conception for the basic structure alone; and third, that it is not formulated in terms of any comprehensive doctrine but in terms of certain fundamental ideas viewed as latent in the public political culture of a democratic society.

However, like Nussbaum, I think Rawls is incorrect to claim that this (or any) political conception can exist without a comprehensive moral doctrine.

4. Martha C. Nussbaum, "In Defense of Universal Values," p. 13. Page numbers in parentheses indicate subsequent references to Nussbaum's chapter in this volume.

5. Possibilities include: Thomas Nagel, *Mortal Question* (New York: Cambridge University Press, 1979); Stuart Hampshire, *Innocence and Experience* (Cambridge, Mass.: Harvard University Press, 1989); David Gauthier, *Morals by Agreement* (New York: Oxford University Press, 1986); Bernard Williams, *Ethics and the Limits of Philosophy* (Cambridge, Mass.: Harvard University Press, 1985); Michael Walzer, *Spheres of Justice* (New York: Basic Books, 1983); Iris Marion Young, *Justice and the Politics of Difference* (Princeton, N.J.: Princeton University Press, 1990). On the politics of narratives of "the human," see Donna J. Haraway, *Simians, Cyborgs, and Women: The Reinvention of Women* (New York: Routledge, 1991).

6. Martha C. Nussbaum, *Women and Development: The Capabilities Approach*, unpublished manuscript, chapter 1, p. 44.

7. In addition to the works cited in note 5, a cursory glance at recent varieties of feminist ethics and critical race theory offers evidence for the falsity of these claims. See, for example, Jane Flax, "Displacing Woman: Toward an Ethics of Multiplicity"; Maria Lugones, "Purity, Impurity and Separation," *Signs* 19, no. 2 (Winter 1994): 458–79; Melissa Orlie, *Living Ethically, Acting Politically* (Ithaca, N.Y.: Cornell University Press, 1997); and Nancy Fraser, *Unruly Practices: Power, Discourse and Gender in Contemporary Social Theory* (Minneapolis: University of Minnesota Press, 1989); Chantal Mouffe, *The Return of the Political* (New York: Verso, 1993); the authors in *Feminists Theorize the Political*, ed. Judith Butler and Joan Scott (New York: Routledge, 1992); Linda Nicholson, "Interpreting Gender," *Signs* 20, no. 1 (Autumn 1994): 79–105; and Paul Gilroy, *The Black Atlantic: Modernity and Double Consciousness* (Cambridge, Mass.: Harvard University Press, 1993).

8. Among the many (varying) advocates of this approach, see Cornel West, *Race Matters* (Boston: Beacon, 1993); Bernice Johnson Reagon, "Coalition Politics: Turning the Century," in *Home Girls: A Black Feminist Anthology*, ed. Barbara Smith (New York: Kitchen Table:

Women of Color Press, 1993), 356–68; Biddy Martin and Chandra Talpade Mohanty, "Feminist Politics: What's Home Got to Do With It," in *Feminist Studies/Critical Studies*, ed. Teresa de Lauretis (Bloomington, Ind.: Indiana University Press, 1986), 191–212; and Iris Marion Young, "Gender as Seriality: Thinking about Women as a Social Collective," *Signs* 19, no. 1 (Autumn 1993): 713–38.

9. For similar arguments, see Sheldon S. Wolin, "The Liberal/Democratic Divide: On Rawls' *Political Liberalism*," *Political Theory* 24, no. 1 (February 1994): 97–111; Wendy Brown, "Rights and Losses," in her *States of Injury: Power and Freedom in Late Modernity* (Princeton, N.J.: Princeton University Press, 1999): 96–134; and Bonnie Honig, *Political Theory and the Displacement of Politics* (Ithaca, N.Y.: Cornell University Press, 1993).

10. On commodity fetishism, see Karl Marx, *Capital: Volume One* (Moscow: Progress Publishers, 1965). Annette Baier makes a similar argument in regards to rights talk. See particularly "Claims, Rights, Responsibilities," in Annette C. Baier, *Moral Prejudices* (Cambridge, Mass.: Harvard University Press, 1994), 224–46.

4

Essence of Culture
and a Sense of History

Martha C. Nussbaum

"Where are the men?" I asked her.
"In their proper places, where they ought to be." [The Sultana tells her that in her country it is women who are secluded.]
"But, dear Sultana, how unfair it is to shut in the harmless women and let loose the men. . . . Suppose some lunatics escape from the asylum and begin to do all sorts of mischief to men, horses, and other creatures: in that case what will your countrymen do?"
"They will try to capture them and put them back into their asylum."
"And you do not think it wise to keep sane people inside an asylum and let loose the insane?"
"Of course not!" said I, laughing lightly.
"As a matter of fact, in your country this very thing is done! Men, who do or at least are capable of doing no end of mischief, are let loose and the innocent women shut up in the zenana! . . . You have neglected the duty you owe to yourselves, and you have lost your natural rights by shutting your eyes to your own interests."[1]

As the argument of my paper will have made evident, I agree with more or less everything Flax says.[2] She argues convincingly that it is a bad mistake, both theoretically and politically, for feminists to endorse simple stereotypes of "Western" and "non-Western" cultures, false to the variety and complexity of the cultures actually being described. Besides being suspect in that they are artifacts of colonialism, such categories obscure the fact that all cultures are highly variegated, and are scenes of contest and struggle. Often, moreover, the cultural "essentializer" ends up accepting as the essence of a culture what is really the view of a group of dominant, and usually male, leaders; this external validation of oppressive norms can do real harm to women in their struggle for equality.

Consider my epigraph, written in 1905 by Muslim feminist Rokeya Sakhawat Hossain, an early campaigner against veiling. She remained to her death a pious Muslim woman, deeply immersed in not only Indian but specifically Muslim traditions. And yet, like many Indian women of her day and this day, she resisted prevalent cultural norms and demanded change. Any feminist who represents "Indian culture"—or the Islamic religion—in a way that omits this dimension of internal criticism, is making a most unfortunate mistake. I am particularly troubled by the tendency in some recent feminist writings to represent Muslim women as passive victims of a cruel patriarchal order.[3] This picture is not only false, it is also politically unfortunate, in that it equates Islam with fundamentalism, exactly what fundamentalists want. It also endorses negative stereotypes of Islam purveyed by Hindu fundamentalists, again playing into the hands of reactionary politics.[4]

Even when a cursory inspection of a local community suggests that its members are in agreement about a set of male-favoring values and practices, this should not be taken as the last word about what people's real views are. If a woman who has no property rights under the law, who has had no formal education, who has no legal right to divorce, and who will very likely be beaten if she seeks employment outside the home, says that she endorses traditions of modesty, purity, and self-abnegation, it is not clear that we should think this is the last word on the matter. Women's development groups typically encounter resistance initially, because women are afraid that challenging the status quo will make things worse. A group of women I met in a desert area of Andhra Pradesh in southern India told me that they had initially resisted participating in a national government project, Mahila Samakhya, which formed women's collectives to demand better working conditions and better services from local government.[5] They thought the collectives would be a waste of time and would cause conflict with their husbands. Over time, however, they saw that many advantages could be gained by collective discussion and action. They got a health visitor and a teacher who really showed up, and they won better working conditions from the landlords in whose fields they worked. Ultimately, the men welcomed these changes, and they have new respect for their wives, seeing them articulating their demands with clarity and winning concessions from local government. Women even reported that their husbands washed more often, in order to impress them!

In short, traditions of deference that once seemed good quickly cease to seem so, when space for critical dialogue and resistance is created. In fact, a large proportion of the cases in which women seem to acquiesce in their own oppression are cases of a collective action problem. Isolated from one another, they are unable to mount a successful challenge against tradition, and they fear even trying. One voice alone is not heard. To this extent an external catalyst (a non-governmental organization [NGO], or a government program) may prove extremely valuable, giving women space to organize and encouraging them to let their voices be heard.

I also agree with Flax that feminists need to recognize and stress the dynamism of cultures, rather than treating traditions as though they never evolved. Again—to fail to recognize dynamism and change is historically wrong; it is also politically insensitive and potentially harmful to women in their struggle for equality. This is particularly important when we are thinking about religious traditions, for male religious leaders often suggest that any change in regard to the position of women will be a deathblow to that tradition.[6] Religious traditions contain plurality and contention, as Rokeya's campaign; and they evolve in response to both internal struggles and external cultural and legal influences. Thus, norms of religious tolerance and respect for difference, introduced into Indian law by the emperor Ashoka in the third century B.C., shaped the evolution of the Hindu tradition; so, too, did related projects pursued during the Moghul Empire in the fifteenth and sixteenth centuries.[7] Feminists are on solid ground, then, if they remind coreligionists that their own proposals for change are no more alien than these other instances of change, and that any living tradition always undergoes change, as its members search for more adequate understandings and ways of life.

Finally, I agree with Flax that it is mistaken to conjure up a unitary image of "the Third-World woman," usually a passive victim, and usually contrasted to the image of a happy, well-fed American woman. (Indeed, I would urge Flax to consider dropping the term "Third-World," which she occasionally uses in her own voice. Development agencies typically no longer use this term, precisely because it suggests a homogeneous misery. The more accepted term, "developing countries," suggests progress and hope.) American feminists need to learn to think more about problems that occur much more often in developing countries, such as female illiteracy, high maternal mortality, and child marriage. We also need to know comparative statistics—for example, the facts that only thirty-five percent of women in India are literate, and that, in some regions of rural Bihar, the sex ratio is seventy-five women to one hundred men, suggesting a staggering problem of female malnutrition and probably infanticide.[8] So we do need to know statistics that inform us of differences between the problems faced by women in developing countries and problems of women in our own nation. The *Human Development Reports* of the United Nations Development Programme should be required reading in every feminist classroom. But we also need to insist that many of the worst problems facing women in developing countries—domestic violence, for example, and sexual harassment in the workplace—are also extremely common in our own nation.

How should these errors about other cultures be combated? Flax offers good arguments, and good argument is surely one way in which error can be dispelled. I would suggest that fieldwork with NGOs addressing women's issues is a good way to further expand one's horizons. In my own experience, going around with a good NGO and seeing what they are doing is an invaluable way of becoming aware of what working-class women in India think about and are striving for. In my own fieldwork, I have chosen to focus on a single nation, because I feel that this is a good way to see issues arising in a specific historical and political context. I chose India because I love it and because I had United-Nations-based connections there that led productively to other connections. Others may prefer to focus, instead, on a single set of issues that arise in all nations, such as prostitution, or domestic violence—although they will need to be careful not to decontextualize the problem as they cross from one nation to another.

But the problem of culpable ignorance of the variety of world cultures is hardly unique to American feminists. Indeed, feminists probably err far less in this regard than do most Americans, because they are usually curious about how women are actually living. Ignorance of world history and cultures is a pervasive problem in American culture. Our systems of primary, secondary, and higher education all need radical reform if we are to have citizens who can think well and subtly about the variety of cultures that may actually touch their lives. In *Cultivating Humanity*,[9] I have made some curricular recommendations for colleges and universities that should, if adopted, help to address the clueless ignorance of so many Americans about religions, cultures, and regions other than their own. But obviously this problem is difficult to solve if children are not led to think about the entire world far earlier—through myths and stories, songs and poems, and then gradually by historical and political fact, presented in an imaginative way. We have a large task to undertake, and feminists should help as and where they can (on school committees, college curriculum committees).

A second source of cultural ignorance is our media. We do far less well than most European nations in media coverage of developing countries. No major national newspaper carries intelligent and regular coverage of India, for example. Television is much worse: during the flurry of brief attempts to say something about India apropos of the fiftieth anniversary of the democracy in 1997, I actually heard a respected national commentator refer to "Hindu India and Muslim Pakistan"—a phrase to whose false, inflammatory, and politically partisan character he was entirely oblivious. High-ranking media leaders to whom I've complained about poor coverage reply that they fear low ratings. I consider this a scandalous and totally unacceptable response. They are rich enough to take a loss for the public good; and it might not even be a loss, if they stuck with the project long enough to cultivate an educated audience and used enough imagination to delight that audience. Arundhati Roy's wonderful novel has educated more Americans about India than the networks ever have—because it is *interesting*. So, let us tell the media that we think they are behaving badly, and let us not stop telling them until things change!

So far, both Flax and I have focused on descriptive matters. In conclusion, I would like to address the issue of cross-cultural norms. Of course it is irresponsible to propose any norms at all until we get the description right. For example, how could any intelligent development agency propose a project to implement in India if it did not first do all that Flax suggests, getting an accurate picture of the variety of struggles women are waging in a variety of settings? But once we describe the variety correctly, we still must ask how far it is legitimate to propose a set of cross-cultural bench-marks for women's development, or to implement them in development projects of many types.[10]

Obviously enough, the sheer existence of variety doesn't show that singleness at the normative level is wrong: some of the divergent practices may be evil. Thus, the prevalence of marital rape and domestic violence doesn't give feminists any good reason not to work for international unanimity against these practices. But when we consider seeking an international treaty establishing any single set of norms as benchmarks for women in all nations, we do face serious issues surrounding plural-ism, paternalism, and democracy. Who are these international bodies, it will be asked, to try to impose something on people who have their own ways of doing things? Doesn't such a way of proceeding show disrespect for them and treat them like chil-dren?

This objection to paternalism does not lead us in the direction of cultural rela-tivism; in fact, as Flax sees, it is incompatible with cultural relativism. If we are re-ally concerned about respecting people and their opportunity to lead diverse lives of their own choice, we must support, cross-culturally, certain important spheres of freedom and choice for all citizens, such as freedom of assembly, religious freedom, freedom of contract, and freedom from bodily violence. Many real-life cultures do not respect these spheres of freedom. Indeed, most are highly paternalistic, especially toward women: they do not give them these spheres of freedom, at least not on an equal basis. The only way to correct this situation is to insist on the importance of certain spheres of choice and freedom for all citizens. Nonetheless, any project that does defend a set of cross-cultural norms as goals for global political action owes us an account of how it proposes to show adequate respect for pluralism and choice. In conclusion, let me summarize briefly the ways in which my capabilities approach tries to solve this problem. How, then, does my project make room for people's di-versity, and for their freedom of choice as citizens?

First, *multiple realizability*: each of the capabilities may be concretely realized in a variety of different ways, in accordance with individual tastes and/or local circum-stances and tradition. Second, *capability as goal*: the basic political principles focus on promoting capabilities, not actual functioning, in order to leave to citizens the choice of whether to pursue the relevant function or not. Third, *liberties and practi-cal reason*: the content of the capabilities list gives a central role to citizens' powers of choice and to traditional political and civil liberties. Fourth, *political liberalism*: the approach is intended as the moral core of a specifically political conception, and the object of a political overlapping consensus among people who have otherwise very different comprehensive views of the good. Fifth, *constraints on implementation*: the approach is designed to offer the philosophical grounding for constitutional principles, but the implementation of such principles must be done, for the most part, by the internal politics of the nation in question, although international agen-cies and other governments are justified in using persuasion—and in especially grave cases, economic or political sanctions—to promote these developments.

NOTES

1. Rokeya Sakhawat Hossain, *Sultana's Dream and Selections from The Secluded Ones* (1905), ed. and trans. by Roushan Jahan (New York: Feminist Press of the City University of New York, 1988).

2. My *Women and Human Development: The Capabilities Approach* (Cambridge, Mass.: Cambridge University Press, 2000) has many discussions that parallel Flax's arguments.

3. See my response to Susan Okin's lead essay in *Multiculturalism and Women*, ed. J. Cohen (Princeton, N.J.: Princeton University Press, 1999). I am grateful to Zoya Hasan for conversation on this point; she is currently engaged in a large research project aimed at attaining a more accurate picture of the variety of Muslim women in India, their quality of life, and their opinions.

4. For examples of such stereotypes, and the difficulties they create for Muslim women seeking equal treatment under the law, see chapter 3 of *Women and Human Development*.

5. The state government of Andhra Pradesh is notoriously corrupt and inefficient; the national government, therefore, chose that state as one of the focal points of its new women-collectives program.

6. This happens especially often in India, where the religions control the entire system of family law and property law: see my *Women and Human Development*, chapter 3.

7. I choose this example to reinforce Flax's point about the West and the non-West: we need to remember that ideas that we associate with the European Enlightenment had much earlier origins in Indian culture. See Amartya Sen, "Human Rights and Asian Values," *The New Republic* (July 10–17, 1997).

8. Personal communication, Viji Srinivasan of Adithi, an NGO working in northern Bihar. Statistics produced by the state government seemed unreliable, so Adithi did its own census.

9. See my *Cultivating Humanity: A Classical Defense of Reform in Liberal Education* (Cambridge, Mass.: Harvard University Press, 1997), especially chapters 2 and 4.

10. Most NGOs that deal with women's issues are transnational in some respect. They are either transnational agencies themselves (such as UNICEF or OXFAM, or WIEGO, the recently formed group that seeks improved conditions for women in the informal sector), or are indigenous groups that get grants from abroad (such as every group I have ever visited in India—money coming above all from Sweden and the Netherlands). I have worries about the dominance of internationally funded NGOs, even excellent ones. Although they often do better work than would be done by the government of the nation in question, and although they provide a mechanism for morally required transfers of wealth from richer to poorer nations, the bypassing of duly elected governments raises grave issues of democratic accountability.

Section II

Justice, Care, and Evils

5

Caring Relations and Principles of Justice

Virginia Held

THE CONTROVERSY

The question of whether impartial, universal, and rational moral principles must always be given priority over other possible grounds for moral motivation continues to provoke extensive debate. David Velleman has recently added his defense of Kantian ethics to those offered by others against recent challenges to the priority of impartial rules. The challenges have come from Bernard Williams, among others, and especially from certain advocates of a feminist ethic of care. An example of the controversy was a session of the American Philosophical Association in Philadelphia in December 1997 where Velleman gave a paper called "Love and Duty," and defended Kantian ethics against the kind of challenge presented by Bernard Williams (Velleman). Like most such defenses of the priority of universal moral rules, Velleman said nothing about the feminist critique, but other defenders of Kant and of the priority of universalistic principles have begun to address the feminist challenge. They have offered a variety of answers to the feminist critique of claims about the adequacy of moralities built on universal principles of rational impartiality. It is the feminist challenge that I will largely discuss and defend against these responses.

Velleman concentrates on the case that Bernard Williams discusses, originally put forward by Charles Fried and much discussed since, of whether a man may justifiably save his wife rather than a stranger, if he can save only one (Velleman). Williams suggests that if the man stops to think about whether universal principles could permit him to give special consideration to his wife rather than treating both persons impartially, the man is having "one thought too many" (Williams). Velleman argues that Kantian principles would include, not deny, that we have special responsibilities for the members of our families and that these can be consistently universalized, so there need be no conflict here. One commentator, Thomas Hill, changed

67

the example to avoid any sexist stereotypes involved, but agreed with the defense of Kantian impartiality against this kind of attack (Hill). Harry Frankfurt, another commentator, gave more support to Williams's critique (Frankfurt), but none of the three addressed the feminist versions of the challenge to Kantian principles, which resemble Williams's in some respects and differ from it in others.

Williams's arguments are presented from the point of view of a man with a set of projects, the sorts of projects that make life worth living for this man. The image, like its Kantian alternative, is still that of an individual deliberator. Williams pits the individual's particular goals—to live life with his wife or, in another case, to be a painter—against the individual's rational and impartial moral principles, and he doubts that the latter should always have priority. Williams disputes the view that our particular projects must always be constrained by universal principles requiring that we should only pursue what universal principles permit (Friedman). If a man's life would be worth living only if he put, for example, his art ahead of his universalizable moral obligations to his family, Williams is not willing to give priority to his moral obligations. In the example of the man and the drowning others, the man's wife may be his project, but the dilemma is posed in terms of an individual's own particular goals versus his universal moral obligations. At a formal level it remains within the traditional paradigm of egoism versus universalism. Williams is unwilling to yield the claims of the ego, especially those that enable it to continue to be the person it is, to the requirements of universalization. But he does not reject the traditional way of conceptualizing the alternatives. Like Thomas Nagel in *The Possibility of Altruism*, and most other philosophers before him, the problem is seen as pitting the claims of an individual ego against those of impartial rules.

The feminist challenge to Kantian moralities does require a change in this paradigm. It does not pit an individual ego against universal principles, but considers a particular relationship between persons, a caring relationship, and questions whether it should always yield to universal principles of justice. It sees the relationship as not reducible to the individual projects of its members. When universal principles conflict with the claims of relationships, the feminist challenge disputes that the principles should always have priority. The feminist critique of liberalism as moral theory and of Kantian morality gives us reason to doubt that, in terms of how the debate has been framed, justice should always have priority over care.

In his new book, *Justice as Impartiality*, Brian Barry devotes a considerable portion of Chapter 10 to the feminist critique of impartiality. He attributes it to misunderstandings. Thoroughly disparaging the work of Lawrence Kohlberg, the psychologist of moral development criticized by Carol Gilligan, Barry blames Kohlberg for the confusions that he thinks are responsible for the feminist critique of impartiality. Barry fails to see that much of what feminist moral philosophers have written about feminist morality and the ethics of care has little to do with Kohlberg, but does have a great deal to do with the kind of justice as impartiality defended by Barry.

Barry advocates what he formulates as second-order impartiality. This kind of impartiality requires that the moral and legal rules of a society be such that they are "capable of attaining the . . . assent of all" taken as free and equal individuals (Barry, p. 191). This does not require or imply first-order impartiality, the kind of impartiality that dictates that we should not be partial to our own friends and family members. Barry argues that as long as we can all accept the rules, these rules can, of course, permit us to give special consideration to our friends and families.

Barry points out that most second-order impartiality theories, such as John Rawls's theory of justice, are designed for judging institutions, not the actions of persons in personal situations, and for judging institutions in "nearly just" societies. This renders them of little use for recommending actions in the context of the seriously unjust conditions of currently existing institutions. According to Barry, there can be second-order impartiality theories that support the morality of breaking some bad laws rather than merely waiting for them to change. Thus, his arguments for impartiality are an improvement over many others. But Barry supports the position of impartialists generally in holding that justice, now formulated as second-order impartiality, always has priority over considerations of care, not just in legal but in all moral contexts. In Barry's view, care can justifiably be the basis of choice only after the demands of justice as impartiality have been met. He argues that there can be no genuine conflicts between the rules of justice and considerations of care: they deal with different matters. We are morally obligated to fulfill the requirements of impartiality, and then, we can be moved as we choose by our feelings for friends and family.

This interpretation of the issues sidesteps rather than addresses the arguments of many defenders of the ethics of care. The latter question the priority of justice as impartiality (including second-order impartiality) and are not willing to relegate care to an optional choice about preferences once all the requirements of justice have been satisfied (Baier). These advocates of care deny that we are simply talking about different matters; they hold that those who defend the priority of justice and those advocating an ethic of care are, at least sometimes, both talking about the same topic—morality—and are disagreeing about it. The debates have often seen the issues as being about which kind of approach would be better for a given problem: the approach of justice or the approach of care? And they reject the view that considerations of care are appropriate only in personal relations after the rules of justice have decided them to be permissible. Questions of care can appropriately arise in public as well as personal contexts, and we can wonder at fundamental levels whether we should always treat people as if the liberal assumptions of impartial justice take priority in our dealings with them. Sometimes the points of view of care and of justice provide different moral evaluations of and recommendations for the same problems and matters. When they do, we need to choose between them rather than simply talking past each other.

Stephen Darwall is another philosopher who has tried to address the challenge presented by feminist ethics. He finds that the ethics of care usefully calls attention to the actual relationships that are such an important part of our lives. But he denies that the ethics of care really presents an alternative opposed to the moralities of impartial universal principles, the moralities of Kant and utilitarianism. He argues that we arrive at the basic idea of utilitarianism, "that everyone's welfare matters and matters equally" (Darwall 1998, p. 226), by thinking about why we value an actual particular child who engages our attention. We realize that it is because the particular child we care about is "someone with a conscious life that can be affected for good or ill," and that the sympathy we feel for a particular child is something we can feel for any other. Similarly, according to Darwall, Kantian respect for persons "involves recognizing an individual's dignity or value in himself, but it is grounded in features that a person shares with any other moral agent" (p. 227). Hence, we extend to all persons the kind of respect we can recognize that an individual we know deserves. To Darwall, then, the ethics of care is a "supplement" to "morality as conceived by the moderns" (p. 228), but both aim at the same ideas of equal concern and respect.

This interpretation, like Barry's, fails to recognize the challenge to moralities of universal, impartial principles that the ethics of care, or Bernard Williams, present. And to an advocate of an ethic of care, Darwall's interpretation of what it is in our child that leads us to value or respect him is rather questionable in terms of descriptive persuasiveness. What a parent may value in her child may well not be what makes this child like every other, but the very particular relationship that exists between them such that she is the mother of this child, and this particular person is her child. If we think of how we would respond to the question "Why do you care about this child?" asked perhaps by an official of a hypothetical regime threatening to take the child for adoption by more favored parents, or for a scientific experiment authorized by the regime, we are probably more likely to imagine our response being "because she is my child" than "because she has a conscious life, like all children." This does not mean that we associate our child with our property, thinking of her as belonging to us, or thinking of ourselves as individuals who own our children as well as our property. Nor does it mean we think the reasons the government should or should not take our child are like the reasons it should or should not appropriate our property. The relationship we have with our child is very different from the relationship we have to our property. We might favor policies that would allow governments to appropriate significant amounts and kinds of property in ways that would be fair, yet strongly oppose policies that would sever bonds with our children, even if they would be fair.

In elaborating the reasons that the two kinds of cases are different, we might refer to the conscious life of our child and all other children, or to Kantian principles against treating persons as means. But the relationship between a particular child and a particular parent is a more plausible source of the valuing of each by the other than are the features they share with all other children and parents. And so if the moral recommendations grounded on this relationship ever conflict with the moral recommendations derived from universal moral principles, the problem of which has priority remains, despite Darwall's efforts to dissolve it.

DIFFERENCES AMONG FEMINISTS

Martha Nussbaum is another philosopher who argues for liberal universalism against the ethics of care; she believes that the kind of liberalism for which she argues will be better for women than care ethics and should be embraced by feminists. She acknowledges that some of the feminist critique of liberalism can conflict with what she sees as the "norms of reflective caring that are preferred by liberalism" (Nussbaum, p. 30). The latter norms would demand that love or attachment be based on an uncoerced choice from a position of equality, whereas an ethic of care recognizes that many of our attachments cannot or need not be based on such choice. A most obvious example is that no child can choose her parents, who are for many years more powerful than she. Though Nussbaum does not acknowledge it, many defenders of an ethic of care favor reflective care over blind care, but they part company with Nussbaum in not seeing care primarily in terms of individual interest or choice, as does Nussbaum. Nussbaum cites Nel Noddings's description of the maternal paradigm of care and writes: "Liberalism says, let them give themselves away to others— provided that they so choose in all freedom. Noddings says that this is one thought too many—that love based on reflection lacks some of the spontaneity and moral value of true maternal love" (p. 30). To Nussbaum, such a view does present a challenge to the Kantian liberalism she defends. But she thinks the position of the ethics of care should be rejected; she thinks it is bad for women. Her reasons, in my view, are based on too limited a view of the ethics of care, a view that identifies it unduly with its earliest formulations.

Many feminists who criticize the liberal individualist view of persons do not deny, as Martha Nussbaum implies, the importance of rights for women who lack them (see Held 1998). When women are denied, as they are in many parts of the world, an equal share of the food or education available to a family, when women are subject to marital rape and domestic violence, extending liberal rights to women is, of course, enormous progress. So is it when, as is still widely the case in the United States, women receive equal shares of basic necessities but are still expected and pressured to make greater sacrifices for their children than are men. The point that feminists often make, however, is that the progress should not stop with equal rights and that the liberal individualist way of formulating the goals of morality is one-sided and incomplete. Nussbaum claims that "what is wrong with the views of the family endorsed by [many liberals] is not that they are too individualist, but that they are not individualist enough" (p. 15) because they do not extend liberal individualism to gender relations within the family as Nussbaum thinks they should. Contrary to Nussbaum's characterization of them, however, most feminists, including those who defend an ethic of care, agree with her that various individual rights should be extended to gender relations in the family. The right not to be assaulted, for instance, should protect women and children in the family, and women should assert rights to a more equitable division of labor in the household. But those who advocate an ethic of care have a very different view from liberal individualists of what gender relations, relations between children and parents, relations of friendship, and human relations generally, should be like even when these rights are extended to those previously left out from the protections they provide.

The feminist critique of liberalism that a view such as Nussbaum's misses is the more fundamental one that turning everyone into a complete liberal individual leaves no one adequately attentive to relationships between persons, whether they be caring relations within the family or social relations holding communities together. It is possible for two strangers to have a so-called "relation" of equality between them, with nothing at all to bind them together into a friendship or a community. Liberal equality doesn't itself provide or concern itself with the more substantial components of relationship. It is in evaluating and making recommendations for the latter that an ethic of care is most appropriate. As many feminists argue, the issues for moral theory are less a matter of justice versus care than of how to appropriately integrate justice and care, or care and justice if we are wary of the traditional downgrading and marginalizing of care. And it is not satisfactory to think of care, as it is conceptualized by liberal individualism, as a mere personal preference an individual may choose or not. Neither is it satisfactory to think of caring relationships as merely what rational individuals may choose to care about as long as they give priority to universal, and impartial, moral principles.

Marilyn Friedman calls attention to when partiality is or is not morally valuable. "Personal relationships," she writes, "vary widely in their moral value. The quality of a particular relationship is profoundly important in determining the moral worth of any partiality which is necessary for sustaining that relationship" (Friedman, p. 40). Partiality toward other white supremacists on the part of a white supremacist, for instance, does not have moral worth. When relationships cause harm, or are based on such wrongful relations as that of master and slave, we should not be partial toward them. But when a relationship has moral worth, such as a caring relationship between parents and children, or a relation of trust between friends and lovers clearly may have, the question of the priority, or not, of impartiality can arise. And as moralities of impartial rules so easily forget, and as Friedman makes clear, "close relationships call . . . for personal concern, loyalty, interest, passion, and responsiveness to the uniqueness of loved ones, to their specific needs, interests, history, and so on. In a word, personal relationships call for attitudes of partiality rather than impartiality" (Friedman).

Evaluating the worth of relationships does not mean that universal norms have priority after all. It means that from the perspective of justice, some relationships are to be judged unjustifiable, often to the point that they should be ended to the extent possible, although this is often a limited extent. (For instance, we will never stop being the sibling of our siblings, or the ex-friend or ex-spouse of the friends or spouse with whom we have broken a relation). But once a relationship can be deemed to have value, moral issues can arise as to whether the claims of the relationship should or should not be subordinated to the perspective of justice. And that is the issue I am examining. Moreover, the aspects of a relationship that make it a bad relationship can often be interpreted as failures to appropriately care for particular others, rather than only as violations of impartial moral rules. Certainly, avoiding serious moral wrongs should take priority over avoiding trivial ones, and pursuing highly important moral goods should take priority over pursuing insignificant ones. But this settles nothing about caring relations versus impartial moral rules, now that we know enough to reject the traditional view that what men do in public life is morally important while what women do in the household is morally trivial. Some caring relations are of the utmost importance, morally as well as causally—human beings cannot flourish or even survive without them—while some of the requirements of impartial moral rules are relatively insignificant. And sometimes it is the reverse.

The practice of partiality, as Friedman well argues, cannot be unqualified.

> When many families are substantially impoverished, then [various] practices of partiality further diminish the number of people who can achieve well-being, integrity, and fulfillment through close relationships. . . . Partiality, if practiced by all, untempered by any redistribution of wealth or resources, would appear to lead to the integrity and fulfillment of only some persons . . . (Friedman, 59).

But this only shows, as defenders of the ethics of care usually agree, that partiality and the values of caring relationships are not the only values of concern to morality. The social conventions through which partiality is practiced need to be evaluated and justified, and impartial moral principles can be relevant in doing so. But a morality of impartial principles will be incomplete and unsatisfactory if it stops with impartial evaluations of what individuals are forbidden or permitted to do. Morality needs to evaluate relationships of care themselves, showing, for instance, how shared consideration, sensitivity, and trustworthiness enhance them and increase their value, while also showing how they can degenerate into mere occasions for individuals to pursue their own interests, or to reluctantly fulfill the duties imposed on individuals by impartial rules. When relationships are valuable ones, moral recommendations based on them may conflict with moral recommendations that would be made from the point of view of impartiality.

A LOOK AT SOME CASES

Let me now try to examine in greater detail what is at issue between an ethic of care and a morality built on impartiality, and why a satisfactory feminist morality should not accept the view that universal, impartial, liberal moral principles of justice and right should always be accorded priority over the concerns of caring relationships, which include considerations of trust, friendship, and loyalty. The argument needs to be examined both at the level of personal relationships and at the level of social policy. Advocates of an ethic of care have argued successfully against the view that care—within the bounds of what is permitted by universal principles—is admirable in personal relations, but that the core value of care is inappropriate for the impersonal relations of strangers and citizens. I will explore issues of both kinds.

Consider, first, the story of Abraham. It has been discussed by a number of defenders of an ethic of care (Noddings) who do not agree with the religious and moral teaching that Abraham made the right decision when be chose to obey the command of God and kill his infant son. (That God intervened later to prevent the killing is not relevant to an evaluation of Abraham's decision for anyone but a religious consequentialist). From the perspective of an ethic of care, the relationship between child and parent should not always be subordinated to the command of God or of universal moral rules. But let's consider a secular case in which there is a genuine conflict between impartialist rules and the parent-child relation. Barry's and Darwall's attempts to reshape the Bernard Williams and the feminist problems so that there is no conflict merely deal with a different kind of case and fail to address the question of what has priority when there is a conflict.

Suppose the father of a young child is by profession a teacher with a special skill in helping troubled young children succeed academically. Suppose now that on a utilitarian calculation of how much overall good will be achieved, he determines that, from the point of view of universal utilitarian rules, he ought to devote more time to his work, staying at his school after hours and so on, letting his wife and others care for his own young child. But he also thinks that from the perspective of care, he should build his relationship with his child, developing the trust and mutual consideration of which it is capable. Even if the universal rules allow him some time for family life, and even if he places appropriate utilitarian value on developing his relationship with his child—the good it will do the child, the pleasure it will give him, the good it will enable the child to do in the future, etc.—the calculation still comes out, let's say, as before: he should devote more time to his students. But the moral demands of care suggest to him that he should spend more time with his child.

I am constructing the case in such a way that it is not a case of the kind Barry suggests where impartial moral rules that all can accept permit us to favor our own children, within bounds set by impartial rules. Rather, I am taking a case where the impartial rules that all could accept direct the father to spend more time practicing his profession, but considerations of care urge him to spend more time with his child. It is a case where the perspective of impartiality and the perspective of care are in conflict.

No doubt there could be ways of interpreting the problem that would avoid a conflict between impartial moral rules and the pull of the relationship between parent and child, but then the problem would not be the one I am considering. Instead,

I'm examining a case where the moral agent must choose whether impartiality or care should have priority. And moral philosophers must consider whether the decision such an agent might make in such a case can be normatively justified.

If there is an objection that this is not the way such calculations would in fact come out, my response is that, in evaluating alternative moral theories, we can be interested in imagined situations where it would be the case that the calculations came out a certain way. The force of the deontologists' objections to utilitarianism can appropriately rest on such arguments as that if, on a utilitarian calculation, a torture show would produce more pleasure for those who enjoyed it than pain for its victims and critics, then it would be morally recommended. That is enough of an argument against utilitarianism; we don't also need to show that the example is empirically likely.

The argument for impartiality might go something like this: Reasoning as an abstract agent (Darwall 1983), I should act on moral rules that all could accept from a perspective of impartiality. Those rules recommend that we treat all persons equally, including our children, with respect to exercising our professional skills, and that when we have special skills we should use them for the benefit of all persons equally. For example, a teacher should not favor his own child if his child happens to be one of his students. And if one has the abilities and has had the social advantages to become a teacher, one should exercise those skills when they are needed, especially when they are seriously needed.

But the father in my example also considers the perspective of care. From this perspective his relationship with his child is of enormous and irreplaceable value. He thinks that out of concern for this particular relationship he should spend more time with his child. He experiences the relationship as one of love and trust and loyalty, and thinks in this case that he should subordinate such other considerations as exercising his professional skills to this relationship. He thinks he should free himself to help his child feel the trust and encouragement his development will require, even if this conflicts with impartial morality.

He reflects on what the motives would be in choosing between the alternatives. For one alternative, the motive would be: because universal moral rules recommend it. For the other, the motive would be: because this is my child and I am the father of this child and the relationship between us is no less important than universal rules. He reflects on whether the latter can be a moral motive and concludes that it can in the sense that he can believe it is the motive he ought to act on. And he can do this without holding that every father ought to act similarly toward his child. He can further conclude that if Kantian and utilitarian moralities deny that such a motive can be moral, then they have mistakenly defined the moral to suit their purposes, and, by arbitrary fiat, excluded whatever might challenge their universalizing requirements. He may have read Annette Baier's discussion of the possible tendency of women to resist subordinating their moral sensitivities to autonomously chosen Kantian rules. Baier writes:

What did Kant, the great prophet of autonomy, say in his moral theory about women? He said they were incapable of legislation, not fit to vote, that they needed the guidance of more 'rational' males. Autonomy was not for them; it was only for first-class, really rational persons. . . . But where Kant concludes 'so much the worse for women,' we can conclude 'so much the worse for the male fixation on the special skill of drafting legislation, for the bureaucratic mentality of rule-worship, and for the male exaggeration of the importance of independence over mutual interdependence (Baier, p. 26).

The father in my example may think fathers should join mothers in paying more attention to relationships of care and in resisting the demands of impartial rules when they are excessive.

From the perspective of all, or everyone, perhaps particular relationships should be subordinated to universal rules. But from the perspective of particular persons in relationships, it is certainly meaningful to ask: Why must we adopt the perspective of all and everyone when it is a particular relationship that we care about at least as much as "being moral" in the sense required by universal rules? This relationship, we may think, is central to the identities of the persons in it. It is relationships between people, such as in families, which allow persons to develop and to become aware of themselves as individuals with rights. And it is relationships between people that sustain communities within which moral and political rights can be articulated and protected. Perhaps the perspective of universal rules should be limited to the domain of law, rather than expected to serve for the whole of morality. Then, in my example, the law should require gender fairness in parental leaves. Beyond this, it might allow persons with professional skills to work more or fewer hours as they choose, but the case as I developed it was to consider the moral decision that would still face the father in question after the law had spoken. Even if the law permitted him to work less, would it be what he morally ought to do? From the perspective of universal impartial utilitarian rules, the answer is no. But, from the perspective of care, the answer is yes. And it is this moral issue I am trying to explore. What I am arguing is that in the ethics of care, the moral claims of caring are no less valid than the moral claims of impartial rules. This is not to say that considerations of impartiality are unimportant; it does deny that they should always have priority. This makes care ethics a challenge to liberalism as a moral theory, not a mere supplement.

THE REACH OF JUSTICE

The concern expressed by liberals such as Nussbaum that every person is a separate entity with interests that should not be unduly subordinated to the "good of the community" can be matched by a defender of care who maintains that relationships of care should not be unduly subordinated to universal rules conferring equal moral rights and obligations and designed for contexts of conflict. The law and legalistic approaches should be limited to an appropriate domain, not expanded to the whole of human life and morality.

Susan Mendus, in a discussion of Brian Barry's *Justice as Impartiality*, notes that the issues are often about the scope of justice: how widely should impartiality be expected to apply? (Mendus). Barry himself thinks it would be absurd to apply it in one's choice of friends, where we choose our friends because we enjoy their company, and discretion is permissible. But he holds that this is only because impartial rules have already been given priority, and some of them permit us to be partial to our friends up to a point.

Where to put justice first and where to consider it secondary or out of place is often the issue between those who argue for moralities of impartial rules, and their critics. The critics often want to shrink the reach of justice, recognizing that the values of caring relationships have been greatly neglected by traditional moralities. They resist the priority of impartiality in personal relationships, and then, having explored the moral priorities in these domains, they consider extending the values of caring, of trust, of solidarity, beyond personal relationships. Political and social life also needs to be rethought in the light of an ethic of care. It is here that those arguing for an ethic of care may meet up with communitarians. However, since the latter have so seldom dealt with the ethics of care, and since care ethics have serious disagreements with most forms of communitarianism, there is by no means a match between an extended ethic of care and communitarianism as so far developed (Frazer and Lacey; Friedman).

"Liberalism," Nussbaum writes, "holds that the flourishing of human beings taken one by one is both analytically and normatively prior to the flourishing" of any group (Nussbaum, p. 11). But Marxian and other arguments that human beings are social beings show how artificial such assumptions are, as we see how the material and experiential realities of any individual's life are fundamentally tied to those of others, and how the social relations in which persons are enmeshed are importantly constitutive of their "personhood." Feminist arguments that take into account the realities of caretaker/child relationships show how misleading this liberal individualist assumption is, ignoring as it does how, for any child to become a liberal individual, it must have been enmeshed in the caring social relations of caretakers and children for many years (Kittay). The adult liberal individual regarding himself as "separate" is formed as well by innumerable social bonds of family, friendship, professional association, citizenship, and the like. Certainly we can decide that for certain contexts, such as a legal one, we will make the assumption that persons are liberal individuals. But we should never lose sight of the limits of the context for which we think this may be an appropriate assumption, nor of how unsatisfactory an assumption it is for more complete conceptions of "persons." Nussbaum's revealing endnote on her experience of motherhood and of the essential separateness of herself and her daughter sidesteps many of the issues and is in no way conclusive.[1] It could well mark the beginning of a debate rather than a conclusion. A statement such as "My child and I are separate individuals" overlooks the relation between a mother and a child. In the absence of a debate about how it is or is not true, the liberal assumption remains an ideological and unexamined starting point with no more support than its familiarity.

Children do not develop adequately when others merely go through the motions of meeting their basic needs; children need to experience social relations of trust and caring. Arguably, then, caring relations are in some sense normatively prior to individual well-being in families. But the priority is not just developmental or causal. Without the social relations within which people constitute themselves as individuals, they do not have the individuality the liberal seeks. At the level of larger groups, persons do not constitute themselves into political or social entities unless social relations of trust and loyalty tie members together into a collectivity of some kind. As Neil MacCormick observes in a discussion of *Justice as Impartiality* and of Adam Smith, "justice matters to people who are already in community with each other" (MacCormick, p. 309). Arguably, then, social relationships of persons caring enough about one another to respect them as fellow members of a community are normatively prior to individuals being valued as holders of individual rights, or to citizenship in a liberal state, and the like. And perhaps gradually, the community within which such ties must be developed so that members can be respected as having human rights is the global, human community.

We might conclude, then, that what has priority are relationships of care or fellow-feeling within which we seek rules that can be agreed on by all for treating each other with equal concern and respect and for those kinds of issues where impartial rules will be appropriate, recognizing that much that has moral value in both personal and political life is "beyond justice." Such a view denies that the rules of impartial morality always have priority, and that we ought only to pursue what other values these rules permit. The outlook within the context of law is that law "covers" all behavior, allowing whatever it does not forbid, and demanding compliance on all that it does forbid. The view that moral rules of impartiality always take priority over considerations of care expands this outlook to the whole of morality. But we generally recognize a distinction between law and morality, and can well argue that morality has normative priority. Then, at the moral level, on my argument we have good reasons not to give priority to moral rules of impartiality, but to acknowledge the claims of caring relations as no less fundamental. This view argues that, at the moral level, justice is one value among others, not always the highest value. Care and its related values of relationship and trust are no less important.

Susan Mendus, discussing Bernard Williams's argument about the man saving his wife, writes that the force of the argument is "that it is not merely impractical and politically inexpedient to force this extension of the scope of impartiality: it is also, and crucially, a deformation of concepts such as love and friendship, which are what they are precisely because they are not underpinned by completely justificatory explanations. In the example of the man saving his wife, willingness to pose the justificatory question is, in part, an acceptance of this deformed model" (Mendus, p.

323). This way of putting the point assumes that "justification" can only be in terms of impartial rules, whereas a broader concept of justification might not be limited to just such forms. But from the perspective of an ethic of care, Mendus is entirely right to argue that accepting the demand to apply rules of impartiality is, in many cases of love and friendship and caring relations, to accept a "deformed model" of these.

MODELS OF MORALITY

At the level of morality, we need to decide which "models" are appropriate for which contexts. Many of the arguments of recent decades about the priority of justice were developed against a background of utilitarian ascendancy. Rawls's theory of justice and its many offshoots are good examples (Rawls 1971). Against utilitarian calculations subordinating all other considerations to the goals of general utility, or claiming that rights can only be justified on the basis of how well they serve overall welfare, arguments are persuasive that such views misunderstand what is inherent to rights. In Dworkin's memorable formulation, rights "trump" general utility, and just what we mean by a person having a right is that this claim is justified whether or not it promotes general utility: rights must stand firm against such maximizing calculations (Dworkin). Basic to democratic theory, for instance, is the view that individual rights must be respected even when this does not maximize the satisfaction of majorities. Similarly, it has been argued, at the moral level, justice and rights have priority over general utility.

From the perspective of an ethic of care, however, this debate can be interpreted as being largely internal to the legal-political context. Rawls has explicitly confined his theory to the domain of the political and has argued that it should not be interpreted as a full-fledged moral theory (Rawls 1993). Dworkin is explicitly a legal philosopher. Utilitarians have not shown comparable modesty, but one may argue, as I have done elsewhere, that utilitarian calculations can be useful and appropriate for recommending various public policy choices even though they are inappropriate for judicial decisions and for a wide range of other kinds of choices (Held 1984; Goodin). Perhaps, then, neither rights theory nor utilitarianism has the capacity to be made into a comprehensive moral theory. And many of those who have continued to argue for Kantian ethics have interpreted Kant in ways that move the theory far beyond rules of impartiality (Baron).

The moral supremacy of the state and its associated demands is an artifact of history. With a more satisfactory morality than one composed of rules of impartiality, the supreme state and its laws might shrink to more justifiable proportions. A culture liberated from commercial domination, for instance, might become the preferred domain of moral discourse out of which might come moral recommendations that could generally be accepted and acted on without the compulsions of legal enforcement (Held 1993). And these recommendations could include acceptance of the plurality of values, and of the primacy of trust and caring relations in various contexts.

An ethic of care suggests that the priority of justice is at best persuasive for the legal-judicial context. It might also suggest that calculations of general utility are at best appropriate for some choices about public policy. A moral theory is still needed to show us how, within the relatedness that should exist among all persons as fellow human beings, and that does exist in many personal contexts and numerous group ones, we should apply the various possible models. We will then be able to see how we should apply the legal-judicial model of impartiality to given ranges of issues, or the utilitarian model of concern for the general welfare to another range of issues, all the time recognizing other issues, such as those that can be seen most clearly among friends and within families and in cases of group solidarity, for which these models are inappropriate or inadequate. And we will see how the model of caring relations can apply and have priority in some contexts, and how it should not be limited to the personal choices made by individuals after they have met all the requirements of justice. A comprehensive moral theory would show, I believe, how care and its related values are not less important than justice. Whether they are more important remains to be argued, but not in this paper.

NOTES

This chapter was presented as a paper on March 28, 1998, in an Invited Symposium at the Pacific Division of the American Philosophical Association's meeting in Los Angeles. I am grateful to Barbara Andrew, Heidi Malm, Claudia Card, and various members of the audience for their comments on that occasion. It was presented at a philosophy colloquium of the City University of New York (CUNY, Graduate School) on February 3, 1999, and I also thank those who commented at that time.

1. Nussbaum's note 98 reads:

> Perhaps I am handicapped by the fact that I simply do not recognize my own experience of motherhood in Noddings's descriptions of fusing and bonding. My first sharp impression of Rachel Nussbaum was as a pair of feet drumming on my diaphragm with a certain distinct separateness, a pair of arms flexing their muscles against my bladder. Before even her hair got into the world a separate voice could be heard inside, proclaiming its individuality or even individualism, and it has not stopped arguing yet, 24 years later. I am sure RN would be quite outraged by the suggestion that her own well being was *at any time* merged with that of her mother, and her mother would never dare to make such an overweening suggestion [italics added]. This liberal experience of maternity as the give and take of argument has equipped me ill to understand the larger mysteries of Noddings's text.

REFERENCES

Baier, Annette C. *Moral Prejudices: Essays on Ethics.* Cambridge, Mass.: Harvard University Press, 1994.

Baron, Marcia W. "Kantian Ethics." In *Three Methods of Ethics*, edited by Marcia W. Baron, Philip Pettit, and Michael Slote. Oxford: Blackwell, 1997.

Barry, Brian. *Justice as Impartiality.* Oxford: Oxford University Press, 1995.

Darwall, Stephen. *Impartial Reason.* Ithaca, N.Y.: Cornell University Press, 1983.

Darwall, Stephen. *Philosophical Ethics.* Boulder, Colo.: Westview Press, 1998.

Dworkin, Ronald. *Taking Rights Seriously.* Cambridge, Mass.: Harvard University Press, 1977.

Frankfurt, Harry. Comment on David Velleman's "Love and Duty," delivered at the annual meeting of the American Philosophical Association, Eastern Division, Philadelphia, Penn. December 30, 1997.

Frazer, Elizabeth and Nicola Lacey. *The Politics of Community. A Feminist Critique of the Liberal-Communitarian Debate.* Toronto: University of Toronto Press, 1993.

Friedman, Marilyn. *What Are Friends For? Feminist Perspectives on Personal Relationships and Moral Theory.* Ithaca, N.Y.: Cornell University Press, 1993.

Goodin, Robert E. *Utilitarianism as a Public Philosophy.* Cambridge, Mass.: Cambridge University Press, 1995.

Held, Virginia. *Rights and Goods. Justifying Social Action.* New York: The Free Press/ Macmillan, 1984.

Held, Virginia. *Feminist Morality. Transforming Culture, Society, and Politics.* Chicago: University of Chicago Press, 1993.

Held, Virginia. "Rights: Moral and Legal." In *A Companion to Feminist Philosophy.* Edited by Alison Jaggar and Iris Young. Oxford: Blackwell, 1998.

Hill, Thomas. Comment on David Velleman's "Love and Duty," delivered at the annual meeting of the American Philosophical Association, Eastern Division, Philadelphia, Penn. December 30, 1997.

Kittay, Eva Feder. "Taking Dependency Seriously." *Hypatia* 10, no. 1 (1995): 8–29.

MacCormick, Neil. "Justice as Impartiality: Assenting with Anti-Contractualist Reservations." *Political Studies* XLIV (1996): 305–10.

Mendus, Susan. "Some Mistakes about Impartiality." *Political Studies* XLIV (1996): 319–27.

Nagel, Thomas. *The Possibility of Altruism.* London: Oxford University Press, 1970.

Nagel, Thomas. *The View From Nowhere.* New York: Oxford University Press, 1986.

Nussbaum, Martha C. *The Feminist Critique of Liberalism.* The Lindley Lecture. The University of Kansas, 1997.

Rawls, John. *A Theory of Justice.* Cambridge, Mass.: Harvard University Press, 1971.

Rawls, John. *Political Liberalism.* New York: Columbia University Press, 1993.

Velleman, J. David. "Love and Duty." Paper presented at the annual meeting of the American Philosophical Association, Eastern Division, Philadelphia, Penn. December 30, 1997.

Williams, Bernard. *Moral Luck: Philosophical Papers 1973–80.* Cambridge, Mass.: Cambridge University Press, 1981.

6

Inequalities versus Evils

Claudia Card

The dichotomizing of justice and care is problematic, as I have argued elsewhere.[1] That is, neither justice nor care may be properly intelligible as an ethical concept entirely independently of the other one. In particular, an ethic of care without justice is ill-equipped to confront evil. Yet there are elements of justice that do abstract from care. Equality is such an element. We can, of course, specify equality in caring treatment. But the bare ideas of equal rights under law and of the even-handed administration of policies include no more substantive an idea of care than simply being concerned to be consistent and to avoid arbitrariness. The moving force behind both utilitarianism and care ethics often seems to be the concern to oppose evils people suffer from others' wrongdoing. The concern to avoid arbitrariness is not the same and is less important, or so I will argue.

One need not be committed to either utilitarianism or a care ethic to prioritize opposition to evils, although I do not argue that here. I have no interest in defending utilitarianism or even a utilitarian understanding of "harm." But the historical focus of utilitarians on what are genuinely serious harms, I suspect, may account for its continuing attraction among its many adherents. Here, I simply explore and support the idea that opposition to evils deserves priority over opposition to inequality. I defend the view that, in particular, opposition to inequalities should be less essential to feminist ethics than opposition to evils and that it is not fruitful to try to recast the concern to address evils simply as a concern with fundamental equality.

EQUALITY FEMINISM VERSUS FEMINIST OPPOSITION TO OPPRESSION

Many would identify American feminism with the pursuit of women's equality. Equality feminism has often meant, in practice, equal rights for white middle-class

83

women and white middle-class men, the generally unstated but implied comparison classes. The comparison classes have seldom been women and men globally, white
women and men of color, nor middle-class women and working-class, jobless, or
homeless men. Women who are either not white or not middle class have often been
less focused on gender inequalities than on other injustices.

Yet there is also a long history of feminist activism that has not prioritized equality but has sought relief from oppression. Media publicity for women's equality or
gender equality (which sometimes focuses on men rather than on women) unfortunately tends to draw attention away from the most serious evils of oppression. It
easily trivializes feminism by focusing on opposition to inequalities that are not
particularly oppressive, some that may not be oppressive at all, and some that may
actually be needed to redress injustices to women. Legal scholar Catharine
MacKinnon approaches some of these issues by contrasting inequality as difference
with inequality as dominance, pointing out rightly that of these, domination (and
the peculiar "differences" that it produces) has been feminism's appropriate target
of criticism.[2] Martha Minow, also a legal scholar, points to what she calls "the dilemma of difference," noting that both treating women the same as men and offering special treatment to women on account of women's special needs can have the
effect of re-entrenching "differences" that are oppressive to women.[3]

I have not found that the concept of dominance, highlighted by Catharine
MacKinnon, makes the ethically critical point as well as the concept of oppression
does. The reason is that oppression (by its very nature) damages and distorts, whereas
dominance—a superior power position—may not actually do damage even when it
is unjustifiable. Dominance has the potential to be oppressive, and when it is, we
can subsume it under oppression. The point is that the most serious practices to be
resisted are those that do major harm.

My thinking about equality and its forms and relative importance is in the tradition of those who insist on the centrality to feminism of resisting oppression. Oppression is a paradigm evil, although not all evils are instances of oppression. Oppression is of something (a people, a group, or an individual) that survives in a
damaged form. The evil of genocide is beyond oppression (and murder is beyond
individual oppression, although institutionalized murder is a common form of group
oppression). I find that the ethically critical point that feminists who target oppression can make with regard to the relative importance of equality can be articulated
more generally, clearly, and directly by using the language of evil. That is what I attempt to do.

Inequalities, I will soon argue, are not in themselves evils, although some inequalities can give rise to evils, and they often accompany evils. If inequalities are not in
themselves evils, it is a mistake to focus on inequality as the basic wrong to be addressed by feminism and by other movements against social oppression. Some inequalities, however, can facilitate the perpetration of evils or interfere with addressing them effectively, which then gives them a special importance.

Although I do not regard eliminating inequalities as top priority, I do think feminists should take inequalities seriously, especially gross inequalities of power. I think Catharine MacKinnon is right about that. Yet I understand that concern as not necessarily prioritizing inequalities that discriminate against women. Most feminists today are rightly concerned (at least in principle) with racial equality, antilesbian and antigay discrimination, and many economic inequalities, even when those inequalities are not obviously at the same time gender inequalities. These become appropriate concerns of feminism because the principles and values underlying feminist opposition to discrimination against women and girls apply with equal force to many kinds of discrimination, and there is often no reason to find the discrimination against women and girls worse; sometimes other discriminations are worse.

In my view, however, feminism's—or any political activism's—most important concern should be evils, not inequalities (or their related discriminations and biases). That inequalities should not be feminism's paramount concern is actually a fairly modest claim, however startling it may sound in the context of American feminism. To clarify that, we need to distinguish evils from what is bad, undesirable, or even unfair or unjust although not evil.

EVILS AND OPPRESSION

And so I turn to the concept of evils. In his genealogy of morality, Nietzsche distinguished between evil (*bose*) and bad (*schlecht*) as belonging to two distinguishable modes of valuation. In *Beyond Good and Evil,* he wrote of master and slave moralities.[4] Later, he ceased referring to master moralities in favor of a noble or aristocratic mode of valuation. Judgments of badness belong, he maintained, to the noble or aristocratic mode of valuation (originally, he speculated, the mode of those in power, who regarded themselves as outstanding—lucky, beautiful, strong, and the like—looking down on others as "bad" by contrast). Judgments of evil, he maintained, belong to what he called the slave, common, or "herd" mode of valuation (originally, he speculated, the mode of the powerless, oppressed, unfortunate masses, who condemned their powerful terrorizers as "evil").[5] Whereas "bad," on Nietzsche's view, appears to mean basically "ordinary," "low," or "inferior" (unlucky, ugly, etc.), and thereby worthy of contempt or even pity, "evil" appears to mean "willfully harmful or hurtful" (or dangerous) and thereby rightly to be hated. What is judged evil, as Nietzsche noted, elicits fear and the impotent anger, or *ressentiment*, of those unable to protect themselves or to fight it. Attitudinally, judgments of evil carry a seriousness missing from judgments of mere inferiority. Those who judge others to be evil tend to be focused on and heavily occupied with those they judge, whereas those who judge others to be inferior are not especially occupied with those they judge.

The distinction I wish to call attention to, between what is evil and what is bad or undesirable without being evil, is similar in some ways, but not quite the same as Nietzsche's distinction, despite the sameness of terminology. Yet it is a commonly recognizable distinction, one commonly described in just those terms, and it shares some important features of Nietzsche's distinction. However, there is a difference regarding to whom or to what the negative judgement is applied. Nietzsche was concerned with judgments about agents (as either evildoers or inferiors). In contrast, my concern is primarily with evils as things that are undergone or suffered—what is done to people—although the evil nature of what is undergone or suffered derives in part from wrongdoing that is implicated in its genesis, maintenance, or aggravation. Thus, evildoers are not irrelevant to judgments of evil in the sense with which I am concerned, but neither are they the focus.

On the other hand, a similarity is the heaviness or seriousness that Nietzsche notices, an important common element between his understanding and mine. It is an emotional clue to differences between what is evil and what is undesirable or bad but not evil.

A second difference is that for Nietzsche it was, at least initially, an open question as to whether what is evil is also bad. He took seriously the proposition that many agents who have been judged evil were not bad (he mentions Napoleon and ancient Romans), but were actually superior individuals. For me, it is not an open question whether what is evil is also bad. In what follows I hope to make clear why not. I understand what is evil as bad both because of the immorality in its genesis (or maintenance or aggravation) and because of what it means for the basic well-being of those who suffer it. Nietzsche was arguably concerned, in his genealogy of morality, to contrast "evil" as a moral judgment with non-moral judgments of negative value.[6] My concern is, rather, to draw a contrast within morality between what is evil and what is merely bad or undesirable (including some injustices) but not evil. But I think Nietzsche was right in some of the things he observed about judgments of evil. I think he was right in observing that not only are such judgments marked by seriousness or heaviness, but also that we tend to fear and hate (at least initially) what we regard as evil. Evils command our attention in a way that what is merely inferior does not. We try to rise above what is merely inferior, not let it occupy our attention too much, not take it too seriously, that is, not take it more seriously than it is worth. Evil, however, we find worth taking seriously. We may question the humanity of anyone who does not.

For those who suffer them, evils present special challenges. With regard to past evils that are incapable of adequate reparation or reversal, and where adequate compensation is impossible, there is the challenge of how to go on with life and what attitudes to take toward perpetrators.[7] With regard to continuing evils, there is also the challenge of how to stop or mitigate them. For potential evils, there is the challenge of how to prevent the actualization of the potentiality. These challenges are often urgent. With regard to what is merely bad or disappointing, the challenges are less serious. What is bad but not evil does not ordinarily force us to confront the question of how or whether to go on with our lives. We may wish to prevent or mitigate many bad things where we can easily do so. However, often we judge that they are not worth a great investment of energy or other expense, and sometimes we think people should just learn to take their knocks, get used to it or get over it. ("If you can't stand the heat, get out of the kitchen." "Into each life some rain must fall.") In contrast, we are not surprised if someone cannot just "get over" evils they have suffered. One's ability to deal with evils is not on a par with being a good sport. Rain we expect, but not acid (even though acid is somewhat predictable, too).

The sense of "evil" that I intend marks the worst sorts of wrongs, those that people hope never to have to experience directly: slavery, torture, murder, sustained battering and stalking, forcible rape, mass rape, gang rape, certain betrayals, severe poverty, and certain of the illnesses, disabilities, and physical or mental disorders that either result from or are aggravated by social injustice and oppression. These are things that we think no one should have to experience, no matter what it does for anyone else. To adapt a formulation from John Rawls regarding primary goods, we might say of such experiences that everyone can be presumed to want to avoid them, no matter what else they might want.[8] It is difficult to imagine anyone freely choosing to undergo any of these things for the sake of something else that they wanted, although in a context already structured by evil, such as a death camp, one may be forced to choose among evils.

Evil in this sense does not just mean "very bad" in the sense of ranking way down on a scale of rational preferences. Nor does it simply mean "very inferior" in the sense of rating extremely poorly in level of performance or utility. Although evils can be presumed to rank low on the preference scales of those who suffer them, and some surely rank lower than others, it is not simply their preference rating that distinguishes them as evils. It matters on what the preference is based. There is an urgency about evils that derives from their relation to such things as the possibility of trust, the depth and permanence or lastingness of damage to the health and well-being of individuals and relationships, the impossibility of reparation or even containment of damages, and the impossibility of adequate or meaningful compensation. One can fail to appreciate evils as such, if one fails to perceive those kinds of connections, which may partially explain why martial rape was not publicly recognized as an evil until recently. Evils are a grave attack on basic sources of well-being. They are grave, both in the centrality to well-being of what is attacked, and in that the damage tends to persist and to infect a whole life or a whole community or environment, or substantial portions of it. They assault our humanity and dignity. They are the sorts of assault from which one may never fully recover. Inequalities, on the other hand, can rightly be sources of resentment without being attacks on basic well-being or on the possibility of a life with dignity.

ARE SOME INEQUALITIES EVILS?

It may be argued that some unjust inequalities—inequalities that might not in themselves be evils if they were merely sporadic or isolated incidents in a life that is otherwise flourishing—can become evils if they are very systematic. Being arbitrarily excluded from an activity that one enjoys and for which one even has an aptitude might be an example. Such exclusions, when systematic, may come to symbolize a social judgment of inferiority regarding one's humanity. They may thereby assault the basic self-esteem and human dignity of those who suffer the injustice. The historical examples of South African apartheid and racial segregation in the United States come readily to mind.

But how is it that such inequalities come to be an assault on the dignity of those who suffer the injustice? It is difficult to be clear empirically about the extent to which it is the quality—that is, the nature—of the treatment, as distinct from the inequality of its distribution, that is responsible for the assault on dignity. In the examples of South African apartheid and racial segregation in the United States, "inequality" grossly under-describes the situation. Blacks in both areas were subject to unspeakable violence, terror, poverty, and degradation.

And yet perhaps the basic point remains that the symbolic meaning of a form of treatment can turn it into an assault on dignity that makes it an evil. That point would hold, however, regardless of whether the treatment in question was systematic or an isolated instance. Deprivations that might in other contexts be annoyances or inconveniences—such as being denied access to a restroom or drinking fountain or being made to sit in the back of the bus—become evils when they acquire the power to symbolize a social judgment of inferior humanity in those so restricted, which then serves, in effect, to license inhuman treatment of them. Arbitrary (unequal) deprivations may be most likely to have that power when institutionalized and supported by the sanctions of law and when they are associated with a natural feature (such as skin color) or an imposed feature (such as badges or readily identifiable clothing). When one's entire life becomes permeated by such discriminations, they can take on an importance that they might not otherwise have had. Thus, inequalities that look superficially like inconveniences may in fact contribute significantly to indignity in those who suffer the discrimination.

Still, there are distinctions to be made. Not every indignity is an evil. The following is a case that involves a certain indignity. Yet I would not go so far as to consider it an evil. When I was a graduate student at Harvard in the early 1960s, I was routinely denied access to the Lamont Library, the undergraduate men's library, for no other reason than that I was female. (I tested the policy that excluded women by attempting more than once to enter that library). Men, however, were welcomed into the Radcliffe Library, the undergraduate women's library, on the first floor, which enabled them to check out any books they wished. Women were not allowed even through the front door to Lamont Library. I resented that. A few of my course assignments were even in books obtainable only in the Lamont Library. I could have asked a male friend to check them out for me. (The library did not provide men to offer this service to women). But I generally did not, because it was embarrassing to have to make the request. This affront to my dignity, however, was compensated to no small extent by the privilege of being accepted to study at Harvard in the first place. Being excluded from the Lamont Library was not something I thought about much or got worked up about, even though the difference between the Lamont and Radcliffe Library policies did symbolize the judgment that females were less important members of the university than males. Nor was this an isolated instance of discrimination against females on that campus, although it was remarkable for being so overt. Women received markedly less encouragement to participate in class discussions, although that was not (to my knowledge) an official policy. And undergraduate women were not supposed to appear on the streets in pants unless they wore a long coat. Still, none of these discriminations was what I would regard as an evil. None of them had the consequence of licensing anyone to treat me as though I was subhuman. They did not touch the basics of my life, such as necessary transportation, drinking water, or having access to bathrooms. Not every affront to dignity is an evil, however wrong. There are degrees of seriousness even here, as marked, for example, by the difference between an affront (or slight) and an assault (or attack). Not all injuries to dignity leave permanent or deeply disfiguring scars, even if they leave permanent memories and are rightly cause for resentment.

In the matter of prioritizing, evils deserve the first attention of those who are in a position to alleviate or prevent them, before attending to lesser insults, disappointments, discomforts, and even many sources of resentment, however painful, even many unfairnesses or injustices. When an inequality actually becomes an evil, the evil, strictly speaking, is the serious damage brought about by wrongdoing. As Philip Hallie argues in his posthumously published *Tales of Good and Evil, Help and Harm,* "evil does not happen only inside moral agents" but involves an "intimate linkage between the moral agents of evil and the sufferings and deaths those moral agents willingly perpetrate."[9] Citing Lewis Carroll's parable of the walrus and the carpenter, Hallie argues that Carroll was right to teach the importance of attending more to the harm done than to the feelings of its perpetrators.[10] A similar point can be made about attending to a perpetrator's scruples regarding consistency and the avoidance of arbitrariness.

Still, some inequalities that symbolize inferior humanity may count among evils. Not just any kind of inequality, however, can come to symbolize a social judgment of inferiority in a way that is deeply and lastingly damaging.

EVILS AND IMMORALITY

I turn next to the moral character of evils. Evils in the sense with which I am concerned are moral phenomena in that someone's morally faulty behavior is implicated in their genesis, aggravation, or continuation. Not every serious deprivation of well-being counts as an evil in this sense. Unforeseeable earthquakes, for example, may inflict death and irreparably gross injury. But they are not, morally, evils in the sense that I have in mind. They are not evils even if we judge that the victims did not morally deserve to suffer as severely as they did. The appeal to desert of good or ill is one of the ways that evils have been distinguished as moral, by contrast with merely natural, in religious discussions of the theological problem of evil. But such an appeal is neither necessary nor sufficient for what is suffered to be evil in a moral sense of that concept. There must, however, be a perpetrator or perpetrators who could have, and should have, done otherwise. There must be one or more agents whose wrongful behavior brought about, failed to prevent, or otherwise contributed significantly to what is suffered.

Another thing that is not necessary, however, is that the perpetrator's motive or intention be to make anyone's life intolerable. There need be only a wrongful intention or the wrongful absence of a right intention. On this point, I agree with John Kekes, who finds in his *Facing Evil* that most evil is not motivated by anything like wickedness or sadism, that most evildoers are not monstrous in that sense, not extraordinary or hair-raising but, on the contrary, all too ordinary and even ugly.[11] It is not necessary, for example, that the perpetrator intends to cause serious suffering or deprivation or takes any pleasure or satisfaction in the spectacle thereof. This distinguishes the sense of evil with which I am concerned from a sense of evil that animates the traditional Christian conception of the devil. It may also help to distinguish the evils with which I am concerned from Nietzsche's focus. For where a perpetrator's motives or intentions are not plausibly regarded as wicked or sadistic, hatred of the evildoer may not be a very natural response. We may hate what has been done to us or hate the fact that it was done to us without finding it possible or easy to hate the doer. In fact, an evildoer may have as much in common, in terms of character, with those whom Nietzsche's ancient nobles had judged to be bad (inferior) as with those their "slaves" condemned as evil.

The motives and intentions of many perpetrators of evil are often, as Hannah Arendt observed of Adolph Eichmann, utterly banal.[12] From this, however, it does not follow that evil is banal.[13] What perpetrators of evil bring about, or fail to prevent, is not at all banal. It appeared (at his trial) that some of Eichmann's motives and intentions in making the actions, decisions, and choices that significantly furthered the Holocaust, were ordinary, mundane (his ambitions to be promoted to a higher office, for example, or to be recognized for his efficiency), although there was nothing banal about their upshot. I would not say that Eichmann's character on the whole was banal, however, because he was not ignorant of the destinations of his shipments, of the conditions of life and death in the camps, nor of the part he was playing in Hitler's "final solution." Hatred of those, such as Ilse Koch or Ivan the Terrible, who appear to have been motivated by sadism or by a hatred of Jews may arise more spontaneously than hatred of petty-minded Philistines like Eichmann. But it was the Eichmanns who did more evil.

This account of evil can easily be extended to the sufferings undergone in other lives besides those of human beings, with a certain modification. Instead of referring to an assault on one's humanity, we can think more generally of an assault on the basic well-being and dignity of living beings and their relationships. Many of the worst evils tolerated in contemporary North America are done (by people who are not especially sadistic) to non-human vertebrate animals, especially those raised for human luxury foods and those tortured and destroyed in commercial and military experiments.[14] A point analogous to my earlier point about inequality can also be made about feminism and evils—feminists are rightly concerned about evils in general, not just those evils that are clearly implicated in sexist practices. Thus, feminists are rightly concerned about the evils of racist and class oppression, even when there is not a special story to be told about how they intersect with or are causally related to the evils of sex oppression. For the same principles and values that underlie opposition to sex oppression apply with equal force to other oppressions, and sex oppression is not always the worst. Sometimes other oppressions are worse. What is feminist about feminist opposition to oppressions that are not themselves instances of sex oppression, is the history or origin of the appreciation and concern to address the evils in question, the likelihood that one will find it natural to draw analogies with sex oppression, and so forth.

To summarize thus far, evils, in the sense with which I am concerned here, have two aspects. One aspect is that they constitute the most serious harms—the profoundest, most lasting, least containable, least remediable—to one's well-being or dignity. They tend to make life intolerable for those who suffer them. The other is that the harm results from or is aggravated or supported by wrongdoings (which can take the form of culpable omissions, as in carelessness, recklessness, or callous indifference). Inequalities are often not among the most serious harms, even when they are wrong, although evil can be inflicted unequally, and some inequalities can facilitate the perpetration of evils or hinder attempts to alleviate them. And when they are, I suspect that what makes them evil is not the inequality of their distribution, but the harm suffered by their victims. In that case, calling them "inequalities" puts the focus on the wrong aspect of what is the matter, even though it is not false.

SOME APPLICATIONS AND IMPLICATIONS

Murder is an evil, although theft may not be, and some murders are more evil than others. Systematic murder (short of genocide) or other terrorism (such as institutionalized rape, martial or "civilian") is profoundly oppressive to groups so targeted. Other examples of evil that have given rise to feminism include domestic battery and other intimate partner abuse, sexual slavery, and "incest" when that term refers to prolonged child rape by a trusted adult, or by an adult who has authority over the child, or when it refers to rape of a very young child, regardless of frequency. These are the more obvious sexual evils suffered primarily by women and girls. Others threatening women in misogynist societies include (forcible) imprisonment in insane asylums or nursing homes and homelessness. Imprisonment can be an evil in itself. But also, it renders inmates vulnerable to further evils, such as the lobotomies to which women like Frances Farmer were subjected in the United States in earlier decades of this century. Homelessness exposes the homeless to poor sanitation and increased risk of disease. Men also suffer such evils, although less frequently than women. Rebellious women in patriarchy are more often than men judged insane by men with power over them. The elderly include more widows and spinsters than widowers or bachelors. Many widows, divorcees, and escapees from domestic abuse have been left without health insurance, Social Security benefits, or the means to earn a livelihood. Historically, men in power have been less concerned about remedying inhumane conditions suffered primarily by women.

Many things suffered by women and girls that have been identified as inequalities are, more importantly, evils. Perhaps they are commonly identified as inequalities because it is easier to accuse those in power of discrimination than to accuse them of evildoing. "Unfair" is a less harsh judgment than "evil." But there is the risk in thus tempering one's judgment of trivializing the object of one's concern. Women inmates in prison have, historically, had to do the laundry for both women's and men's prisons. However unfair, that is not an evil. The rape of female inmates by prison guards is an evil. That is not simply discrimination. If it is pointed out that male inmates get raped, too (they do, by other inmates), that does nothing to mitigate the evil of the rape of female inmates. The rapes of both sexes are evils.

A few years ago, a TV ad, "If you let me play sports . . . " sponsored by a popular maker of athletic clothing, was aired frequently on ESPN during women's basketball games. It is one of my all-time favorite commercials. In it girls one after another tell of the evils they will be better equipped to avoid or defend themselves against if they have sustained athletic experience in their youth. ("I will be less likely to be depressed," "I will be more likely to leave a man who beats me," "I will be less likely to have breast cancer," etc.). At first, I disliked "let me" and wanted to change "let me play sports" to something like "encourage me to play sports." "Let me" seemed to endorse patriarchal authority to give females permissions to do what we should not need permission to do. But then, listening to myself say it with the substituted words, I realized that "encourage me" sends a less powerful message because it conveys that girls do not already have a natural desire to play sports. The "let me" conveys that the only thing holding girls back is sexist prohibition. "Let me" in this context just means "don't stop me" or "don't hold me back." It is "let me" more in the sense of "leave me to" than in the sense of "permit me to."

What makes this ad powerful is not that it is a plug for Title IX, that is, not its appeal to equality in government-supported educational programs. Rather, its power comes from its connection of the evils women suffer in a misogynist society with girls' deprivation of opportunities for sustained athletic development. What is at stake here is a basic health issue, mental and physical. If we press the question, how much opportunity for athletic development should girls have, the answer "they should have as much as boys have" does not really get at the basic issue. Maybe some boys have too much. Maybe others have too little. The right kind of answer should relate the amount of opportunity for athletic development to health and well-being, or at least to the evils that such opportunities can easily prevent.

I think feminism's priorities should be to address the evils to which a misogynist environment exposes people and other living beings and to address the evils of oppression generally. In a society in which nobody else is prioritizing them, perhaps women should give special attention to the evils to which females are especially vulnerable and the evils to which misogyny exposes anyone. The reason I have been drawn to radical feminism is that it has seemed to me to have the right priorities (including addressing the evils done to non-human animals and ecosystems) and to have prioritized evils that others have either ignored or subordinated. Socialist feminists could no doubt say the same thing about why they have been drawn to socialist feminism, although my concern regarding socialist feminism is a fear that it will tend to neglect evils that are not ultimately economic. Radical feminists have prioritized violence against women and girls and other living beings (who are often described in the language of femininity), evils that tend to cut across social class differences or simply not be comprehended under the evils produced by social class. The work of Mary Daly in *Gyn/Ecology*, of Susan Griffin in *Woman and Nature*, of Audre Lorde, Andrea Dworkin, Maria Lugones, Catharine MacKinnon, Adrienne Rich, and many others exemplifies this concern.[15] By contrast, I found it impossible to develop anything like the same energy and enthusiasm for the Equal Rights Amendment during the 1980s (not to deny that its defeat was a profound, if predictable, insult), even though some may have seen that amendment as instrumentally important to combating the evils that have concerned me.

A reason that would make sense of why many women of color are not enthusiastic about joining forces with white feminists is the fear that white feminists will prioritize lesser injustices to white women over genuine evils suffered by people of color. Such fears are not unjustified. There seems to be something timid about equality feminism. It suggests the idea that the way to begin is by trying to right a wrong, the pointing out of which will not (or perhaps should not) cause very much offense or disturbance in those who are responsible for the perpetration or maintenance of the wrong, in the faith that success is more likely in such modest beginnings and in the hope that in such beginnings might lay the foundation for more important social changes down the road. Yet the net result of that strategy is to prioritize what is least important and to delay into the never-to-be-concluded future what is most important. Not only should evils receive priority over lesser injustices but also evils that are not, or not particularly, sexist should receive priority over sexist injustices that are not evils (such as some salary inequities among tenured professors).

DOES RESPECT FOR HUMANITY IMPLY BASIC EQUALITY?

It is not that inequality is unimportant. The point is, rather, about priorities. Relieving and preventing evils is more important than achieving equality. One might object, however, to that very opposition on the ground that it presupposes that evils do not essentially already involve any significant inequality. Suppose one were to object that an important sort of inequality is always at the root of evil, namely, the failure to treat someone with the basic respect that everyone deserves. I, myself, have characterized evils in terms of what anyone can be presumed to want to avoid and what no one should have to suffer. Do these terms "anyone" and "no one" import a significant ideal of equality into the very concept of evil?

If they do, it is not a sort of equality that I find it objectionable to prioritize over other inequalities. But neither do I find it helpful to say that what is basically wrong here is a fundamental sort of inequality. What seems to me genuinely helpful is to identify the kind of treatment that no one should have to endure. Further, there are dangers that emphasizing equality can lead one to tolerate evils that should not be tolerated. Consider the following.

When evils are unequally distributed, it is no improvement to inflict them on those who have escaped thus far, so as to even things out, when doing so would not significantly lessen the burden on everyone who suffers the evils in question. When it is not possible to give equal attention to all who equally deserve relief, or even to make sure that all who are equally deserving have an equal opportunity to obtain relief, the best course is not to withhold relief from everyone alike so as to avoid perpetrating any unfairness. Better to help some arbitrarily, if that can be done without subjecting others to comparably serious evils, than to use the impossibility of fairness as an excuse to do nothing. At least, when it is a question of relieving evils, rather than distributing a luxury or removing an inconvenience, it is better to help some arbitrarily. There may be something to be said for withholding from everyone a luxury or relief from inconvenience rather than bestowing it arbitrarily. It may be more important there to avoid envy generated by the inequality. But resentment of unavoidable inequalities in alleviating evils can be misplaced or petty.

It may be objected that equality does become important when resources are limited although not so limited that it is impossible to do at least something for everyone. If there are not enough resources to make everyone safe from domestic battery, then the question arises as to how much protection anyone should have a right to. Thus, when resources are limited, the question of how to distribute them is a fair one. Equality is one answer. But suppose we were then to conclude that women's physical and moral safety in the home should receive as much resource allocation as men's physical and moral safety in the home: an equal number of shelters, for example, for women as for men. If what is necessary to men's safety is taken as the defining standard, this will not help women much. If what women need is taken as the defining standard, no one will want to spend comparable resources on unnecessary shelters for men when there are genuine needs to be met elsewhere. But men may then resent the "extra" resource allocation for women and allow that resentment to reinforce existing condescending attitudes toward women. This will not help women much, either. Here we seem to have an example of what Martha Minow calls "the dilemma of difference." The way out, she rightly perceives, is to not take the inequality of needs and the existing social values associated with them as givens, but to consider what gives rise to differential needs, what they mean, and what gives rise to such things as the values underlying condescension toward women.

Equal resource allocation is also how the University of Wisconsin has been forced to deal with women's safety on campus at night in regard to free emergency evening transit programs; such transit must be equally available to men and to women. Equal resource allocation is how Title IX deals (or is supposed to deal) with female development in government-supported educational institutions. It prohibits discrimination. It does not otherwise mandate programs.

As in the case of domestic battery, this kind of policy often offers women no significant relief at all. In a misogynist environment women need more protection than men in order to be equally safe. Because male students have less to fear in the way of assault by women students than women have to fear in the way of assault by men, an emergency transit system that paid no attention to the genders of drivers, escorts, or co-riders would put women at greater risk of assault. And it still seems to me that the focus should be not on equal safety (which is compatible in principle with everyone in fact being quite unsafe) but, rather, on achieving certain minimum standards of safety.

The defender of equality as a basic value might then try to clarify that position as supporting a special kind of equality, namely, a guaranteed minimum standard of well-being for all. This returns to a focus on what everyone should have or what no one should have to suffer. Depending on how we understand the implementation of this utopian ideal, it may be compatible with my concern to prioritize evil. But I am not sure. Here is a lingering concern that I have.

How important is the "equality" (or "for all") idea in situations where it is possible to offer relief to some but not to all and there is no fair way, or no uncontroversially fair way, to determine who gets the relief? It may be, for example, that if one takes time to try to be fair in this way, the "relief" will come too late, as in the case of people seeking immigration as asylum from an oppressor. On the level of individual decision making in everyday life, this kind of situation seldom becomes much of a problem. If I can help a specific individual who is suffering by spending a lot of time and energy doing things that make it impossible for me to help someone else who is suffering similarly, I ordinarily think it is a good thing to help at least one of them even if I cannot help both. If I have no special prior relationship to either, I would hardly pause to draw straws or debate the merits of helping this one rather than that one, although I might easily engage in such reflection (as Virginia Woolf did in *Three Guineas*) with respect to sending money to charitable or political organizations that aim to relieve evils.[16] When I am confronted directly with an individual facing an evil that I can alleviate, it is much less natural for me to raise the question of whether someone else might need my help even more.

With regard to extending relief to individuals, I am reminded of the Talmudic verse inscribed inside the ring given Oskar Schindler by his factory workers—that one who saves a single life saves the world entire.[17] Something about this seems very right to me and seems to have enormous moral and political implications about what it is and is not right to do. The idea is not to excuse us from saving fewer lives than we might have simply because it is enough to have saved one. Instead, the idea seems to sanction the saving of those whom we could save, even though there were also many others equally in need, and even though there may be, from that point of view, something arbitrary about our having saved the ones that we did save.

CONCLUDING OBSERVATIONS

There is an indirect way in which less serious inequalities may be justifiably given a political priority that would not otherwise be justified. Attention to equality in resource distribution may become instrumentally important to securing the cooperation of those whose labors are needed to create the further resources needed or helpful for addressing genuine evils. Thus, even when the evils ultimately to be addressed are more important, it may become important for political decision-makers to take very seriously equality in resource distribution so as to be able effectively to elicit cooperative efforts required to address genuine evils. But it does not cease thereby to be the case that, ethically, the more important concern is to address the evils.

I suspect that the plausibility of Carol Gilligan's popular dichotomy between an ethic of justice and an ethic of care may have roots in a tension that is internal to the idea of justice. Justice is both personal and institutional. It is concerned with addressing evils as well as arbitrariness. And its concern with arbitrary inequalities can come into conflict with its more basic concern to address and redress evils.

I have not clarified what it means to prioritize. This is, of course, an important question. To deal with it adequately would require another essay. I do not, however, understand prioritizing evils to imply that no resources whatever should be devoted to other matters until all evils have been satisfactorily addressed. That understanding would no doubt require that all our resources be devoted to addressing evils and to nothing else, for there may never come a day when there are no more evils. I do have in mind giving first attention to evils, recognizing that they are most important to address, but not with the implication that we may not then devote some attention to other things as well.[18]

ACKNOWLEDGMENTS

I am grateful to David Weberman for comments on a very early draft of this paper, which led to substantial revisions. I am also grateful to other colleagues in the Philosophy Department at the University of Wisconsin, to conference participants at the University of San Diego Law School in December 1997, and to audiences at the Pacific Division American Philosophical Association Convention in March 1998 and at Moorhead State University in 1998, for their many thoughtful questions and comments that led to still more revisions.

NOTES

1. Claudia Card, *The Unnatural Lottery: Character and Moral Luck* (Philadelphia: Temple University Press, 1996), 49–96.
2. Catharine A. MacKinnon, *Feminism Unmodified: Discourses on Life and Law* (Cambridge, Mass.: Harvard University Press, 1987), 32–45.
3. Martha Minow, *Making All the Difference: Inclusion, Exclusion, and American Law* (Ithaca, N. Y.: Cornell University Press, 1990).
4. Friedrich Nietzsche, *Basic Writings of Nietzsche*, ed. and trans. Walter Kaufmann (New York: New York Modern Library, 1968), 394–98.
5. Friedrich Nietzsche, *On the Genealogy of Morals*, trans. Walter Kaufmann and R. J. Hollingdale (New York: Vintage, 1969), 25–55.
6. This view is defended by Maudemarie Clark, "Nietzsche's Attack on Morality" (unpublished Ph.D. dissertation, University of Wisconsin, Madison, 1976).
7. I discuss this kind of challenge in "Living with Evils" in *The Realm of the Spirit: Essays in Honor of Virginia Held*, ed. Mark S. Halfon (Lanham, Md.: Rowman & Littlefield, 1998). See also John Kekes, *Facing Evil* (Princeton, N.J.: Princeton University Press, 1990) and Norman S. Care, *Living with One's Past: Personal Fates and Moral Pain* (Lanham, Md.: Rowman & Littlefield, 1996).
8. John Rawls, *A Theory of Justice* (Cambridge, Mass.: Harvard University Press, 1971), 62, 92. See also Card, *The Unnatural Lottery*, 90–96.
9. Philip Hallie, *Tales of Good and Evil, Help and Harm* (New York: Harper Collins, 1997), 98–99.
10. Hallie, *Tales of Good and Evil*, 93–101.
11. Kekes, *Facing Evil*, chapters 3–5. Unlike Kekes, however, I am not willing to characterize behavior as immoral unless the perpetrator could have done otherwise.
12. Hannah Arendt, *Eichmann in Jerusalem: A Report on the Banality of Evil* (New York: Viking, 1963).
13. Hallie's discussion (97–99) of Hannah Arendt on Adolph Eichmann is very helpful on this point.
14. See Peter Singer, *Animal Liberation*, revised edition (New York: Avon, 1990), chapters 2 and 3, and Ingrid Newkirk, *Free the Animals! The Untold Story of the U.S. Animal Liberation Front and Its Founder, "Valerie"* (Chicago: Noble, 1992), especially chapters 3–6.
15. Mary Daly, *Gyn/Ecology: The Metaethics of Radical Feminism* (Boston: Beacon, 1978); Susan Griffin, *Woman and Nature: The Roaring Inside Her* (New York: Harper & Row, 1978); Audre Lorde, *Sister Outsider: Essays and Speeches* (Trumansburg, N.Y.: Crossing, 1984); Andrea Dworkin, *Woman Hating* (New York: Dutton, 1974); and *Life and Death: Unapologetic Writings on the Continuing War against Women* (New York: Free Press, 1987); Maria Lugones, "Playfulness, 'World'-Travelling, and Loving Perception," *Hypatia* 2:2 (1987): 3–19, and many other articles; Catharine MacKinnon, *Feminism Unmodified*; and Adrienne Rich, *On Lies, Secrets, and Silence: Selected Prose 1966–1978* (New York: Norton, 1979).

16. Virginia Woolf, *Three Guineas* (New York: Harcourt, Brace & World, 1938).

17. Thomas Keneally, *Schindler's List* (New York: Simon & Schuster, 1992; originally 1982), 368.

18. Thanks to Barbara Bergmann for pressing me on this point at the conference on feminism and law at the University of San Diego Law School, December 1997.

7

Particular Justice and General Care

Claudia Card

Are there cases in which we must decide, ethically, whether to prioritize justice over care or to prioritize care over justice? Professor Held finds that there are and argues that, at least sometimes, we ought to prioritize care.[1] She has in mind cases in which the demands of a particular relationship, such as a parent-child relationship, collide with those of universal rules. My discussion is directed to her argument's presupposition that ethical concerns of care lie outside the scope of justice, and that concerns of justice lie outside the scope of care.

It is difficult to compare care ethics with justice because of the relative imprecision of philosophical accounts of care ethics. Justice has a longer and fuller academic philosophical history than care ethics. The requirements of care ethics are less clear, even if it is sometimes clear what caring for someone requires, or what someone needs for basic well-being, or what a relationship requires to survive or thrive. Whereas principles of justice have been elaborated in detail, the requirements of care ethics tend to be left at an intuitive level. Or, conclusions are drawn about what care requires in particular cases without a clear rationale for why care requires that rather than something else. How does care ethics determine which needs one ought to respond to and in which ways one ought to respond? Perhaps care ethics is not only about responding to needs.

If it is difficult to compare care ethics with justice, it is also true, because of narrow but common assumptions about what justice requires, that relationships between justice and care can seem clearer than they should. Justice is often assumed to be impartial and universal, as though "impartial justice" and "universal justice" were redundancies. Justice, Kantian ethics, and impartial rules are sometimes lumped together, as though they were more or less the same. Yet Kant's ethics includes what Kant called "duties of virtue" as well as his "duties of justice." Kant understands justice as pertaining only to what is appropriately enforceable. His duties of virtue

include such unenforceable matters as gratitude. But even justice narrowly understood (as pertaining to the enforceable) requires more than consistency and impartiality in the application of rules. It matters what the rules are. Justice requires more
than can be captured even by carefully formulated principles and rules. As Aristotle
noted, equity is a kind of justice that eludes codification in rules, and we need equity for those inevitable cases in which correct applications of the rules (no matter
how well designed they are) fail to yield a just solution.[2]

Justice has many strands, some very general and others very particular. A principle of formal justice requires us to treat relevantly similar cases in relevantly similar ways.[3] It directs that we apply rules consistently. But it does not tell us what rules
to have. Other principles of justice, such as those put forward and defended by John
Rawls, are framed as bases for justifying or evaluating general rules (such as those
of a political constitution or legislation).[4] Yet, as Joel Feinberg argued long ago, justice is also a matter of responding to personal deserts.[5] Justice is not concerned only
with impartiality and universality. It is also concerned with treating particular individuals as they deserve, where what they deserve is a less formal matter than their
entitlements (rights) or even qualifications, as determined by general rules. Feinberg
claimed that the bases of desert are characteristics of the deserving individual or
something that the deserving individual has done.[6] Yet what a particular individual
deserves is often deserved from a particular other. When that is the case, it seems to
me that the desert is often (although not always) grounded in a relationship between
them, such as friendship. Justice grounded in deserts is particular justice, by contrast with the justice grounded in universal or impartial principles applying to everyone alike.

Particular justice has received less attention in ethical theory than universal and
impartial justice.[7] John Rawls presents his principles of justice (as Kant does his
Categorical Imperative) as imposing limits on the legitimate pursuit of goals.[8] They
serve as filters or "side-constraints," scruples. Considerations of care, on the other
hand, may seem to set goals for us: the pursuit of human well-being, the maintenance of relationships. But deserts may also impose scruples on the pursuit of goals.
The particular justice of being responsive to deserts may also be a way of caring that
is better understood as a kind of scrupulousness than as the pursuit of certain goals.

The view of justice as imposing scruples and of care as setting goals could account
for a common view, to which Professor Held objects, that justice and care are compatible in the following way: once the requirements of justice are met, we are permitted to act on considerations of care. This view may seem to reduce care ethics to
matters of personal preference, optional deeds. Yet, one could understand care as
imposing requirements also, but requirements that do not come into play until general principles of justice are satisfied. This appears to be Kant's understanding.[9] His
duty to help others is presented as "imperfect." Imperfect duties, he says, must always yield to perfect ones in cases of conflict between them, and duties of justice
are perfect. On that understanding we have a lexical ordering of justice and care,
one that prioritizes justice systematically over care.[10] Professor Held's view is that

care is not always simply optional and that it would be wrong to order its requirements lexically in that way with respect to justice.

I agree that the claims of particular relationships (such as friendships) are not always optional or reducible to matters of personal preference. Such relationships
impose genuine responsibilities (obligations, although usually not correlated with
rights). Although I am not yet persuaded that such responsibilities lie outside the
scope of justice, I do find it plausible that no lexical ordering of universal justice
and particular justice will withstand scrutiny.

Sometimes the demands of a particular relationship or a person for whom one
cares can be momentous, as Professor Held notes, whereas a conflicting demand
based on a general moral rule may be relatively trivial. One may have to break a
promise to meet someone for coffee, for example, in order to render aid to a seriously injured person or just to "be there" for a partner in crisis. Keeping the promise may be naturally understood as a requirement of justice. But isn't the requirement to aid the injured party, or to be there for one's partner, also a demand of justice?

Lest one object that such a case simply illustrates a conflict between two general
rules (keep promises and aid those in trouble), let me vary the case so as to particu-
larize the demand for care more. Suppose that keeping a promise not to reveal a secret
conflicts with the demands of loyalty to a friend, because you have learned, since
you made the promise, how seriously knowledge of that secret could affect your
friend's welfare. It may not be obvious what you should do. But it is possible that
the promisee will not release you, even though the reason you were asked to keep
the secret is relatively trivial, whereas the potential impact on your friend of the
knowledge of that secret is momentous. If your friend's future welfare would be seriously endangered by not knowing the secret, breaking the promise could be the
right thing to do. Does this mean that care would triumph over justice? Or was what
your friend deserved from you a more important demand of justice? Couldn't it be
unjust (to your friend and to the relationship between you) to be a stickler about
promises here?

Deserts of punishment and reward are paradigms of justice. But these are not the
only morally significant kinds of deserts. People can also deserve trust and loyalty.
Betrayal of a friend can be deeply unjust even if no promise was made. If the demands of a particular relationship or individual can be articulated in terms of what
that person or relationship deserves from us, then, even though the same demands
might also be articulated in the language of care, it is misleading to say that we confront a conflict between justice and care. Some demands of justice (those based on
deserts) can be in conflict with others (those based on impartial rules).

Although failing to treat others as they deserve is a paradigm of injustice, it need
not take the form of violating rights. People often deserve rewards, for example, but
seldom have a right to them. Although sometimes rights and deserts may be inter-
changeable, they are not always. Following Feinberg's distinctions, deserts more often
tend to be relatively informal, in contrast with entitlements (rights) and eligibilities

(meeting minimum qualifications). Deserts elude codification in rules—desert of gratitude, for example. Where deserts are relatively informal in this way, it is sometimes more natural to speak of being unfair to someone than to use the language of injustice. Yet the values may be the same. Whether we call it injustice to someone or unfairness to someone, we are honoring what makes an individual special, rather than what all individuals have in common. Where there is no enforcement or even codification of the appropriate conduct, it takes a stronger, more developed, more nuanced sense of justice to do what is required.

Aristotle presented justice as giving each their due. "What is due" did not mean, "what one has a right to." Aristotle appears to have had no conception of rights. "Due" appears to mean something like "deserved." What our children deserve from us is different from what our parents or lovers deserve. We cannot talk about Aristotelian justice without also talking about relationships—not just in an abstract logical sense, but relationships in the sense of connections. Aristotle observes that "friendship and justice . . . seem to be concerned with the same objects and exhibited between the same persons"; that "the claims of justice differ too; the duties of parents to children and those of brothers to each other are not the same, nor those of comrades and those of fellow citizens"; and that "the injustice increases by being exhibited towards those who are friends in a fuller sense; e.g., it is a more terrible thing to defraud a comrade than a fellow citizen, more terrible not to help a brother than a stranger."[11] He continues, saying that "the demands of justice also seem to increase with the intensity of the friendship, which implies that friendship and justice exist between the same persons and have an equal extension."[12] These remarks may seem difficult to reconcile with his earlier observation that "when men are friends they have no need of justice"[13] unless we take it that "needing justice" in that context means "needing enforcement." But he goes on to note that when people are just, they need friendship as well and "the truest form of justice is thought to be a friendly quality." These observations suggest that relationships underlie justice and determine its scope.

Although Feinberg claimed that deserts are based on some characteristic of the deserving person, or on something that person has done, I would point out that deserts often seem grounded more generally in the relationship between the deserving person and the person or persons from whom certain kinds of treatment are deserved. Friends deserve our loyalty, not simply on the basis of their characteristics as individuals or even on the basis of what they have done simply as individuals, but because they are our friends—at least, if they are good friends (or, perhaps, friends in good standing). Benefactors deserve our gratitude; being someone's benefactor—befriending someone—is being in a certain kind of relationship to that person.[14] Repentant wrongdoers may sometimes deserve forgiveness. Rescuers may deserve praise. A lover may deserve one's trust. Because failing to treat people as they deserve can be unjust to them, justice has a wider scope than that of rights. It is not merely a legal or legalistic concept.

These responses—loyalty, gratitude, forgiveness, praise, trust—are also instances of caring, are they not? If so, they show that caring is wider in scope than caretaking, caregiving, or benevolence. Loyalty might require caretaking on some occasions, but I can be loyal on other occasions simply by refusing to betray someone. Caring is often a matter of taking an appropriately supportive or appreciative attitude toward someone, one that shows that you value that person or your relationship with that person in a certain way. Fred Berger argued that gratitude is important because it shows that we value our benefactor not just as a source of our own welfare.[15] Such responses are not deserved by just anyone from just anyone else. They are particularized. They demonstrate concern and appreciation for the individual. They share emotive elements commonly associated with caring. As with caring, generally, it can be difficult to specify what particular acts, if any, are required for having the appropriate response.

Not all responsiveness to deserts exemplifies caring; arguably, for example, responsiveness to desert of punishment and blame do not. But responsiveness to many kinds of deserts that Feinberg classified as "non-polar"—the kinds mentioned above: gratitude, loyalty, trust, forgiveness—does exhibit behavior that is also naturally recognized as caring behavior, and such responsiveness may be essential to the maintenance of relationships such as friendships.

In her "Look at Some Cases," Professor Held comments briefly on the story in Genesis 22 of God's testing Abraham by asking him to sacrifice his son Isaac, a case much discussed by proponents of care ethics. She then presents at greater length her own case of a father who has special skills that could help many other children besides his own, but only at the cost of his leaving the care of his own child largely to others. Regarding Abraham, she notes that "the relationship between parent and child should not always be subordinated to the command of God or of universal moral rules."[16] Yet it seems arbitrary to regard Abraham's relationship with God as giving only the side of justice and not care, and to regard Abraham's relationship with Isaac as giving the side of care but not justice. If there is obvious justice on either side, is it not in the obligation not to kill? Kierkegaard found the claims of universality on the side of not killing when he presented God's demand as a "teleological suspension of the ethical."[17] Actually, Abraham is caught between two special relationships: with God and with Isaac. God tests Abraham's trust, and Isaac trusts Abraham. Insofar as God deserves Abraham's trust, and Isaac deserves to be able to trust Abraham, there are demands of particular justice on both sides. There is also a demand of universal justice on the side of not killing.

Professor Held's case of the father who has special skills in helping troubled young children succeed academically shows, I think, something very wrong with a utilitarian conception of justice. It also illustrates how difficult it can be to identify what appropriate care requires for all those who may make claims on one's care. The father's child has special claims on his attention. Unless he has already accepted a position of responsibility for the care of other children, it is not unjust favoritism to give special attention to his own child rather than others (when he cannot do both). It might be difficult for him to decide whether to take on the responsibility to care for other children where no one else who had the requisite skills was readily available. But saving others the inconvenience of having to look elsewhere for those skills, perhaps at some expense, need not be sufficient to justify his acceding to their demand. He could justifiably refuse on the grounds of his prior commitment to his family. If securing someone else with the requisite skills proved costly (or even impossible), the responsibility would not be simply the father's. The other children's needs are, presumably, the responsibility of a wider community. A problem with utilitarianism is that it distributes responsibility too expediently.

But, further, in this kind of case, as in Abraham's case, there are demands of care on both sides. Corresponding claims of justice argue each way. On one side is what a particular individual, your child, deserves from you, the parent. On the other is the general demand to help others where you can do so without excessive cost. Care is deserved on one side but also demanded on the other (even if not deserved by the other children from this father). To represent only one side as that of care oversimplifies care ethics. Presumably it is not Professor Held's view that, in general, from the point of view of care ethics, the claims of particular relationships (such as fatherhood) always take precedence over the needs of strangers. Yet no rationale is provided for why they do so here. Pointing out that the child is the father's own, as an answer to that question, only suggests that, from the point of view of care, special relationships always take priority. Yet that is not plausible. On the other hand, within the idea of justice, we have a case in which the son's particular deserts are pitted against a more general rule of helping those in need, particular justice against universal justice. To present only the claims of universal justice as "the side of justice" is to suggest, inevitably, that universal claims always win out over particular ones from the perspective of justice. Yet that is also implausible.

The case of the father who has skills reminds me of another case, somewhat similar but also different, documented in Jung Chang's narrative of the Cultural Revolution, *Wild Swans: Three Daughters of China*. Her father, as a public official, refused to take advantage of his access to medical supplies to bring home more than the allotted share of medications for his own family, who needed them badly. He refused on the grounds that doing that sort of thing was just the kind of corruption that had caused so many problems with public life in China.[18] At first, the mother could not understand his attitude, and he could not understand how she could expect him to do such a thing. But eventually, they came to understand each other's point of view without abandoning their own values and principles.

Jung Chang's father, in my opinion, did the right thing. He was not a less caring parent for having so acted. As a public official, he had public responsibilities as well as private ones, and he was not being asked in his public capacity to make his family sacrifice more than other families were expected to do. Other families deserved to receive their share, just as his family deserved his special concerns. But the validity of his special concerns did not mean that his family deserved more than their fair share or that in respecting others' shares, he cared less than he should have for his own family.

It may be tempting to describe the case of Jung Chang's father as pitting care (for his own family) against justice (in administering the rules for distributing medicines) and say that, in contrast with Professor Held's case, here is one where justice wins out over care. Yet, again, I find this misleading, because there is justice on both sides and there are concerns of care on both sides, albeit particularized on the one side and generalized on the other.

The reader by now may be asking what difference it makes which language we use (that of justice or that of care) to describe these conflicts, as long as we appreciate that such conflicts arise and that there is no lexical ordering of values that will yield the right answer in every case. What difference does it make whether we label the demands of particular relationships those of "care" or those of "particular justice"? As long as we find care on both sides, or as long as we find justice on both sides, perhaps it does not matter which language we use. It is important, however, to recognize that there are importantly similar values at work on both sides of such conflicts. In particular relationships, we may be more likely to appreciate those values in a lively way if the relationship engages us positively and if it is especially vital to our well-being. On the other hand, if we have come to take particular relationships for granted and if we self-consciously identify with a more public role (and the more formal relationships that define it), it may be easier to appreciate the values at stake in universal claims. In either case, the likelihood or ease of our appreciation of the relevant values does not, in itself, carry ethical weight. Feminist criticism of ethical theories that pay insufficient attention to the values at stake in particular relationships could exploit the concept of justice to make that point.

NOTES

1. Virginia Held, "Caring Relations and Principles of Justice," in this volume, pp. 67–81.

2. Aristotle, *The Nicomachean Ethics*, trans. David Ross (New York: Oxford University Press, 1925), bk. 10, 132–34.

3. For discussion of this principle and its role in generalization arguments, see Marcus G. Singer, *Generalization in Ethics* (New York: Knopf, 1961).

4. John Rawls, *A Theory of Justice* (Cambridge, Mass.: Harvard University Press, 1971), 60. He offers and defends the following principles: (1) "each person is to have an equal right to the most extensive basic liberty compatible with a similar liberty for others" and (2) "social and economic inequalities are to be arranged so that they are both (a) reasonably expected to be to everyone's advantage, and (b) attached to positions and offices open to all."

5. Joel Feinberg, "Justice and Personal Desert" in *Doing and Deserving: Essays in the Theory of Responsibility* (Princeton, N.J.: Princeton University Press, 1970), 55–94.

6. Feinberg, 58.

7. But see George Sher, *Desert* (Princeton, N.J.: Princeton University Press, 1987).

8. Immanuel Kant, *Groundwork of the Metaphysics of Morals*, trans. H. J. Paton (New York: Harper Torchbook, 1964).

9. Kant, *The Doctrine of Virtue, Part II of The Metaphysics of Morals*, trans. Mary J. Gregor (Philadelphia: University of Pennsylvania Press, 1964). See Kant's "Introduction to the Metaphysics of Morals," 7–28.

10. The concept of a lexical (short for lexicographical) ordering is discussed in Rawls, 42: "This is an order which requires us to satisfy the first principle in the ordering before we can move on to the second. . . . A principle does not come into play until those previous to it are either fully met or do not apply."

11. Aristotle, VIII:9, 207.

12. Aristotle, VIII:9, 208.

13. Aristotle, VIII:1, 193.

14. For more on gratitude and its peculiar obligations, see chapter 6 in Claudia Card, *The Unnatural Lottery: Character and Moral Luck* (Philadelphia: Temple University Press, 1996), 118–39, or Card, "Gratitude and Obligation," *American Philosophical Quarterly* 25:2 (April 1988): 115–27.

15. Fred Berger, "Gratitude," *Ethics* 85:4 (July 1975): 298–309. See especially p. 307.

16. Held, p. 74 of this volume.

17. Søren Kierkegaard, *Fear and Trembling* and *The Sickness unto Death*, trans. Walter Lowrie (New York: Anchor, 1954), 64–77.

18. Jung Chang, *Wild Swans: Three Daughters of China* (New York: Simon & Schuster, 1991).

8

The Language of Evil

Virginia Held

In her contribution to this volume, Claudia Card recommends that we use "the language of evil" to address the most important wrongs that oppressed groups face. I realize, in reading her paper, that 'evil' is a word I never use—at least I cannot remember using it in all the times I've written and spoken on moral issues. Is this a deficiency on my part? Should I change my ways?

Certainly I think that people often act wrongly, even outrageously, that they commit gross injustices through acts that are inexcusable. I think they often fail to respect others' rights, or lack a decent regard for their own humanity or that of others. As I describe and evaluate them, people often bring about results that are morally harmful, shameful, or grievously damaging. I believe that people often fail to meet the requirements of care, and that they are deficient in the forming and maintaining of relationships or in feeling appropriate concern. I often argue that people are responsible for these injustices, bad consequences, and failures to care, and I think I can express as much moral outrage as anyone disturbed by the human history we create.

But 'evil'? It seems to me that we can deal with all the relevant moral considerations without it. If we use it to designate particularly grave cases of injustice or unconcern, I probably have no objections, but am unclear what 'evil' adds to describing moral wrongs as especially severe, inexcusable, or outrageous. And I remain wary of the associations between the language of evil and such questionable positions as that particular persons, or humanity in general, are "inherently" evil, and the many associations between the language of evil and religious doctrines of various kinds. We should all strive, I think, to free the language of morality from its religious entanglements, allowing it to develop independently in ways open to all. And that Nietzsche saw 'evil' as a term of "slave morality" seems to me less than no recommendation. So I doubt that I will transform my style of writing about moral issues, but for this discussion of the issues raised by Card, I will sometimes use 'evil' in what I take to be ways similar to hers.

Card gives priority to care and utility over justice-as-equality because she sees care ethics and utilitarianism as primarily concerned with opposing the evils people suffer, and she sees this as more important than merely avoiding arbitrariness. But this implies that we are comparing the avoiding of severe harms and lacks of care with the avoiding of minor injustices. If we think of utilitarianism as an ethic of preference satisfaction, then it would seem that avoiding a gross injustice such as slavery, or a severe violation of respect for persons such as denying women the right to vote, should clearly take priority over minor raisings in the level of satisfaction of trivial preferences. And though I think that we should see relations of care as the wider and, in some sense, primary concern of morality within which we should seek justice and well-being for persons, not all considerations of care are especially weighty or serious. Grave injustices can thus be more important than minor improvements in care.

Card wants to prioritize opposition to evils, and perhaps we can all agree with this position if we see evils as the most severe forms of whatever wrongs we are attending to. But as I see them, the debates about whether justice or utility or care has priority are about a different set of issues. They concern whether, as between wrongs of a comparable severity, justice and rights, say, should have priority over maximizing utility, or whether considerations of caring relations should have priority over both. Deontologists prioritize rights and justice, and both deontologists and utilitarians prioritize universal rules and rational deliberation over relations of care between actual persons. Some of us dispute these prioritizations. The point of these discussions is greater clarity, better moral theory, and hence, better judgments and practices in all the innumerable efforts we should engage in to make the world less morally awful.

Card argues that opposition to evils based on evaluations drawn from utilitarianism or from the ethics of care should be more important to feminist ethics than opposition to inequalities. But this seems to be because she interprets inequalities as relatively trivial ones in comparison to the very gross harms with which they are contrasted. Despite her efforts to do so, she does not sufficiently, I think, acknowledge how severe inequalities can themselves be evils, if we use that language. She thinks that to describe South African apartheid or racial segregation in the United States as inequalities "grossly underdescribes the situation" that existed (p. 88). This may well be, but the question her discussion seems to need to address is whether the parts of these situations that were severe inequalities were evils, and it seems clear that they were.

She acknowledges that when less severe inequalities such as being made to sit in the back of the bus acquire the power "to symbolize a social judgment of inferior humanity" then they may become evils (p. 88). But then the point of her distinction between inequalities and evils seems questionable. The inequalities against which feminists have fought have almost never been mere differences of treatment. What feminists, including liberal feminists, have often opposed have been the many ways in which certain seemingly minor differences of treatment have symbolized the social judgment of women's inferiority, and the ways in which women's objections to this judgment have been dismissed as a misplaced concern for trivial matters. This doesn't mean we cannot distinguish between the relatively unimportant injustices and the truly gross ones.

If one thinks of the repression of women and girls now occurring in Afghanistan, the inequalities faced by the victims are surely themselves an evil. When severe but avoidable poverty causes all in a group to suffer pains and deprivations, it is an evil. When unjust inequalities within that group cause some to suffer severe indignities and affronts to their self-respect, and still greater pains and deprivations than the dominant group, it is a different wrong, but also an evil. I find it more helpful to distinguish the kinds of injustices and sufferings involved, and their severity, without needing to use the language of evil.

When Card argues that relief from the often violent oppression that women suffer is more important than the often trivial issues of gender equality on which the media focus, it is easy to agree. But as I see it, a major argument for a focus on oppression is that it takes account, in a way that liberal treatments of inequality often fail to, of the social structure that produces or allows oppression, including systematic economic inequalities. Then, when Card claims that "inequalities . . . are not in themselves evils," we may well disagree (p. 84). When severe and structural, inequalities may well be evils. Certainly equality of treatment does not mean literal sameness of treatment: the well and the sick should not receive the same medicine. But philosophers since Aristotle have been able to make this point. When adequate interpretations have been made of what treating persons as equals requires, then gross disregard for these requirements can be unjust and evil.

Card argues that "the most serious practices to be resisted are those that do major harm" (p. 84). But to think that major injustices always cause harm is, in my view, to confuse moral considerations that are best kept distinct. Harm is a consequence often caused by wrong actions, but some actions should be judged wrong regardless of their consequences. If a person intentionally tries to shoot and kill a doctor who performs abortions, but the shot misses and the act's beneficial consequences of strengthening security at abortion clinics outweigh the harmful consequences of increased fear, we could still judge that the person acted wrongly. And if a father tries to coerce his daughter into a life of prostitution, leading her to run away and eventually find a life that is an improvement over the life she would have had if he had not coerced her, we would not judge that he did nothing wrong. And so on. Deontological moral considerations can be as important as consequentialist ones. And so too, in a different and perhaps even more fundamental way, considerations of care can be important.

At the same time, we can agree with Card and Kekes that horribly damaging but avoidable situations can occur even without agents intending them. These can be called evil, but we can still wonder if this adds much more than rhetorical variety to our understanding of them as grievous wrongs. We can evaluate from the perspective of care the failures of both those who commit injustices and of those who contribute to or fail to alleviate avoidable harms. And we can especially, out of concern for those who suffer grievous wrongs, try to build the caring relations that will reduce wrongs in the future.

What Claudia Card calls attention to so well in her paper is that we often need to decide on what should have priority in our moral concern. I agree with her that justice and equality should not always have priority, but neither, I think, should the avoidance of harm or of failures in care always have priority. In general, the serious should have priority over the trivial in our moral efforts, whatever the type of moral consideration. Card's discussion helps us to distinguish these in a variety of particular cases, and to recognize how the distinction is often overlooked.

Section III

Feminism and Philosophy of Science

9

What Does Feminism Contribute to Philosophy of Science?

Janet A. Kourany

It is often said that the aim of philosophy of science is to provide a systematic and comprehensive picture of science, its aims and methods, its foundations and results. Thus, the basic issues it deals with include the nature of scientific observation and experiment and their roles in scientific research; the nature of the claims scientists make (factual statements, empirical laws, theories, and so forth), their explanatory and other functions in science, and the ways they are assessed; the way science, its aims and methods and subject matter, develops over time; the nature of the results of scientific inquiry, whether science provides truth about the world, or only useful information; and the like. The aim of feminism, on the other hand, is to achieve gender equality, and feminists spend their time documenting how far it is from being achieved, and investigating and putting to use the strategies needed to achieve it. What does feminism contribute to philosophy of science? What *can* feminism contribute to philosophy of science?

Start with feminist historians, sociologists, and anthropologists of science, as well as feminist scientists themselves. They have shown that science is not a site of gender equality, and never has been. Thus, we are told, men have controlled Western science right from its beginning, and still do. In the past the control took such obvious forms as denying women with scientific talents access to universities and other centers of scientific learning, denying them all but menial research roles, and denying them membership in prestigious scientific academies and professional organizations.[1] More recently men's control of Western science has taken subtler forms: restrictive admissions quotas for undergraduate and graduate women students, or deliberate recruitment and selection by (masculine) gender; less financial assistance for women students; research positions for women with inferior work space and equipment and pay, and with little authority or possibility of advancement; exclusion of women from the most important scientific meetings and collaborations and

113

information networks, and restricted access to prestigious scientific academies; a system of expectations and rewards structured for the lives that men traditionally have led, free of family responsibilities; and, of course, such newly recognized phenomena as sexual harassment.[2] As a result, we are told, "women have been swelling the lower and middle ranks of science for years, yet still have not managed to pierce the upper scientific strata in anything beyond token numbers."[3]

Men's control of Western science, in turn, has affected its content. Indeed, feminist scientists have pointed out that Western science has tended to leave women largely invisible in its knowledge and research. For example, medical researchers have often failed to include females in animal studies in basic research, as well as in clinical research, unless the research centered on controlling the production of children. This has led, among other things, to drugs not adequately tested for women patients before being marketed and lack of information about the etiology of some diseases in women. Indeed, research on conditions specific to women (e.g., dysmenorrhea, incontinence in older women, and nutrition in postmenopausal women) has received low priority, and research on diseases (like heart disease) that affect both sexes has been primarily concerned with the predisposing factors for the disease in males (in this case, white, middle-aged, middle-class men), while very little research has been concerned with high-risk groups of women (e.g., older women and poor black women who have had several children).[4]

In the social sciences abstract models based on male experience and male perception have been presupposed in the formulation of ongoing research projects. For example, the model of the rational actor in sociology has been "the abstracted model of organizational or bureaucratic man, whose motives, methods, and ego structure are organized by the formal rationality structuring his work role."[5] The model of human nature presupposed by a dominant strand of contemporary political science has been that of a narrowly calculating masculine being "who adapts, conforms, and engages in self-interested behavior, rather than in action with a social as well as a private meaning."[6] And more generally, "political science [in the words of Borque and Grossholtz] 'insists upon a narrow and exclusive definition of politics which limits political activity to a set of roles which are in this society, and many others, stereotyped as male. . . .' Thus, what women do is conceptually excluded from the purview of political science."[7] Again, the model of the healthy, mature, socially competent adult in psychology has been that of a male adult rather than a female adult.[8]

The problem is that social science "often assumes a 'single society' with respect to men and women, in which generalizations can be made about all participants, yet men and women may actually inhabit different social worlds."[9] It is only the men's world that social science takes to be the single social world, however. Thus, for example, in the conceptual schemes of sociology and economics all human activity is either work or leisure, a dichotomy that more accurately describes men's lives than women's. As a consequence, housework and volunteer work, which are not quite work (wage labor, part of the gross national product) and not quite leisure, cannot easily be conceptualized even though they form significant parts of women's experience. Nor can women's more concrete and caring modes of moral evaluation be easily captured within the Piaget-Kohlberg model of moral development in psychology that was originally abstracted from male experience.

When Western science *has* considered women, on the other hand, feminists make clear, it has often portrayed us in negative terms. A favorite theme has been women's intellectual capacity. In the seventeenth century, for example, women's brains were said to be too "cold" and "soft" to sustain rigorous thought. In the late eighteenth century, the female cranial cavity was considered too small to hold a powerful brain. In the late nineteenth century, the exercise of women's brains was thought to shrivel our ovaries. In our own century, the way women process visuospatial information (supposedly by using the left hemisphere of the brain in addition to the right) supposedly makes women inferior in visuospatial skills (including mathematical skills).[10] But comparably negative stands have been taken with regard to many of women's other traits. Indeed, this situation is related to the problem of women's general invisibility, noted previously. That is to say, if men's bodily processes or social world or mode of psychological development, or whatnot, is the described state of affairs in science, the norm or standard, then to the extent that women's situation is different, it is no large step to conceiving of women as deviant, defective, or inferior. In this way women's moral and sexual and social development has been thought to be inferior because it does not fit the model of development applied to men.

And what is the result of all this? The invisibility and negative portrayals of women, and things feminine, in scientific knowledge and research has yielded, or helped to yield, such things as inferior educational and athletic opportunities for women, inferior medical treatment for women, and inferior positions for women in the work place, the family, and every institution of human life.[11] What's more, if women are among those most likely to make women visible and fairly portrayed in scientific knowledge and research, then men's continuing control of science and exclusion of women from the most important activities in science promise to perpetuate the invisibility and negative portrayals of women in science. In turn, the invisibility and negative portrayals of women in science also promise to perpetuate—to "justify"—men's control of science. And just as men's control of science and women's invisibility and negative treatment within science promise to perpetuate—since science so profoundly shapes our attitudes and our world—the inequality women confront in society at large, so too, the inequality women confront in society promises to perpetuate these conditions in science.

Feminist historians, sociologists, and anthropologists of science, as well as feminist scientists themselves, have pointed out, then, that science is not, and never has been, a site of gender equality, and that this promises to perpetuate, and is in turn perpetuated by, a gender unequal society. For their part, feminist philosophers of science have sought to analyze the aspects of science thus revealed.[12] For example, excluding women from the most important activities in science has certainly robbed science of much of its pool of available talent, and thus, of much of its progress. But has it had other effects as well? Would women have made different kinds of scientific contributions from men, leading to a different kind of science, had they been granted the requisite opportunities? Indeed, do women now make different kinds of scientific contributions from men in fields that have a critical mass of women in them? Are the critiques of science furnished by feminist scientists, the ones that show that science is not a site of gender equality, and the new research directions these scientists have frequently embarked on as a result, examples of such different contributions? Relatedly, what are the epistemological bases of these critiques, why have women/feminists been the ones to make them, and why have men frequently resisted them? Are the new research directions pursued by feminist scientists really better than the old, and in what sense or senses (for example, are they leading us to more politically acceptable results, more objective or truer results, etc.)? These are some of the kinds of questions feminist philosophers pursue, and they lead to theorizing on what constitutes good and bad science, the place of values in science, scientific objectivity, and other issues as well. Still, what does all this really contribute to philosophy of science?

THE PRESENCE OF WOMEN

For one thing, feminist philosophers of science, and the feminist scientists and historians and sociologists and anthropologists of science who provide the philosophers with their data, deal very much with the work of women scientists past and present, and this forms an important addition to philosophy of science. After all, philosophy of science, when it deals with concrete scientific work at all rather than with idealized logical reconstructions of science, deals almost exclusively with the work of men scientists—typically famous men scientists like Copernicus and Lavoisier, Newton and Einstein, Darwin and Bohr.[13] But the aim of philosophy of science is to provide a comprehensive picture of science, any and all of it, and there is no reason to suppose (and no research has been done to support) that the work of such men scientists is representative of science in general, including the science done by women, or can be used as a normative model for science in general. What's more, focusing almost exclusively on selected cases of men's science, as philosophy of science does, reinforces our conception of science as a masculine activity. When we think of science, we think of the greatest science of men scientists; and this may make men's control of Western science appear more justifiable. Investigating the work of women scientists in the way feminist philosophers of science have done, on the other hand, helps us to see science as a possible and appropriate activity for women as well as men, one to which women have already made significant contributions.

Feminist standpoint theorists have provided still stronger reasons to applaud the study of women scientists. For one thing, women scientists have generally been excluded from positions of authority in the communities that have produced our scientific knowledge and, being "outsiders" in this way, are in a better position than those more centrally involved to detect the limitations of this knowledge.[14] Regarding, particularly, the scientific knowledge that has tended to leave women largely invisible, and that has often portrayed women, and things feminine, in negative terms when it *has* considered us, women scientists are in a better position to detect limitations in another way as well. Given the division of activities assigned to men and women in society, men scientists generally have little access to women's concrete life experiences, to the child care, dependent care, homemaking, community service, and the rest, that scientific knowledge ignores or distorts. Hence, men scientists are not in as good a position to detect such failures of fit. Women scientists, on the other hand, do have access to these life experiences and to at least many of the life experiences of the men, given that they do "men's work" as scientists as well as "women's work" in other parts of their lives. As a consequence, they can measure their fields' bodies of knowledge against a more complete and diverse set of experiences than their male counterparts, and hence are in a position to be more critical than they.[15]

This is not, of course, to say that all women scientists will be critical of sexist and androcentric contributions to scientific knowledge, or that all men scientists will not be. It is only to say that these women will be in a better position, and the men in a worse position, to be so critical. But there may be other important epistemically relevant differences between men and women scientists as well. Indeed, as philosopher Eve Browning Cole points out, "it would be hard to argue against the claim that experience importantly structures our cognitive capacities, determining which ones we will work hard to develop and which we will ignore."[16] She elaborates:

> Women . . . in many if not most contemporary cultures depend for their livelihood or even survival on being sensitive to the moods and dispositions of those for whom they care and those they serve. This causes them to develop perceptual capacities, communication skills, a facility for emotional management, conflict resolution, discretion, acting skill, and many other behaviors it is the privilege of the ruling class and gender to neglect.[17]

All of these skills give women a special ability to engage in, and contribute to, collaborative enterprises, including collaborative scientific enterprises. In addition, "feminist awareness of the consequences of oppression, our knowledge of what it feels like to be erased, ignored, patronized, and brushed off as a potential knowledge-maker, cannot but encourage the development of non-oppressive, and more inclusive, knowledge-making practices."[18] In short, women scientists may bring special social skills and dispositions, as well as special critical perspectives, to their practice of science, ones that make them especially valuable to the scientific enterprise. And hence, they may be especially important for philosophers of science to investigate. And given that, almost without exception, it is feminists who are investigating them and bringing them to the attention of philosophers of science, feminists are making an important contribution to philosophy of science.

The above is sure to elicit an objection, however. Much of the stated special importance of women scientists, and hence special contribution of feminists to philosophy of science, it will be said, relates to the natural and social sciences. The focus of philosophy of science, however, is the physical sciences, and hence, if women scientists are not in a special position to contribute to the physical sciences, then neither are the feminists who study them in a special position to contribute to philosophy of science. Is there any answer to this objection? Aside from the points already made—for example, that since women scientists are not studied by philosophers of science, no one is in a position to know whether women scientists do or do not make special contributions to the physical sciences—why should the physical sciences be the focus of philosophy of science? The aim of philosophy of science, once again, is to provide a comprehensive picture of science, any and all of it, and there is little reason to suppose (and little research to support) that the physical sciences are representative of science in general, or can be used as a normative model for science in general. What's more, making the physical sciences the focus of philosophy of science without such a justification promotes an unfortunate intellectual climate. Indeed, with so much attention focused in this way on physical science in philosophy of science, women's invisibility and negative treatment within other areas of science become matters of small concern, if noticed at all. After all, women are not misrepresented within physical science, and if there are no gender-related problems within the content and methods of physical science, there are no gender-related problems within "real science," the only area of science that counts. And finally, with so much reverence bestowed on physical science, practitioners of the social sciences cannot but be encouraged to model their research goals and methods and concepts on those of the physical sciences. But this kind of research has yielded negative portrayals of women and other "minorities" as results.

For example, research design in the past in psychology, modeled as it was on that of the physical sciences, tended to emphasize physiological or biochemical variables, and variables defined by performance on psychological tests or manipulation of circumstances in the research situation, and it tended to de-emphasize the background, personal history, and gender of subjects and experimenters, as well as research situations outside the laboratory or in naturalistic settings. And this had the effect (among others) of producing gender bias in the results of that research. In the past it was frequently reported in social psychology texts, for instance, that women are more susceptible to persuasive influences or suggestions than men. More recently, however, this has been corrected by research demonstrating that influenceabilty or suggestibility is affected by a variety of factors, including whether a topic is of concern to a subject, and the gender of the researcher in relation to the topic. It was demonstrated, for example, that women are more suggestible with a male researcher when the topic is socially defined as one of male interest, but that men respond in parallel fashion when a woman researcher tries to influence them on a topic socially defined as interesting to women. The result of this more recent research, research that takes into account such factors as the gender of the researcher, the experimental context, and the interests and self-definition of subjects, is that there is now no basis whatsoever for saying that women are more suggestible or influenceable than men.[19]

But modeling the research methods, concepts, and goals of a discipline like psychology on those of the physical sciences can have other effects than gender bias, as psychologist Mary Brown Parlee has pointed out. For when psychological phenomena are stripped of their sociocultural, political, and personal dimensions to fit patterns appropriate to the physical sciences, the individual is represented "not as an agent who acts for reasons in a social and moral order but as a being subjected in natural-law-like ways to various causal influences conceptualized as variables or factors." And

> To the extent that this representation of persons in mechanistic, agentless, nonmoral language becomes part of public discourse (or part of the discourse of the educated elites), it deprives the general public of the richer linguistic resources for self-interpretation and self-understanding inherent in the everyday language of persons, actions, reasons, motives, and values. These resources enable or even encourage people to experience and think of themselves as agents who can act politically and in other ways in a world of meaning toward ends they value. The mechanistic, pseudoscientific language of psychology thus plays its role in the reproduction of the existing social order by pervading public discourse and the interpretations of ourselves that are shaped by it, displacing a discourse more compatible with the self-interpretations necessary for people to act together for social change.[20]

SOCIAL ACCOUNTABILITY

Feminist philosophers of science, and the feminist scientists and historians and sociologists and anthropologists of science who provide the philosophers with their data, then, deal very much with the work of women scientists past and present, and this forms an important addition to philosophy of science. A second contribution feminists make to philosophy of science is to reveal the epistemological significance of the social dimensions, and in particular the gender dimensions, of science.[21]

As stated at the outset, philosophy of science has traditionally set for itself the task of providing a systematic and comprehensive picture of science as a knowledge-producing activity, and this has traditionally been taken to exclude the social. The program of logical empiricism was most blatant in this regard. Providing a systematic and comprehensive picture of science meant, for logical empiricism, characterizing it within the conceptualizations provided by formal logic and empiricist epistemology. And this resulted in a very abstract, idealized, a very socially detached picture of science. Indeed, logical empiricism portrayed only the "logic of science": disembodied "observations" and "observation statements," "experiments" isolated from the individuals and groups who design them, fund them, and carry them out, "scientific explanations" detached from their proponents, their purposes, their audiences, their effects. Thus, a scientific theory was an axiom system together with a set of rules that partially defined selected nonlogical terms of the system ("theoretical terms") by terms defined on the basis of observation ("observational terms"). A scientific explanation was the (deductive or inductive) logical derivation of a statement to be explained (the "explanandum") from a set of general laws and statements of initial conditions (the "explanans"). The process of evaluating a hypothesis consisted in logically deriving observation statements ("predictions") from the hypothesis in conjunction with statements of initial conditions, and comparing these with statements describing the results of observation or experiment. Scientific development consisted in the extension of scientific knowledge (e.g., the addition of new empirical laws or theories to existing ones) and, especially, in the greater (deductive) systematization of that knowledge—the (deductive) explanation of scientific laws and theories by more general theories, and the (deductive) reduction of scientific theories, and even whole disciplines, to other theories and disciplines. And so on. All social details—who is doing what, who has been excluded from doing what, whose questions are being settled by what mechanisms, and with what effects—were antiseptically removed. And with them, all details of gender were removed. But this characterization of science was, nevertheless, held to be a comprehensive picture of science, its aims and methods, its foundations and results, or, at least, everything that was important to science as a knowledge-producing activity.

The effect[22] of the logical empiricist picture, of course, was to protect science from social critique. Indeed, if science as a knowledge-producing activity was "pure"—purely logical and empirical, purely non-social—then there could be no place for social critique. The protection went much further than this, however. The characterization of science provided by logical empiricism functioned more as a prescription to science than as a description of it: it told us what scientific explanations, theories, empirical laws, processes of hypothesis evaluation, instances of scientific development, and the rest, were, *in the sense of* the logical and empirical conditions statements or inferences had to fulfill to *be* scientific explanations, theories, empirical laws, processes of hypothesis evaluation, instances of scientific development, and the rest. The program of logical empiricism was, thus, a very normative program: it served to describe what ideal science was, and what actual science was aspiring to be—and sometimes was, if it was truly science at its best. And, of course, the foundation of this normative program was formal logic and empiricist epistemology. This foundation, however, made any other prescriptive role toward science problematic. In particular, its empiricist criterion of meaning analyzed moral and political prescriptions as devoid of cognitive significance—useful for expressing (venting) attitudes and emotions, perhaps, but not for critiquing and improving science. In consequence, logical empiricism doubly protected science from social critique, first by providing a picture of science that made the social invisible, and then by disarming social critique itself.

The "new" historicist program of philosophy of science ushered in by Thomas Kuhn, Paul Feyerabend, Norwood Russell Hanson, Stephen Toulmin and others in the early 1960s largely continued the protection. For although the program was now to examine the actual processes and products of scientific research, past and present, and to characterize science accordingly, this did not extend to the social. Consider Kuhn,[23] who did more than anyone else to define the new program, both by the work he produced and by the influence he exerted on others. Kuhn sought to provide a general descriptive account of science—its fundamental components and the process by which they develop, as well as the process by which they undergo fundamental change. According to this account, paradigms—scientific theories and the concrete applications ("exemplars") that accompany them—are the mainstay of science, rather than the observation statements and logic of the logical empiricists. Indeed, it is paradigms that determine the research agenda of science, in the form of problems the paradigms' first appearance leaves unsolved or incompletely solved; it is paradigms that provide the methods to be used in solving these problems, and the standards to be used in assessing the solutions; and hence, it is paradigms that determine what counts as "scientific success" and "scientific progress." It is even paradigms that shape what is observed and determine how what is observed is to be described. So once again science is portrayed as independent of the social and its economic/political/cultural—including gender—and other modes of influence, not because it is claimed that observation and logic are powerful enough to construct science all by themselves, as logical empiricism suggested, but because it is claimed that *paradigms* are[24]—or "research programmes," or "research traditions," or "scientific domains," or any of the other central players of the "new" philosophy of science.[25] And once again we are discouraged from engaging in a social (moral, political) critique of science, not because the empiricist criterion of meaning renders such a critique devoid of cognitive significance, as logical empiricism suggested, but because the actions that such a critique enjoins are likely to impede "scientific progress"—as the intervention of social needs impedes the internally directed development of the social sciences for Kuhn[26]—or worse, are likely to be "irrational."[27] As a consequence, science is doubly protected from social critique now by the "new" philosophy of science as well as the old.

Of course, the "new" philosophy of science is exceedingly diverse.[28] It explores the whole gamut of traditional issues in philosophy of science and some new ones as well, and in order to develop and support its views of science it makes use—in addition to case studies in the history of science and contemporary science—of a wide spectrum of resources, from mathematics (for the semantic approaches to scientific theories, for example) to the cognitive sciences (for the cognitive theory of science). But the limitations I have discussed and illustrated in the work of Kuhn are entirely general, and they are matched by comparable limitations in other current work in the philosophy of science that continues to show the influence of logical empiricism.

All this contrasts sharply with the picture of science provided by feminists. Indeed, as stated at the outset, feminists have shown not only that men control Western science, and have from its beginning, but that this control has affected its content.

Thus, it was said, in fields such as biology and psychology and medical research, economics, political science, anthropology, and sociology, men's ("androcentric") interests and values and experiences have shaped the science that has been done— the kinds of questions pursued and assumptions made, the kinds of concepts and hypotheses suggested as answers, and the kinds of observations considered relevant to those answers and the ways they are expressed. Even basic criteria of scientific evaluation such as simplicity and external consistency, philosopher Helen Longino has pointed out, have had a "political valence" supportive of men.[29] Thus, the criterion of simplicity in its most common ontological version is the preference for theories that postulate fewer entities or processes—for example, the preference for theories that postulate only one kind of causally efficacious entity, or that treat apparently different entities as merely different versions of a single, standard kind of entity, or that treat differences as eliminable through decomposition of entities into a single basic kind, over theories that grant parity to different kinds of entities. This criterion has grounded preference for theories that treat women's bodily, social, psychological, and moral dissimilarities from men as signs of women's inferiority to men, where men are taken as the norm or standard of comparison, rather than as signs of women's differences fom men, where women and men have equal standing. Again, the criterion of external consistency is the preference for theories that are consistent with presently accepted theories, over theories that differ in significant ways from presently accepted theories, whether in the kinds of entities the theories postulate, or the kinds of explanation they offer, or the kinds of concepts or metaphors they employ. This criterion has grounded preference for theories that continue in the same androcentric and sexist theoretical directions as the past. Feminist scientists, Longino notes, have moved toward different criteria from these, criteria such as novelty (the preference for theories that differ in significant ways from presently accepted theories) and ontological heterogeneity (the preference for theories that grant parity to different kinds of entities). These different criteria ground more egalitarian theoretical preferences.

Feminists have shown, then, not only that men control Western science, but that, in fields such as biology and psychology and medical research, economics, political science, anthropology, and sociology, this control has shaped both the science that has been done and the criteria used to evaluate it—in short, the knowledge that has been accepted. Not only that, feminists have shown the effects of such knowledge on women's lives—the inferior educational and athletic opportunities for women mentioned at the outset, inferior medical treatment for women, and inferior positions for women in the workplace, the family, and every institution of human life. Feminists have thus done much to sketch into philosophy of science's picture of science the social details so long invisible, their epistemological consequences, and the social significance of those consequences in the society at large. They have thereby begun a social critique of science that can furnish the basis of science's enlarged social accountability.

A MODEL

Feminists have done more than provide a social critique of science, however. They have also provided suggestions for reform. Consider, for example, Helen Longino on the question of achieving scientific objectivity.[30] Claiming that, in an important sense, scientific objectivity has to do with limiting the intrusion of individual subjective preferences into scientific knowledge, and hence has to do with the extent to which community criticism of individuals' scientific work, and responses to that criticism, are possible, Longino offers a number of conditions a scientific community should strive to fulfill. First, the members of the community should have recognized avenues—such as journals, conferences, and the like—for the criticism of evidence, methods, assumptions, and reasoning. Second, the members of the community should share standards—substantive principles as well as values—that critics can invoke. Third, the community as a whole should be responsive to the criticism. That is, the beliefs of the scientific community as a whole and over time—as measured by such public phenomena as the content of textbooks, the distribution of grants and awards, and the flexibility of dominant worldviews—should change in response to the critical discussion taking place within it. Fourth, intellectual authority should be shared equally among qualified members. And fifth,[31] alternative points of view that can serve as sources of criticism should be represented in the community, the more numerously the better.[32] A science will be objective, then, to the degree that it satisfies these conditions—to the degree that it permits what Longino calls "transformative criticism."

It follows that present science is not objective. Indeed, since (upper- and middle-class white) men have controlled Western science right from the start, Longino's fourth condition for scientific objectivity has never been satisfied. That is to say, when women have been permitted to engage in science at all, or when they have simply done so on their own, they usually have not been granted intellectual authority commensurate with their abilities and achievements. Nor have most of the other conditions for scientific objectivity been fully satisfied. Thus, regarding the fifth and first conditions, though women in science have frequently brought with them alternative points of view, at least regarding issues related to women and the feminine, in the past they were allowed little or no access, and still typically are allowed unequal access, to conferences, journals, information networks, and other avenues for publicizing their points of view and criticizing the dominant points of view. And regarding the third condition, when women have managed to present their views and criticisms nonetheless, in the past they were most frequently simply dismissed or ignored, and frequently still are not taken as seriously as they should be.[33] To work toward the satisfaction of the first, third, fourth, and fifth conditions for scientific objectivity would thus be Longino's suggestion for rectifying the problems in science feminists have disclosed.

Other feminists would add other suggestions. For example, Longino's second condition stipulates that the members of a scientific community should share standards—substantive principles as well as values—that critics can invoke, but will *any* shared standards ensure scientific objectivity, or do we need to specify the kinds of shared standards that will be necessary? Some feminists would answer that the shared standards necessary here would have to include, at the very least, feminist values. The reason they would give is that feminist values function as methodological controls, to weed out unjustified assumptions. Indeed, cases have been presented—for example, in cell biology—to show that the use of such controls has actually led to better science.[34] Thus, the Biology and Gender Study Group concludes:

> We have come to look at feminist critique as we would any other experimental control. Whenever one performs an experiment, one sets up all the controls one can think of in order to make as certain as possible that the result obtained does not come from any other source. One asks oneself what assumptions one is making. Have I assumed the temperature to be constant? Have I assumed that the pH doesn't change over the time of the reaction? Feminist critique asks if there may be some assumptions that we haven't checked concerning gender bias. In this way feminist critique should be part of normative science. Like any control, it seeks to provide critical rigor, and to ignore this critique is to ignore a possible source of error.[35]

There is another reason the shared standards demanded by Longino's second condition ought to include feminist values. Society—both women and men—ultimately pays for science. And society is deeply affected by science: science shapes our lives, not least of all by shaping our consciousness of ourselves.

> The truth of a theory about man is either creative or irrelevant, but never merely descriptive. A theory about the stars never becomes a part of the being of the stars. A theory about man enters his consciousness, determines his self-understanding, and modifies his very existence. The image of a man affects the nature of man. . . . We become what we think of ourselves.[36]

It follows that the needs of society ought to deeply constrain the aims of science, and hence, the critical standards used in measuring progress toward those aims. But one of the needs of society—of both women and men—is justice, and feminist values articulate one aspect of that justice. Thus, values that promote a more just society, including feminist values, ought to be included among the standards that the members of a scientific community use to evaluate their science.

There is still another reason the shared standards demanded by Longino's second condition for scientific objectivity ought to include feminist values: a potential problem with her fifth condition is thereby averted. Longino's fifth condition stipulates that alternative points of view that can serve as sources of criticism should be represented in the community, the more numerously the better, but as stated it provides no limitations on the points of view to be represented. For example, in a thoroughly reformed, nonsexist science, will scientific objectivity demand the presence of sexist points of view, and hence the hiring, funding, promotion, and so forth, of blatantly sexist scientists? The addition of feminist values in Longino's second condition justifies a negative answer to this question, and with no ill effects. For no legitimate points of view will thereby be excluded.[37]

Philosopher Sandra Harding would further specify the kinds of shared standards necessary for scientific objectivity. As she points out,

> It is not individual, personal, 'subjective' error to which feminist and other social critics of science have drawn attention, but widely held androcentric, Eurocentric, and bourgeois assumptions that have been virtually culture-wide across the culture of science. . . . These assumptions have constituted whole fields of study, selecting their preoccupying problems, favored concepts, hypotheses, and research designs; these fields have in turn lent support to male supremacist assumptions in other fields.[38]

Not *any* shared standards, therefore—not, for example, androcentric, Eurocentric and bourgeois assumptions—will ensure scientific objectivity when used as a basis for community criticism. But which standards, then? How do we know which standards are the ones that do not simply express the interests and values of the most powerful groups in society? Take androcentric values, for example. Harding reminds us that these values directly benefit men (especially white men), whereas they oppress women. As a consequence, women are more likely than men to be critical of such values. "They have less to lose by distancing themselves from the social order; thus, the perspective from their lives can more easily generate fresh and critical analyses."[39] But similar things can be said about Eurocentric and bourgeois values. Thus, only by adopting a standpoint outside that of the most powerful groups in society— thus, inside the lives of women of different races, ethnicities, classes, and sexualities—will we arrive at standards that provide "a critical edge for generating theoretically and empirically more accurate and comprehensive accounts."[40]

The above are just some of the suggestions feminists have offered to increase the objectivity of science. But much work still needs to be done, not only to further develop these suggestions—for example, to clarify just how we ought to "start thought from women's lives," or how else we might specify the needed shared standards for scientists—but also to extend the suggestions to deal with important social dimensions of science other than gender. After all, as the work, especially, of Sandra Harding makes clear, the interests and values and experiences of white, privileged, heterosexual scientists (both men and women) have shaped science just as much as the interests and values and experiences of men. What's more, science is shaped by the interests and values of its funders (the military and the agricultural, pharmaceutical, chemical, biotechnological, and oil industries, for example), its interest groups (animal rights activists and antiabortionists, for example), and its publishers, as well as by the interests and values of scientists. If feminists have done much to sketch gender into philosophy of science's picture of science, together with its epistemological consequences and the social significance of those consequences in the society at large, there is much of the social still to sketch in to complete the picture, and hence much still to do to provide a full understanding of science's epistemic/social responsibilities. What feminists have done, however, is provide a model of how to proceed, a kind of pilot project for how to do socially responsible philosophy of science.

A NEW PROGRAM FOR PHILOSOPHY OF SCIENCE

So, what does feminism contribute to philosophy of science? Attention to the work of women scientists and to the control of science wielded by men, attention to the epistemological and social consequences of men's control of science and to suggestions for reform, the promise of greater social accountability . . . but most of all, a new program for philosophy of science and a model of how to pursue it. For whereas the primary aim of logical empiricism was to *prescribe* to science, and the primary aim of the "new" historicist philosophy of science has been to *describe* science, the primary aim of this new kind of philosophy of science is equally descriptive and prescriptive. Its prescriptions are grounded, moreover, not simply in descriptions of great science (which is part of the "new" historicist philosophy of science), nor simply in logic and epistemology (which is part of logical empiricism), but in a complicated mix of these sources with moral and political philosophy, and especially feminist philosophy, as well. Such a descriptive/prescriptive kind of philosophy of science is thus not morally and politically neutral. Indeed, it presses, in philosopher Joseph Rouse's words, for "better knowledge and a better world, together."[41] But neither are the old prescriptive and the "new" descriptive philosophies of science morally and politically neutral, the programs that have kept the gendered nature of Western science, and its damaging effects on women, invisible and intact. And what of its lack of moral and political neutrality?! Moral and political neutrality is not an asset in an immoral world, and in any case, the descriptive/prescriptive kind of philosophy of science exhibited here aims to do what philosophy has *traditionally* aimed to do—capture and clarify the established order, question it, and suggest alternatives to it. And such a descriptive/prescriptive kind of philosophy of science might actually do some good—might actually get scientists (and others) to view their research in as informed, as systematic, and as critical a way as the objects of that research, so that scientists no longer see science and themselves as "fast guns for hire," "institutions and individuals that are, insofar as they are scientific, . . . studiously unconcerned with the origins or consequences of their activities or with the values and interests that these activities advance."[42] At least the descriptive/prescriptive philosophy of science will do more of this than its two predecessor programs in philosophy of science. It should thus be an important and needed addition to the various (descriptive) social studies of science, something that cannot clearly be said of the current descriptive program in the philosophy of science.

NOTES

This chapter is dedicated to Jim Cushing, who has pressed the title question with considerable verve.

1. Londa Schiebinger, *The Mind Has No Sex?* (Cambridge, Mass.: Harvard University Press, 1989); Margaret Rossiter, *Women Scientists in America* (Baltimore: Johns Hopkins University Press, 1982); H. J. Mozans, *Woman in Science* (Notre Dame, Ind.: Notre Dame University Press, 1991).

2. B. Vetter, "Women in Science," in *The American Woman 1987-88*, ed. S. Rix, (New York: W. W. Norton, 1987); H. Zuckerman, J. Cole, and J. Bruer, eds., *The Outer Circle* (New York: W. W. Norton, 1991); L. Dix, ed., *Women: Their Underrepresentation and Career Differentials in Science and Engineering* (Washington, D.C.: National Academy Press, 1987); Committee on Women in Science and Engineering, National Research Council, *Women in Science and Engineering: Increasing Their Numbers in the 1990s* (Washington, D.C.: National Academy Press, 1991); Vivian Gornick, *Women in Science*, revised edition (New York: Simon and Schuster, 1990); L. Hornig et al., "Women in Technology," *Technology Review* 87 (1984): 29–52; Naomi Weisstein, "'How can a little girl like you teach a great big class of men?' the Chairman Said, and Other Adventures of a Woman in Science," and Evelyn Fox Keller, "The Anomaly of a Woman in Physics," in *Working It Out*, eds. S. Ruddick and P. Daniels (New York: Pantheon Books, 1977); and Carey Goldberg, "M.I.T. Issues Report Acknowledging Sex Discrimination," *The New York Times*, March 23, 1999.

3. Natalie Angier, "Women Join the Ranks of Science But Remain Invisible at the Top," *The New York Times*, May 21, 1991. See also Phyllis Goldberg, "Creeping Toward Inclusivity in Science," in *Women in Science and Engineering: Choices for Success,* ed. Cecily Cannan Selby (New York: The New York Academy of Sciences, 1999).

4. Sue Rosser, "Re-visioning Clinical Research—Gender and the Ethics of Experimental Design," *Hypatia* 4:2 (1989).

5. Dorothy Smith, "A Sociology for Women" in *The Everyday World as Problematic* (Boston: Northeastern University Press, 1987); see, as well, "Women's Perspective as a Radical Critique of Sociology" in *Feminism and Methodology*, ed. Sandra Harding (Bloomington, Ind.: Indiana University Press, 1987).

6. Jean Elshtain, "Methodological Sophistication and Conceptual Confusion: A Critique of Mainstream Political Science," in *The Prism of Sex: Essays in the Sociology of Knowledge*, ed. J. Sherman and E. Beck (Madison: University of Wisconsin Press, 1979).

7. Joan Tronto, "Politics and Revision: The Feminist Project to Change the Boundaries of American Political Science," in *Revolutions in Knowledge: Feminism in the Social Sciences*, ed. S. Rosenberg Zalk and J. Gordon-Kelter (Boulder, Colo.: Westview Press, 1992), p. 95.

8. Beverly Walker, "Psychology and Feminism—If You Can't Beat Them, Join Them," in *Men's Studies Modified*, ed. Dale Spender (Oxford: Pergamon Press, 1981).

9. Marcia Millman and Rosabeth Kanter, "Introduction to *Another Voice: Feminist Perspectives on Social Life and Social Science*," in *Feminism and Methodology*.

10. See Schiebinger, *The Mind Has No Sex?*

11. See, for example, Anne Fausto-Sterling, *Myths of Gender* (New York: Basic Books, 1985).

12. Of course, feminist scientists have also contributed to this venture, and feminist philosophers of science have also contributed to exposing sexism in science.

13. David Hull is one of the very few exceptions. See his *Science as a Process* (Chicago: University of Chicago Press, 1988) in which he deals with the work of ordinary scientists as well as extraordinary ones, and women scientists as well as men.

14. See Harding, *Whose Science? Whose Knowledge?* (Ithaca, N.Y.: Cornell University Press, 1991), 124, for a further discussion of this point.

15. This more critical perspective may extend to areas other than those directly related to women. See, for example, Sarah Blaffer Hrdy, "Empathy, Polyandry, and the Myth of the Coy Female," in *Feminist Approaches to Science*, ed. Ruth Bleier (New York: Pergamon Press, 1986).

16. Eve Browning Cole, *Philosophy and Feminist Criticism* (New York: Paragon House, 1993), 92.

17. Cole, *Philosophy*, 91.

18. Cole, *Philosophy*, 91.

19. Carolyn Sherif, "Bias in Psychology," in *Feminism and Methodology*.

20. Mary Brown Parlee, "Feminism and Psychology," in *Revolutions in Knowledge: Feminism in the Social Sciences*, 35.

21. Sociologists of scientific knowledge have done much to reveal the epistemological significance of the social dimensions of science, but have not generally included gender as an aspect of the social.

22. Though not necessarily the aim. That is a completely separate issue.

23. Thomas Kuhn, *The Structure of Scientific Revolutions* (Chicago: University of Chicago Press, 1962).

24. This holds, of course, only for "normal science," the usual goings-on of science for Kuhn. It has never been quite clear what determines or explains "scientific revolutions" for Kuhn, or in what way scientific revolutions can constitute "scientific progress," but certainly he does not rule out the social or psychological in his treatment of scientific revolutions; see, for example, Thomas Kuhn, "Objectivity, Value Judgment, and Theory Choice," in *The Essential Tension: Selected Studies in Scientific Tradition and Change* (Chicago: University of Chicago Press, 1977), and *The Structure of Scientific Revolutions*.

25. See, for example, Imre Lakatos, "Falsification and the Methodology of Scientific Research Programmes," in *Criticism and the Growth of Knowledge*, ed. Imre Lakatos and Alan Musgrave (Cambridge, Mass.: Cambridge University Press, 1970); Larry Laudan, *Progress and Its Problems* (Berkeley, Calif.: University of California Press, 1977); William Newton-Smith, *The Rationality of Science* (Oxford: Routledge and Kegan Paul, 1981); Dudley Shapere, *Reason and the Search for Knowledge* (Dordrecht, Holland: D. Reidel, 1984). (But also see, for important exceptions, Mary Hesse, *Revolutions and Reconstructions in the Philosophy of Science* (Brighton: Harvester Press, 1980); and Ernan McMullin, "Values in Science," in *PSA 1982*, Volume 2, ed. Peter Asquith and Tom Nickles (East Lansing, Mich.: Philosophy of Science Association, 1983), and "The Rational and the Social in the History of Science," in *Scientific Rationality: The Sociological Turn*, ed. James Brown (Dordrecht, Holland: D. Reidel, 1984). The social *can*, and on occasion *does*, intervene in science according to these analyses, of course, but when it does, the science is "irrational," that is to say, contrary to the rationality defined by the analyses: ". . . The sociology of knowledge [i.e., explanation in terms of social factors] may step in to explain beliefs if and only if those beliefs cannot be explained in terms of their rational merits." (Laudan, *Progress and Its Problems*, 202)

26. See, for example, Kuhn, *The Structure of Scientific Revolutions*, 37.

27. See note 25.

28. For an indication of how diverse, see, for example, *The Process of Science: Contemporary Philosophical Approaches to Understanding Scientific Practice*, ed. Nancy Nersessian (Hingham, Mass.: Martinus Nijhoff, 1987), and Werner Callebaut, moderator, *Taking the Naturalistic Turn or How Real Philosophy of Science is Done* (Chicago: University of Chicago Press, 1993).

29. See Helen Longino, "Gender, Politics, and the Theoretical Virtues," *Synthese* 104 (1995); "In Search of Feminist Epistemology," *The Monist* 77 (1994), and "Cognitive and Non-Cognitive Values in Science: Rethinking the Dichotomy," in *Feminism, Science, and the Philosophy of Science*, ed. Lynn Hankinson Nelson and Jack Nelson (Dordrecht, Holland: Kluwer Academic Publishers, 1997). See also Sue Rosser's "Women's Ways of Knowing" in her *Female-Friendly Science* (Elmsford, N.Y.: Pergamon Press, 1990).

30. See her *Science as Social Knowledge: Values and Objectivity in Scientific Inquiry* (Princeton, N. J.: Princeton University Press, 1990), especially 76–81.

31. Longino cites only four conditions for objectivity in *Science as Social Knowledge* as well as more recent publications, but makes clear in her surrounding discussions that a fifth is also needed. See, for example, *Science as Social Knowledge*, 78 and 80.

32. In her "Cognitive and Non-Cognitive Values in Science: Rethinking the Dichotomy," Longino speaks instead of "all relevant perspectives" being represented. See p. 40.

33. See for the latter, for example, Sue Rosser, "Good Science: Can It Ever Be Gender Free?", *Women's Studies International Forum* 11:1 (1988): 13–19.

34. See, for example, The Biology and Gender Study Group, "The Importance of Feminist Critique for Contemporary Cell Biology," *Hypatia* 3:1 (1988): 61–76.

35. The Biology and Gender Study Group, "The Importance of Feminist Critique," 61–62.

36. A. J. Heschel, *Who is Man?* (Stanford: Stanford University Press, 1965), 7, quoted in "The Importance of Feminist Critique for Contemporary Cell Biology," 73.

37. If Longino's fifth condition demands, instead, that "all relevant perspectives" be represented (see note 32), then the inclusion of feminist values in her second condition would help to specify what the relevant perspectives are.

38. Sandra Harding, "'Strong Objectivity': A Response to the New Objectivity Question," *Synthese*: 104:3 (1995): 339.

39. Sandra Harding, *Whose Science? Whose Knowledge?*, 126. See chapter 5 for a helpful discussion of feminist standpoint epistemology.

40. Sandra Harding, "'Strong Objectivity': A Response to the New Objectivity Question," 344.

41. Joseph Rouse, "Feminism and the Social Construction of Scientific Knowledge," in *Feminism, Science, and the Philosophy of Science*, 210.

42. Harding, *Whose Science? Whose Knowledge?*, 158–59.

10

Sorry, Virginia, There Is No Feminist Science

E. R. Klein

Science it would seem is not sexless; she is a man, a father and infected too.
—Virginia Woolf[1]

Once upon a time a newspaper journalist responded to a little girl who questioned the editor of the (now defunct) *New York Sun* about the existence of Santa Claus.[2] The girl's name was Virginia O'Hanlon, and every Christmas since then, perhaps because of the time of the year, perhaps because of the power of nostalgia itself, the article is rerun in papers and magazines all over the country.

Today's more sophisticated parents are more likely to stick to the truth and attempt to instill in their children the "real meaning" of the Christmas holiday. Santa, they say, is merely a symbol of gift-giving—of love, friendship, even justice. (Don't forget, bad boys and girls get coal in their stockings.)

This brave new age of enlightened honesty has yet to dawn on some fields of academia, however. One would think that if parents can come clean with their own children about something like Santa, academicians could summon the courage to break the news to dreamy feminist theorists: Sorry, but despite the optimism of the past two decades, despite the many attempts to discredit classical[3] science while simultaneously trying to develop a science of its own, science has not only survived but has prevailed. Along the same line, a recent cover story in *TIME*[4] somewhat mournfully reports that many aspects of contemporary feminism may be dead.

No matter, though; for death becomes her. Like some B-movie horror flick zombie, feminism still walks the halls of academia, feasting on the soft, chewy brains of our young students, as well as the seasoned gray matter of politically charged professors and administrators. Although it is true that the critiques of feminism (more precisely, challenges to the legitimacy of feminist research) have not, in fact, "been subjected to the kind of criticism that parallel biases in other fields have received,"[5] the amount of actual criticism is of little consequence. For no matter how many times she is killed,[6] no matter how many nails seal her coffin,[7] feminism somehow manages to rise again.

THE REASON MYTH

Much of feminism's uncanny ability to stay alive despite criticism is due to the fact that she simply goes about ignoring her critics while continuing to repeat the same old false stories to her followers until they become, like religious lore, unquestioned dogma. One much-cited example surrounds the supposed historical fact, documented ostensibly by Genevieve Lloyd,[8] that the entire history of philosophy created a "male account of reason and evidence"—the keystones to modern scientific methodology.

It is often claimed that "in *The Man of Reason*, for example, Genevieve Lloyd makes a historical argument that the concept of transcendence, the ability of reason to transcend material and temporal limits, is male centered. . . ."[9] "In *The Man of Reason*, Genevieve Lloyd traces the historical development of Western ideals of Reason. Although variously articulated, these ideals are markedly consistent in defining themselves by contrast with and exclusion of traits, values, and attributes unquestioningly marked 'feminine'."[10] "In Lloyd's *The Man of Reason*, Lloyd argues that central philosophical terms—'reason' in particular—are defined so as to affirm masculinity and to silence and exclude femininity."[11]

> Lloyd's careful analysis of the history of conceptions of reason [in *The Man of Reason*] . . . argues that the latent conceptual connections between reason, masculinity, truth and the intellect, on one hand, and sense, femininity, error and emotion, on the other, are so entrenched and pervasive in the history of philosophy that they virtually prohibit women from reason.[12]

> As Genevieve Lloyd has told the story, what has been taken to characterize the man of reason may have changed from historical period to historical period, but in each, the character ideal of the man of reason has been construed in conjunction with a rejection of whatever has been taken to be characteristic of the feminine.[13]

These quotations are only the tip of the myth's iceberg. Lloyd's work is mentioned in almost every feminist work challenging every possible classical concept, even those never addressed by Lloyd herself, such as 'objectivity,' for example. "These concepts—[speaking of objectivity] like reason in Lloyd's analysis—have their operative meanings so saturated with the androcentered specificities of their histories that they have to be respecified, retold whenever they are employed in revisionary projects."[14] Finally, in literally hundreds of other feminist publications, Lloyd's book is cited directly following the author's own exaggerated claim that feminist theory proved beyond a shadow of a doubt that reason is inherently male. But such grand posturings are far from true.

While it is true that Lloyd clearly aims at showing that the "maleness of Reason . . . is no superficial linguistic bias,"[15] she is unable to do anything more than suggest that one could, if one is a committed feminist, read sexism and dichotomizing into the language of Plato,[16] Bacon,[17] Augustine,[18] Aquinas,[19] Descartes,[20] Kant,[21] and Hegel.[22] However, Lloyd's own linguistic bias should be taken into account, and it should, therefore, be recognized that one need not read any of these great philosophers as inherently sexist.

Oddly, this is something Lloyd ultimately admits. On the last page of *The Man of Reason*, Lloyd claims that readers should not be led to believe something as radical as that "the principles of logical thought valid for men do not hold also for female reasoners"; but they should believe that "philosophers can take seriously feminist dissatisfaction with the maleness of Reason without repudiating either Reason or Philosophy."[23] In other words, in the final analysis, reason is not inherently male. This claim, of course, is directly contradictory to the hysterical belief held by most feminists that reason is inherently male-biased.

Rumors, however, having once taken hold, are sometimes harder to dispel than fact. And Lloyd, whose book has been successful in the marketplace, has done little to dispense with the myth that she has single-handedly unmasked the evil male commitment to reason and evidence that has infected the entire history of philosophy and contemporary scientific inquiry.

THE MCCLINTOCK MAZE

With the above deception in mind, it is time to look at the leading argument for sexism in science (and the philosophy of science) and the hallmark experiment that is supposed to have both proved beyond a shadow of a doubt that science is inherently male-biased and founded a positive feminist methodology for science. The Barbara McClintock story, as told by Evelyn Fox Keller,[24] has become the foundation for all feminist philosophy of science to date. Contemporary feminists do not move a critical muscle against science (or philosophy of science) without appealing to Keller and her account of the McClintock story. Again, however, the story is, at best, exaggerated; and the lessons for the future are less than revolutionary.

First, simply, Barbara McClintock attended Cornell to become a geneticist. "Plants were the subject of choice when McClintock arrived at Cornell, and she chose corn."[25] McClintock eventually won the Nobel Prize for her DNA research on maize. McClintock's ostensibly unorthodox (and, therefore, later touted as feminist) methodology was "not that she did not use the micro techniques,"[26] of the day; for she did. Instead the myth was born because she believed that it was important to "know" your organism, to "just let the material tell you."[27] In other words, Keller claims, McClintock took "the time to look . . . at the hidden complexity"[28] of the organism; to be aware of the "oneness of things,"[29] "the magnificent integration of cellular processes."[30]

The phrase cited by feminists as having summed up McClintock's approach to science is that she, supposedly unlike any other (male) scientist before her, had a "feeling for the organism." This statement has become, for the feminist philosopher of science, the mantra of McClintock's work as well as Keller's main reason for claiming that classical science is inherently sexist—the reason most feminists (still) cite Keller to make any case against traditional science. The "feeling" mantra has also become the foundation for the contemporary feminist belief that any future philosophy of science must rework scientific methodology so that it now has such "feeling."

THE USE OF MYTH

To document the rampant use of the McClintock myth about maize, one need not look far. In chronological order, I list the following testimonials.

> Evelyn Fox Keller is another biographer whose work does not fit the traditional historical mold. In *A Feeling for the Organism: The Life and Work of Barbara McClintock*, though she retains the focus on an exceptional woman, Keller does not simply measure McClintock against traditional male standards . . . Keller uses this story as a vehicle for evaluating current methods of experimental science. Keller emphasizes that McClintock's relation to her material in her genetic research was characterized not by the conventional practice of distinguishing subject and object, but rather by the merging of self with the material—a feeling for the organism. McClintock's unconventional style, arising in part from individual idiosyncrasies and in part from the isolation she experienced as a woman in a man's world, reflects a unity with and a deep reverence for nature. . . .[31]

> Consider, for example, Evelyn Fox Keller's investigation of Nobel-Prize-winning scientist Barbara McClintock's way of doing science. According to Keller, McClintock did not aim, in her conceptualizations of the objects of her research, to reduce nature to simplicity in an effort to master it, to predict and control its behavior.[32]

> Keller points to many non-macho elements in the history of science. One of the themes of her intellectual biography of Barbara McClintock is the transcendence of gender in McClintock's scientific problematic, concepts and theory, and methods of research. McClintock's "feeling for the organism," her respect for the complexity of difference between individuals, her need to "listen to the material" all exemplify non-masculine tendencies that can also be detected elsewhere in the history of science . . . McClintock's work does not provide a feminist science, Keller argues, exactly because it transcends gender (though McClintock may have been more easily led to a deviant formulation of molecular biology, Keller speculates, because of her own status as a woman, as an outsider, a deviation, within science).[33]

In McClintock's work, Keller finds a subject-object relation premised on respect rather than domination, "in which respect for difference in her specimens shapes the research and conclusions she draws."[34] Even the most famous of all feminist philosophers of science, Sandra Harding, has bought into the myth. Citing Keller, Harding states that:

> One consequence of the prevalence of this sort of preference [for certain scientific methods which carry masculinist meaning or avoid feminist ones] is that scientists become less able to understand those aspects of nature that are not detectable through such methods and models. For instance, if Barbara McClintock's noninterventionist observation of patterns of growth in corn is associated with distinctively nonmasculine styles of interaction, it will be less used and appreciated by people who over-value masculinity and devalue femininity.[35]

And finally, straightforwardly, "Evelyn Fox Keller suggests in her discussion of Barbara McClintock's work in genetics that it was because McClintock was not a man that she had to develop a nonmasculinist practice of science."[36]

THE MAZE OF ABUSE

All of this, however, overdramatizes the facts. First, it is important to note that McClintock got plenty of recognition and honors for her work on maize, both during her lifetime and posthumously.

> Despite a widespread reading of Keller's biographical study as implying that in some way McClintock was not adequately recognized in science, there is little solid evidence of this . . . McClintock had long been an acknowledged member of the scientific elite, and she was, as Keller points out, early spoken of as a genius [by her colleagues] . . . the outside world had the strong suspicion she was a genius, and scientific honors continued to be bestowed on her, from a non-residential chair at Cornell in 1965 to the Kimber Genetics Medal of the National Academy in 1967 and, in 1970, the National Medal of Science.[37]

McClintock also had no less than twelve honorary degrees. In 1983, she won the coveted Nobel Prize; and in honor of her 90th birthday, her students and colleagues wrote essays on her work, which were collected and published.[38] Despite Keller's whining on her behalf, McClintock does not seem to be a woman who was discriminated against in any sense, let alone for being a woman.[39]

In addition, it is important to point out that some feminists, including Keller herself, admit that McClintock "explicitly denied that her way of doing science was feminine,"[40] claiming that science is a place where "gender drops away."[41] Parenthetically, this very unfeminist approach to her work manifested itself in the fact that

McClintock's Nobel Prize acceptance speech mentions nothing about either her sup-posed struggles as a woman or the celebrated-as-feminist implications of her work.[42]

It may be that the novelty of McClintock's ideas caused her to make the discov-eries she made and to have the distinguished career she did, in fact, have, but there is no reason to think that such ideas either sprang from her being a woman or were in any way especially feminist. It seems that Keller has a long way to go to show that McClintock's way of thinking about the holistic interaction of organisms, even if viewed as "a more mystical" or Eastern way of thinking[43]—thinking that Keller acknowledges was taken seriously by great men like Einstein, Schrodinger, Bohr, and Oppenheimer—is any more gynocentric than some other less holistic approach.[44] Having "feeling for the organism" does not a feminist make.[45]

Finally, this turn to a more holistic, active, and animistic model of the organism, even if it is more feminine (despite its male history) is not scientifically remarkable. For one thing, Barbara McClintock's self-organizing and strongly interactive "mod-els of transposition and gene action . . . [can] in the end, be understood in tradi-tional reductionistic (i.e., male) terminology."[46] For another, in the long run her account may not have the predictive success of its more linear sister or some other future account. It seems that McClintock's corn and the myth it established were nothing more than a feminist maze planted by Keller.

THE KELLER MYTH

Keller, however, is on a rampage against male, that is, classical science. And her next move is to blame the lack of recognition for her own empirical work on the same sexism that, as demonstrated above, she erroneously claims haunted McClintock. Keller argues that the McClintock story was primarily about the fight between male linear thinking and female holistic thinking; between the old male view of DNA acting under a "Master Molecule" model, and the new feminine view of aggrega-tion without the need for hierarchy or designating any particular cell as the "pace-maker."[47]

Keller's own scientific research focused on cellular slime mold aggregation—that is, how *Dictyostelium* progressed through its life cycle, including reproduction (see diagram). When viewed in slow motion, at a very intense magnification, hundreds of slime mold spores will aggregate to create one single organism.[48] The question Keller asked, while working as an empirical scientist, was: "What triggers the aggre-gation?"[49] No answer was forthcoming.

Once Keller started emphasizing feminist theory, however, the question changed. Now Keller asked: "Why, when both linear reductionist and interactionist perspec-tives are available, the scientific community preferred the linear or 'master molecule' theory that understands natural process as controlled by a single dominant factor?"[50] This time an answer was easy. The reason could not have been the objective em-pirical power of the reductionist over the interactionist model—its predictive suc-

Figure 10.1

DICTYOSTELIUM LIFE CYCLE

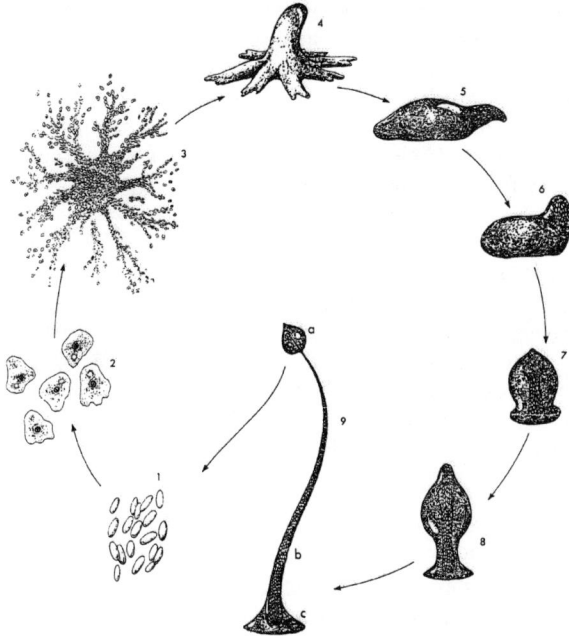

1. Spores	7. Beginning of sorophore formation
2. Myxamoebae (feeding stage)	8. Elevation of sorogen
3. Aggregation	9. Sorocarp
4. Pseudoplasmodium	a. Sorus
5. Migrating slug	b. Sorophore
6. Return to erect position	c. Basal disc

Carolina Biological Supply Company, Burlington, North Carolina 27215

Printed in U.S.A. © 1967 Carolina Biological Supply Company

Bioreview® Sheet
8310

Special thanks to Mr. Daniel E. James, V.P., for his permission to reprint.

cess, its ability for additional explanatory power, its consistence with the rest of accepted science, or any other classical "male" scientific desideratum. For Keller the answer had to be that the reductionist model uses a masculine language and is, therefore, subjectively enticing to the male-dominated scientific community. In other words, Keller wants her readers to believe that the sole reason the reductionist model is preferred by science is because science is inherently sexist.

THE USE OF METAPHOR

And so the myth continues to infect the feminist literature:

Evelyn Fox Keller also discusses the importance of the ideas of power, control, and domination, both over nature and other humans, in the goals, theory, and practice of modern Western science. . . . The themes of domination permeate the sciences both as explicit principles of social organization assumed to exist among primates and other species of animals, as though inherent in nature, and also as metaphoric assumption, such as in the "Master Molecule" concept of the action of genes. Through this concept, Keller nicely illustrates two different ways of conceptualizing and approaching the investigation of natural phenomena. In the face of a dominant paradigm in the field of molecular biology that posits linear hierarchy in the genetic DNA codes and transmits all instructions for cellular development, the research of biologist Barbara McClintock, who spoke to Keller of her scientific approach of "letting the material speak to you" and having "a feeling for the organism," led her to a different view. In this view, DNA is "in delicate interaction with the cellular environment"; master control is not found in a single component of the cell; rather, "control resides in the complex interactions of the entire system." The focus of importance is on the organism and its environment, not on a Master Molecule.[51]

The evidence for male bias in science continues to be invented, now using the supposed "concrete illustration"[52] via the "problem of slime mold aggregation."[53]

Unlike McClintock, who wanted nothing to do with this kind of feminist theorizing, Keller strengthens her relationship with, and makes a name for herself in, the tight-knit circle that is feminist theorizing. Keller boldly claims that "science bears the imprint of its genderization not only in the ways it is used but in the description of reality it offers. . . ."[54] And, "the most immediate issue for a feminist perspective on the natural sciences is the deeply rooted popular mythology that casts objectivity, reason, and mind as male, and subjectivity, feeling, and nature as female."[55] Therefore, claims Keller, "the 'laws of nature' are more than simple expressions of the results of objective inquiry . . . they must be read for their personal—and by tradition, masculine—content."[56]

The myth of male bias continues to grow, and now the feminist's new mantra becomes much more generalized: "Science it would seem is not sexless, she is a man, a father and infected too."[57] Despite an admittance that the evidence for male bias is primarily metaphorical, as the citations below demonstrate, that admittance is generally ignored.

Evelyn Fox Keller and other historians of science have noted that reliance on metaphors and models of both nature and research processes which center forms of order and relationships that are idealized in bourgeois, Western notions of masculinity result in partial and distorted descriptions and explanations of nature and social life.[58]

Some historians of science [citing Keller] have brought to our attention the persistent presence of metaphors of gender politics in the formal and informal thinking of scientists from the emergence of modern science through the present day.[59]

METAPHOR MONGERING[60]

However, the appeal to metaphor as the most fundamental form of evidence of the inherent sexism of science qua scientific methodology is weak to say the least. Elsewhere, I have labeled this move the "hermeneutical fallacy."[61] When the lion's share of the evidence for the inherent sexism of science, specifically scientific methodology, is based solely on one's interpretation of texts, one should cautiously proceed with any admonishments. For when the interpretation of the text is performed by a feminist, it seems that the male-biased boogeyman can be found everywhere.

This kind of "metaphor mongering," is, to put it simply, illegitimate. First, metaphor in general allows for a multiplicity of interpretations. For Keller to assume that any one particular interpretation, that is, the one that demonstrates inherent sexism, is the correct one, completely misses the point of employing metaphor to begin with. In the Quinian[62] vernacular, if there is one sexist interpretation, there are many. Moreover, there is no reason to think that the feminist reading of male bias in science, reading every negative metaphor as female and every positive metaphor as male, is anything more than their particular brand of verbal "cross-dressing."[63]

Setting aside the fact that Keller never cites the writings of any contemporary scientists, let's look at one of Keller's examples of sexism in science, an infamous quotation by Francis Bacon: "let us establish a chaste and lawful marriage between Mind and Nature. . . . It is Nature herself who is to be the bride, who requires taming, shaping, and subduing by the scientific mind."[64] Considering the fact that the rest of the quotation states that "for man is but the servant and interpreter of nature . . . nor can nature be commanded except by being obeyed,"[65] one must wonder whether any single quotation citing a metaphorical use of the sixteenth-century conception of marriage can possibly be charged with the serious crime of having made all of contemporary science—its methodological commitments to objectivity, evidence, reason, and logic—inherently sexist?

In the first place, such evidence, by Keller's own lights, depends on the interpretation of the reader; and, as stated above, when the reader is steeped in the feminist mystique, it is not hard to guess that male bias will be found. Second, for every metaphorical quotation that can be viewed as masculine, one can just as easily find metaphors with a feminine curve.

For example, a contemporary of Bacon's, and a great scientist in his own right, Johannes Kepler, uses what Keller must consider a feminine metaphor—music. In his famous astronomical piece entitled "The Harmonies of the World," Kepler actually composes pages of music to accompany the different voices of the planets and their moons to help him understand, explain, and predict the motions of the celestial bodies in our solar system. It can be nothing less than male-bashing that feminists cite Bacon's few pat comments about marriage, take these to be foundational to the belief that all of nature is viewed through masculine eyes, and then jump to the theoretical conclusion that all of scientific methodology since Bacon is inherently male biased; at the same time ignoring Kepler's extremely committed interpretation of nature—via music—as feminine. Kepler believed that nature not only follows the harmonic compositions of music, but he believed it for no other reason than he felt like it: "I do not know why but nevertheless this wonderful congruence with human song has such a strong effect upon me that I am compelled to pursue this part of the comparison, also, even without any solid natural cause."[66] Talk about a male scientist who had a feeling for, and listened to, the organism.

Nor is it the case that women, or all things feminine, are perceived in a negative light by the history of science. For example, in an interesting subchapter of *The Descent of Man,* entitled "Secondary Sex Characteristics of Mammals," Charles Darwin writes that the picking of a male mate by the female (quadruped) is anything but haphazard. As a matter of fact, there seems to be a serious decision-making process prior to, as well as a considerable loyalty factor after, a mate is chosen. Darwin cites a case

> in which a valuable and wonderfully-intelligent female terrier loved a retriever belonging to a neighbor to such a degree . . . she would never acknowledge the courtship of any other dog. . . . From these facts there can be no doubt that, with most of our domesticated quadrupeds, strong individual antipathies and preferences are frequently exhibited, and much more commonly by the female than by the male.[67]

Unless decision making and loyalty are viewed as negative characteristics, it seems that name-calling is all that is evident with feminist theorizing. However, metaphor, and a biased choice at that, is all Keller offers her readers in her warlock hunt for sexism in science. By focusing on the language of scientists concerned with the analysis of cellular slime mold aggregation, specifically the use of the term "Master Molecule," as opposed to the empirical results of classical scientific methodology on the organism (not to mention the incredible predictable success of past science in general), Keller was able to strengthen and propagate the myth that science always has been and always will be inherently male-biased.

Such evidence is clearly conceived in sin and, hopefully, unconvincing to anyone outside the quilting bee that is feminism. Perhaps Keller and other feminists should heed Keller's own advice and cease imposing "on nature the stories [specific readers] like to hear."[68] At the very least, feminist theorists should stop making theoretical mountains out of mold [*sic*] hills.

In the final analysis, either metaphorical evidence is enough or it is not. If it is enough, then science, if it must be gendered at all, may be gendered male when reading Bacon; but if so, it must be gendered female when reading Kepler and Darwin. Each metaphor from every work of any scientist will have to be judged independently. If, however, metaphorical interpretation is not enough to condemn all of classical contemporary science as inherently sexist, then the feminist critics must offer something more, or cease and desist from making further accusations.

IS SCIENCE INHERENTLY MALE-BIASED?

Without the abuse of history or the misuse of metaphor, there is little evidence that science either has always been, or always will be, a boys' club where its members act as one-dimensional, linear-thinking automatons who treat their subjects of study in such a way that they would joyfully misconstrue the evidence in a sexist manner just to maintain the masculine status quo, and would ultimately use their findings to harm women. Of course the history of science is a history of male scientists and their discoveries, but this is merely a descriptive fact of human culture in general, not, in any way, an insight into some insidious conspiracy to bias evidence and keep scientific methodology out of the reach of the supposed "women's ways of knowing."[69]

As a matter of fact, the history of science, even in brief, reveals that in many cases unwanted or unexpected evidence alone motivated the theory-making of those scientists that posterity still reveres.

Many of the men who have contributed to the great changes in science have really been very unhappy over what they have been forced to do. Kepler, who loved spheres, discovered ellipses; Planck, with his famous quantum of action, introduced an element of discontinuity into physics, which seemed to him absolutely and intolerably strange and ugly. Einstein, who was able to live with the theories of relativity and regretted only very few aspects of them, also contributed to the development of quantum theory; he proposed the idea of light quanta, but never could reconcile himself to quantum theory logically built up from this basis. And de Broglie, who discovered that there are waves that are associated with material particles, could never reconcile himself to their interpretation as waves that only represented information and not some disturbance in a corporeal medium.

These changes are forced on physicists somewhat reluctantly because "we are both traditional and conservative and at the same time a little too adventurous."[70]

A commitment to evidence, it seems, despite the fears of feminists, overrode many a great scientist's subjective desires. Unfortunately, any commitment to objective criteria, including the hard facts provided by empirical investigations, is viewed by feminists, at the next level of epistemological subterfuge, to be yet another male trick to oppress women.[71]

FEMINIST BEEF

To rehash, when the feminist critiques of science over the past two decades are distilled, the following are four ways in which contemporary science is viewed as masculine by feminist theorists:

(1) Men have controlled it [science] right from the start, (2) The enterprise [of science] has tended to leave women largely invisible in its knowledge and research, (3) [Science] has often portrayed women, and things feminine, in negative terms when it has considered us, and (4) Western science has sought right from the start to dominate nature conceived of as feminine, with a method characterized by disinterestedness and emotional detachment, aggression and competitiveness.[72]

Given that the first claim is indisputable—after all, the history of science is primarily a history of men—this claim of heredity has no theoretical teeth[73]. Also, given that the second claim wasted all of its political muscle on the McClintock myth and the third claim was reduced to a misguided commitment to metaphor in general— worse yet, a biased commitment to specific metaphors—there is little left for the self-respecting critical feminist to sink her teeth into except the final, methodological, claim. The question now is: Is science inherently male-biased? That is, is science sexist because of its methodological commitments to disinterestedness and emotional detachment?[74]

At the very least, feminism has not made the case that this is so. Classical science's desire for objectivity, in all of its guises—including "disinterestedness" and "emotional detachment"—has been under siege since Keller[75] and has yet to show even a scratch. Even Harding's celebrated attack and her reworking of the concept of objectivity, where she distinguishes "strong" from "weak" objectivity,[76] did little to discredit science and its classical methodological principles, including its commitments to disinterestedness and emotional detachment. In fact there is no reason to believe either that such concepts are inherently male, or, when applied, entail consequences that are harmful to women.[77]

Again, the history of science offers us the exact opposite evidence. Without the so-called "male" desiderata of disinterest and emotional detachment, bad science, or pseudoscience, as well as biased science (for example, Nazi science), seems to flourish. When the physicians in Germany were better Nazis than they were scientists, we ended up with an entire race/religious group of people being exterminated for being "sick." With no non-Nazi criteria, no truly objective criteria to appeal to, the Nazis were free to act as interested and emotionally attached to their misguided theories and practices as they wished. Sexism, if not checked by the facts, would follow suit mutatis mutandis. In a society still plagued by real sexism in the form of unequal treatment, feminist philosophy of science—with its constant condemnation of objectivity and evidence—even if it did exist, would, ironically, not be good for women.

So what is it that feminists find so objectionable about objectivity and evidence? Why do they boldly claim that "to be perfectly blunt . . . [they] do not believe in the 'truth' of scientific theories or representation of nature"?[78] Why, after all these years, do they still not see that what science needs is more, not less, of a commitment to disinterestedness and emotional detachment? Because, I believe, feminists, in their hearts, are relativists at best, sexists at worse.

FEMINISTS QUA RELATIVISTS

There is a great deal of evidence in the literature of the feminist commitment to relativism, specifically the brand made popular by Thomas Kuhn.[79] Putting the unfeminist fact that Kuhn is a man aside, feminists have bought into the "Kuhnian strategy of arguing that observations are theory-laden, theories are paradigm-laden, and paradigms are culture-laden: there are and can be no such things as . . . objective facts."[80]

Although a thorough discussion of Kuhn's arguments against the notion of objectivity would fall outside the scope of this project, there is a vast body of philosophical literature claiming that he has not made his case against objectivity.[81]

Briefly, Kuhn's use of 'incommensurability'—meaning that theories from two different paradigms cannot be compared and, therefore, rationally adjudicated—is at the center of his version of relativism. Because of this, his account of relativism is caught between the horns of a dilemma. Either the thesis, on the one hand, truly embraces incommensurability, or it does not. If the former, then Kuhnian relativism is provocative, for it entails unintelligibility; if the latter, it entails the promise of objectivity and is therefore benign. As Israel Scheffler has pointed out, "objectivity requires simply the possibility of intelligible debate over the comparative merits of rival paradigms."[82]

Although it is not clear that Kuhn ever actually supported the radical reading of the incommensurability claim, it is certain that the feminists cannot simply rest on their Kuhnian laurels. For even if Kuhn is interpreted to be a radical incommensurabilist, feminist critics of traditional science must take the body of criticisms of Kuhnian and, therefore, their own relativism seriously.[83]

And taking the problems of relativism seriously would mean, at the very least, a recognition that embracing such a theory may have problematic consequences for the raison d'etre of feminism itself, that is, the empowerment of women. As one self-critical feminist, Claudia Murphy,[84] has pointed out:

> . . . relativism is unacceptable because feminism is not only an epistemology but also a political ideology.[85] Most feminists abhor the idea that one can take isolated philosophical positions. They believe that one's philosophy is to be lived. And relativism is politically and morally repugnant. To the man who wants to treat me as an object which he owns I will not simply say 'Well, that's your view.' Both views cannot peacefully

coexist. More specifically, relativism is unacceptable because feminists want a stand-point from which they can criticize the dominant view. . . . Feminists want to be able to argue that this view is wrong; and not just politically incorrect or emotionally up-setting but false.[86]

In other words, embracing relativism, and its rejection of any notion of an absolute truth, would mean it would be both impossible for women to rationally resist, or for feminists to rationally argue against, oppression by men. One could, at best, hope for the correct flip of the sex/gender coin, regardless of who's doing the flipping.

FEMINISTS QUA SEXISTS

Some feminists finally began to believe that a commitment to Kuhnian relativism would continue to keep the masculine enterprise of science "invisible and intact,"[87] and, therefore, they took feminism yet one step further, to feminist standpoint theory.

Feminist standpoint theory is an offshoot of the standpoint theory that was in-herent in the Hegelian-Marxist epistemic apparatus[88] and was later appropriated by Sandra Harding. Its main tenet is that because women are an oppressed group, their social experiences, unlike the skewed-by-privilege experiences of men, "can provide the grounds for a less distorted understanding of the world around us."[89] As Harding states, "'the winner tells the tale,' as historians point out, and so trying to construct the story from the perspective of the lives of those who resist oppression generates less partial and distorted accounts of nature and social relations."[90]

With standpoint, however, feminism has jumped out of the relativism pan, and into the fire of sexism. Feminist standpoint, in its attempts to avoid the unseemly consequences of relativism, ends up with a "residual objectivism,"[91] an objectivism that is actually female-biased.

This reverse bias becomes obvious when one examines more closely Harding's standpoint theory. She claims that feminist scientists (and philosophers of science) must adopt standpoint as the only way science can achieve an accurate picture of the world. "It is because women have struggled against male supremacy that research starting from their lives can be made to yield up clearer and more nearly complete visions of social reality than are available only from the perspective of men's side of these struggles."[92] In other words, feminists must fight so-called "male bias" by in-venting female bias.

Of course, at this point the "residual objectivism that informs feminist stand-point"[93] becomes obvious. And this objective foundation is anything but disinter-ested. On the contrary, Harding and all other feminist standpoint theorists have sim-ply replaced the so-called "male" objective perspective with the victimized female perspective. Hierarchy remains, the master/slave dynamic remains, and bias remains; all that changes is who is on top. While feminist science criticizes the tradition of playing king-of-the-scientific-knowledge hill, feminist standpoint theorists have simply declared themselves goddesses of that same hill, thereby ending up, theoretically speaking, "trapped in the epistemological paradigm they meant to deconstruct."[94]

In their desire to demonstrate that the methods of science were inherently sexist, feminists went too far. Unable to unearth any real evidence—non-historical, non-hermeneutical—of bias in science, feminists attempted to undermine the notion of "objectivity" itself, the cornerstone not only of science, but of all rational adjudication. And, ironically, by establishing a feminist standpoint, by using this tactic of fighting fire with fire, feminism has actually ended up burning only itself.

THE "NEWEST" FEMINIST SCIENCE

With the above false starts in mind, Janet A. Kourany attempts a new approach for the development of a peculiarly feminist science by combining what she calls "contextual empiricism" with some of the ideas of feminist standpoint theory.[95] However, in her attempt to avoid both "neutrality," at all costs (something she believes "is not an asset in an immoral world"[96]), and the pitfalls of the standpoint theory described above, Kourany has completely removed anything peculiarly feminist from her program. When Kourany is done articulating her "new" account of feminist science there is nothing left for feminists to claim as their own; nothing, that is, that isn't fundamentally sexist.

Kourany's early feminist commitments, like most of her theoretical ilk, are consistent with the Kuhnian relativism described above. However, Kourany's more recent and more sophisticated account of the philosophy of science finds comfort in something much more esoteric.

Kourany credits Kuhn with having performed an important metaepistemological shift in the way scientists (and philosophers of science) look at scientific methodology. She claims Kuhn offered theorists a way to shift the program of science from one committed to pure prescription, with respect to the establishment of the desiderata for science, to one that incorporates the descriptive accounts of the socially situated lives of scientists themselves—their fears, needs, and desires. In summing up Kuhn with respect to this descriptive/prescriptive issue, Kourany claims that "it was argued [by Kuhn], how could philosophers of science presume to prescribe what science should be like when they had no clear idea what science was like, when their 'characterizations' did not in any way match the sophistication and diversity of actual science?"[97]

Taking this lead, Kourany goes on to argue that a feminist change that could "deeply" affect science would be to make the primary aim of science something that concentrates on both the "descriptive and prescriptive" aspects of science equally.[98]

Kourany, it seems, wants to develop a project that combines both the empirical data concerning the ways in which scientists actually make the discoveries they do—for example, what desires and biases motivated them to form hypotheses—in equal measure with the logical and methodological desiderata to which scientists should appeal to justify those hypotheses.

My first response to this move is: So what? Kourany's self-proclaimed "new" project, if this is all it is, is nothing new. Neither scientists nor philosophers of science ever denied that actual researchers and scholars don't overlap their interests with respect to both the descriptive project of discovery and prescriptive project of justification. Nor do they deny that the two, albeit separate, investigations cannot play some role in the project of the other. Certainly Kuhn is right that philosophers of science creating methodological desiderata should know something about the history of science and its past methodological principles. Likewise, scientists working under the constraints of theory should understand the logic that underlies that theory. Classical science and philosophy of science never had a problem with this kind of cooperation and integration.[99] If this is all that Kourany is saying, it is hardly new, let alone feminist.

More importantly, I must ask why it is that feminists like Kourany saw such "new" promise in the breaking down of the descriptive and prescriptive projects (what Hans Reichenbach[100] coined decades ago as the distinction between the context of discovery and the context of justification)? What did they hope to gain?

If the descriptive project of science (and/or the philosophy of science) is to document the history of working scientists—their beliefs as well as all the "reasons" for their beliefs, no matter how subjective—while the prescriptive project is to assess those "reasons" by attempting to offer metacriteria for legitimizing some "reasons" while condemning others—then if Kourany truly wants to address both projects on equal footing, the old hoary normative questions about the goodness of reasons remain.

As such, feminist theorists must either admit to their relativist commitments—claiming that there is no way to proceed with the prescriptive project and determine which of various "reasons" scientists should embrace—or they must appeal to some extradescriptive or prescriptive reasons for their adjudications. Again, if they appeal to classical normative (ostensibly male) ideals like evidence and logic, then they are not doing anything new, and they are certainly not doing anything particularly feminist. If they appeal, on the other hand, to their "standpoint" as oppressed women, they then have the problem of admitting female bias, or reverse sexism.

Since it is clear that Kourany neither wants to be stuck between the horns of the above dilemma, nor wants to support the prescriptive project over and above the descriptive one, it must be that she secretly supports the descriptive project alone. That is, Kourany and other feminist theorists must really be saying that there is no such thing as the normative project of science (or the philosophy of science) and, therefore, the descriptive project is all there is. With the prescriptive project out of the way, feminist theorists are free to focus solely on the descriptive project. With only one project, all of science (and the philosophy of science) is reduced to the charting of the historical events hallmarking science. And, of course, when this chronology is looked at through the lenses of feminist standpoint theorists, it is not surprising that all that shows through are the sexist behaviors of men running amok, without any constraints on their always evil, or at least fundamentally selfish and sexist, desires.

The argument then, has not only come full circle, it is fundamentally circular. Feminist theorists, by way of assuming a particular standpoint—that the history of science is a history of men and their sexist ways—have, not surprisingly, proven that science is inherently sexist. Nothing could be more vicious.

CONCLUSIONS

Fortunately, one need not buy into feminist science (or feminist philosophy of science) to fight sexism. One can, I believe, fight sexism the old-fashioned way—with the classical tools of logic and a commitment to objective evidence. By maintaining a commitment to the distinction between the discovery of hypotheses (including all of their subjective motivations), nd the actual justification of those same hypotheses (which requires the additional commitment to objectivity and unbiased evidence), any sexism in science will be brought to an end.

In the wake of all of the years of feminist apostasy, I am reminded again of the editorial article that lied to little Virginia so many years ago. The editor offered as evidence of the existence of Santa Claus the following hypothetical question and response: "Did you ever see fairies dancing in the lawn? Of course not, but that's no proof that they are not there."[101]

In parallel fashion, I find feminism having nothing better to say. The theoretical query that comes to mind is: Have feminist philosophers of science offered any real evidence of sexism in science? No, but that does not mean that such evidence can't exist, and since there are no objective normative criteria for determining how one should acquire or justify such evidence, feminists are free to simply invent it. After all, two wrongs always make a right, and isn't that what men have been doing all these years?

On a more practical level I ask: Have feminist scientists (and philosophers of science) offered women any real tools that they can use to fight sexism in the scientific community, or when criticizing science at any level? Again, sadly, the answer is no. At this point, one could decide to stand by feminism and wait for the invention of such tools and see if any can be forged in a way that is not self-destructive. Or, and this is what I recommend, one can throw feminism to the wind and reappropriate the classical tools of logic, reason, and evidence. Call the tools "male" if you wish, but such tools by any name will work just as well.

It seems that feminists want to save their theories no matter what the cost to women. Such nostalgia, however, unlike the Christmas editorial, is neither quaint nor benign. Actually, it is nothing less than patronizing and sexist. Women approaching the 21st century do not believe in Santa or fairies. Virginias everywhere have grown up, and they want to arm themselves with the real weapons of liberation. They don't care about the use of the pronoun "she" instead of "he" in science and philosophy journals, they care about achieving equal opportunity to study, publish in, and edit those same journals. They don't care about the rewriting of the history of science or philosophy so as to eliminate metaphor or unearth some obscure (dead) woman scholar who somewhere said one thing that may be taken to have influenced some aspect of something in science or philosophy. Instead, they care about equal consideration (and pay) for their own accomplishments in those same fields.

It is my hope that grown-up Virginias everywhere are ready to hear the truth: Sorry, there is no feminist science. And, more importantly, despite efforts to infect science with feminism, it must remain sexless.

NOTES

1. Virginia Woolf, *Three Guineas* (New York: Harcourt, Brace, and World, 1938), 212–13. This quote is widely cited (I believe incorrectly, see note 57) as evidence of Woolf's feminism. See, for example, Janet A. Kourany, "A New Program for Philosophy of Science, in Many Voices," in *Philosophy in a Feminist Voice: Critiques and Reconstructions*, ed. Janet A. Kourany (Princeton, N.J.: Princeton University Press, 1998), 231; Hilary Rose, *Love, Power and Knowledge: Toward a Feminist Transformation of the Sciences* (Bloomington, Ind.: Indiana University Press, 1994), 1; Hilary Rose, "Hand, Brain, and Heart: A Feminist Epistemology for the Natural Sciences," in *Sex and Scientific Inquiry*, ed. Sandra Harding and Jean F. O'Barr (Chicago: University of Chicago Press, 1987), 265–82, 265; Sandra Harding, *The Science Question in Feminism* (Ithaca, N.Y.: Cornell University Press, 1986), 135.

2. The journalist was Mr. Francis Pharcellus Church, and the first appearance of the editorial piece was on September 27, 1897.

3. I use the term "classical" here to avoid the now trendy feminist criticism of all that is "traditional." The former term brings to mind the standards of great traditions (for example, in music, painting, or ballet) foundational to, without being at all restrictive toward, the most contemporary arrangements.

4. *TIME* magazine, cover story, June 29, 1998.

5. Iddo Landau, "Good Women and Bad Men: A Bias in Feminist Research," *Journal of Social Philosophy* 28, no. 1 (Spring 1997): 141–50, 146.

6. See, for example, Daphne Patai and Noretta Koertge, *Professing Feminism: Cautionary Tales for the Strange World of Women's Studies* (New York: Basic Books, 1994).

7. See, for example, E. R. Klein, *Feminism Under Fire* (Amherst, N.Y.: Prometheus, 1996).

8. Genevieve Lloyd, *The Man of Reason: 'Male' and 'Female' in Western Philosophy* (Minneapolis: University of Minnesota Press, 1993).

9. Charlotte Witt, "Feminist Metaphysics," in *A Mind of One's Own: Feminist Essays on Reason and Objectivity*, ed. Louise M. Antony and Charlotte Witt, 1991, 119–20.

10. Lorraine Code, *What Can She Know?* (Ithaca, N.Y.: Cornell University Press, 1991), 119–20.

11. Elizabeth Grosz, "Philosophy," in *Feminist Knowledge: Critique and Construct*, ed. Sneja Gunew (New York: Routledge, 1990), 162.

12. Moira Gatens, *Feminism and Philosophy: Perspectives on Difference and Equality* (Bloomington, Ind.: Indiana University Press, 1991), 94–95.

13. Virginia Held, "Feminist Reconceptualizations in Ethics," in *Philosophy in a Feminist Voice: Critiques and Reconstructions*, ed. Janet A. Kourany (Princeton, N.J.: Princeton University Press, 1998), 92–115.

14. Lorraine Code, "Voice and Voicelessness: A Modest Proposal?" in *Philosophy in a Feminist Voice: Critiques and Reconstructions*, ed. Janet A. Kourany, (Princeton, N.J.: Princeton University Press, 1998), 204–30, 224.

15. Lloyd, ix.

16. For example, Lloyd cites the Timaeus as having demonstrated that "the very nature of knowledge was implicitly associated with the extrusion of what was symbolically associated with the feminine [with] . . . intimations of gender differentiation with respect to the exalted conception of cosmic Reason," 4–5.

17. Here Lloyd claims that the "mind's domination of matter . . . was not explicitly associated with the male-female distinction . . . ," 16.

18. On the contrary, Lloyd admits that in Augustine's theorizing, "women's status as a rational mind is equal to man's," 32–33.

19. Again, however, according to Lloyd, "woman does not symbolize an inferior form or lesser presence of rationality," 35.

20. Even Descartes—a favorite whipping boy of the feminists—"offered a method of critical analysis that was supposed to be accessible to women," 48.

21. According to Lloyd, Kant "did not explore the possibility of a sexual differentiation," 67.

22. Lloyd admits that "gender does not figure explicitly in Hegel's story of the development of human consciousness. . . . But the pattern he introduces there lends itself to the accommodation, containment and transcending of feminine consciousness, in relation to more mature "male" consciousness," 72–73.

23. Lloyd, 109.

24. First in Evelyn Fox Keller, *A Feeling for the Organism: The Life and Work of Barbara McClintock* (New York: Freeman, 1983); then in Keller, *Reflections on Gender and Science* (New Haven, Conn.: Yale University Press, 1985).

25. Arthur Zucker, "Evelyn Fox Keller, A Feeling for the Organism," in *Introduction to the Philosophy of Science*, ed. Arthur Zucker (Upper Saddle River, N.J.: Prentice Hall, 1996), 384–85.

26. Zucker, 385.

27. Keller, *A Feeling for the Organism*, 179.

28. Evelyn Fox Keller, "A Feeling for the Organism," in *Introduction to the Philosophy of Science*, ed. Arthur Zucker (Upper Saddle River, N.J.: Prentice Hall, 1996), 386–92, 391.

29. Keller 1996, 390.

30. Keller 1996, 390.

31. Linda Schiebinger, "The History and Philosophy of Women in Science: A Review Essay," in *Sex and Scientific Inquiry?* ed. Sandra Harding and Jean F. O'Barr (Chicago: The University of Chicago Press, 1987), 7–34, 16.

32. Kourany, "A New Program for Philosophy of Science, in Many Voices," 231–62, 245.

33. Lynn Hankinson Nelson, *Who Knows: From Quine to a Feminist Empiricism* (Philadelphia: Temple University Press, 1990), 122.

34. Lorraine Code, *What Can She Know?: Feminist Theory and the Construction of Knowledge* (Ithaca, N.Y.: Cornell University Press, 1991), 151.

35. Sandra Harding, *Whose Science? Whose Knowledge?: Thinking from Women's Lives,* (Ithaca, N. Y.: Cornell University Press, 1991), 45.

36. Bat-Ami Bar On, "Marginality and Epistemic Privilege," in *Feminist Epistemologies,* ed. Linda Alcoff and Elizabeth Potter (New York: Routledge, 1993), 83–100, 90–91.

37. Hilary Rose, *Love, Power and Knowledge: Toward a Feminist Transformation of the Sciences* (Bloomington, Ind.: Indiana University Press, 1994), 162–63.

38. Nina Fedoroff and David Botstein, eds., *The Dynamic Genome, Barbara McClintock's Ideas in the Century of Genetics* (Plainview, N. Y.: Cold Spring Harbor Laboratory Press, 1992).

39. This fact is even recognized by Sandra Harding, who clearly believes that "women have been systematically excluded from doing serious science," but nonetheless believes that "McClintock is the one exception to this rule," Sandra Harding, *The Science Question in Feminism* (Ithaca, N.Y.: Cornell University Press, 1986), 31. As an anecdotal aside, I went into the library and arbitrarily picked out several introductory and advanced texts on genetics. Every one cited McClintock's work. I invite the reader to do the same.

40. Kourany 1998, 249.

41. Evelyn Fox Keller, *Reflections on Science and Gender* (New Haven, Conn.: Yale University Press, 1985), 173; Evelyn Fox Keller, "The Gender/Science System: or, Is Sex to Gender As Nature is to Science," *Hypatia,* vol. 2, no. 3 (Fall 1987): 37–49, 41.

42. Barbara McClintock, *Le Prix Nobel* (Stockholm, Nobel Foundation, 1983) reprinted under the title "The Significance of Responses of the Genome to Challenge," *Science* 226, (1983): 792, 801.

43. Keller 1996, 386–92, 389–90.

44. See, for example, the work of the following men: Gary Zukav, *The Dancing Wu Li Master: An Overview of the New Physics* (New York: Bantam Books, 1979); Fritjof Capra, *The Tao of Physics: An Exploration of the Parallels Between Modern Physics and Eastern Mysticism* (Boulder, Colo.: Shambhala Press, 1975).

45. While I was writing this piece, world-renowned chef Wolfgang Puck, while cooking on the Jay Leno show, July 17th, 1998, stated that in order to be a great cook you must "have a feeling for the food." He said this while holding up a (very dead) soft-shell crab.

46. This was pointed out by Helen Longino, *Science as Social Knowledge: Values and Objectivity in Scientific Inquiry* (Princeton, N.J.: Princeton University Press, 1990), 208.

47. Keller 1985, 150–57.

48. I have seen the Stephen Bonner video that documents this event, and I have also run my own experiments with two separate philosophy of science classes under the tutelage of two different biology professors (one man, one woman) from two different colleges. Although both scientists were quite familiar with *Dictyostelium,* neither had heard of Keller, and neither saw anything sexist in any aspect of the research done in this area.

49. Keller 1985, 151.

50. Helen Longino, "Subjects, Power, and Knowledge: Description and Prescription in Feminist Philosophies of Science," in *Feminist Epistemologies,* eds. Linda Alcoff and Elizabeth Potter (New York: Routledge, 1993), 101–20, 107.

51. Ruth Bleier, *Science and Gender: A Critique of Biology and Its Theories on Women* (New York: Pergamon Press, 1984), 204, 205.

52. Keller 1985, 138.

53. Keller 1985, 150.

54. Keller 1985, 80.

55. Keller 1985, 6–7.

56. Keller 1985, 10.

57. Virginia Woolf, *Three Guineas* (New York: Harcourt, Brace, and World, 1938), 212–13. What is interesting to note is that feminist theorists throughout the years (see note 1) have used this quotation as the battle cry against classical science, yet it seems to have been completely misconstrued. Woolf's point is in no way a condemnation of classical science nor its methodological principles. As a matter of fact, Woolf employs the words of Bertrand Russell to help make her very unfeminist case that the methods of science are not sexist, but that such methodological constraints do not always stop sexist men in the sciences from making themselves ridiculous while employing a variety of pseudosciences for their biased endeavors.

58. Harding 1991, 300–301.

59. Harding 1986, 233.

60. A term coined by Paul R. Gross and Norman Levitt in *Higher Superstition: The Academic Left and Its Quarrels with Science* (Baltimore, Md.: The Johns Hopkins University Press, 1994), 116.

61. E. R. Klein, "Criticizing the Feminist Critique of Objectivity," in *Reason Papers* 18 (1993): 57–70.

62. W. V. Quine, world-renowned philosopher.

63. Tibor R. Machan coins this phrase while trying to flesh out a similar move by feminists in his criticism of Alison Jagger's attacks on the supposed male notion of "justice" in his "Communication From One Feminist," *Journal of Social Philosophy* 28, no. 1 (Spring 1997): 54–61, 58.

64. Keller 1985, 36; Keller, "Feminist Perspectives on Science Studies," *Science, Technology, and Human Values* 13, nos. 3 & 4, (Autumn 1988): 235–49, 235.

65. Francis Bacon, *The New Organon and Related Writings*, ed. F. H. Anderson (Indianapolis: Bobbs Merrill, 1960), 29.

66. Johannes Kepler, "The Harmonies of the World," in *Great Books of the Western World*, 16, ed. Robert Maynard Hutchins et al., (New York: Encyclopedia Britannica, Inc., 1952), 1005, 1085, 1049.

67. Charles Darwin, "The Descent of Man and Selection in Sex," in *Great Books of the Western World*, 49, ed. Robert Maynard Hutchins et al., (New York: Encyclopedia Britannica, Inc., 1952), 252–659, 545.

68. Keller 1985, 157.

69. Mary F. Belenky, et al., eds. *Women's Ways of Knowing: The Development of Self, Voice and Mind* (New York: Basic Books, 1986).

70. J. Robert Oppenheimer, *The Flying Trapeze: Three Crises for Physicists* (New York: Oxford University Press, 1964), 5–6.

71. This idea has been more fully developed in Klein's *Feminism Under Fire*, (Amherst, New York: Prometheus Books, 1996), ch. 2.

72. Kourany 1998, 231–62, 242–43.

73. After all, this is the genetic fallacy—that just because some idea comes from a man, it is a "male" idea. Even feminists have had to admit that "this is not to say that all women

scientists will be critical of sexist and androcentric values and the scientific knowledge they support, or that all men scientists will not be," Kourany 1998, 254.

74. I ignore the supposed desiderata of "aggression" and "competitiveness," since they are goals that are clearly inconsistent with "disinterestedness" and "emotional detachment." One cannot simultaneously accuse men of being both. Furthermore, the history of feminist critiques of science, philosophy of science, and epistemology focus primarily on "disinterestedness" and "emotional detachment."

75. Keller 1985.

76. Sandra Harding, "Rethinking Standpoint Epistemology: What is 'Strong Objectivity?'" in *Feminist Epistemologies*, ed. L. Alcoff and E. Potter (New York: Routledge, 1993), 49–82. See Klein 1996 for a full analysis and critique.

77. For a more detailed criticism of this particular obfuscation of Harding's, see Klein 1996, chapter 1.

78. Evelyn Fox Keller, "The Gender/Science System: Response to Kelly Oliver," *Hypatia* 3, no. 3 (Winter 1989): 149–52, 150.

79. Thomas Kuhn, *The Structure of Scientific Revolutions* (Chicago: University of Chicago Press, 1970).

80. Harding 1986, 102.

81. Just to name a few: W. H. Newton-Smith, *The Rationality of Science* (London: Routledge and Kegan Paul, 1981); Israel Scheffler, *Science and Subjectivity* (Indianapolis: Bobbs Merrill, 1967); Harvey Siegel, *Relativism Refuted* (Dordrecht, Holland: D. Reidel Publishing Co., 1987); Carl R. Kordig, *The Justification of Scientific Change* (Dordrecht, Holland: Reidel, 1971); James F. Harris, *Against Relativism* (LaSalle, Ill.: Open Court, 1992).

82. Israel Scheffler, "Vision and Revolution: A Postscript to Kuhn," *Philosophy of Science*, 39 (1972): 369.

83. See, for example, E. R. Klein, "Can Feminism Be Rational?" *Journal of Interdisciplinary Studies*, X, no. 1/2 (September 1998): 17–29.

84. Claudia Murphy, "Feminist Epistemology," in *Aspects of Relativism*, ed. James E. Bailey (New York: University Presses of America, 1992), 133–40.

85. Some feminists make the much stronger claim that "feminism is, first and last, a political movement," *Feminist Epistemologies,* ed. L. Alcoff and E. Potter, "Introduction," 2.

86. Murphy, 135.

87. Kourany 1998, 242.

88. Master-slave ideology that attempts to argue for the legitimizing of the standpoint of the slave despite the distortions of the overarching master view.

89. Harding 1991, 191.

90. Harding 1991, 126.

91. Daniel W. Conway, "Circulous Vitiosus Deus? The Dialectical Logic of Feminist Standpoint Theory," *Journal of Social Philosophy* 28, no. 1 (Spring 1997): 62–76, 63.

92. Harding 1991, 126.

93. Conway, 69.

94. Conway, 69.

95. Kourany 1998, 255.

96. Kourany 1998, 256.

97. Kourany 1998, 239.

98. Kourany 1998, 256.

99. Harvey Siegel, "What is the Question Concerning the Rationality of Science?" *Philosophy of Science* 52 (1985): 513, 37.

100. Hans Reichenbach, *The Rise of Scientific Philosophy* (Berkeley, Calif.: University of California Press, 1959).

101. Francis Pharcellus Church, "Yes, Virginia, There Is a Santa Claus," *The New York Sun* (September 27, 1897).

11

A "New" Program for the Philosophy of Science?

E. R. Klein

Kourany's new "new" program for the philosophy of science claims to have as its primary aim the creating of a philosophy of science that is "equally descriptive and prescriptive,"[1] with the emphasis on "equal." The "old" program of philosophy of science (what she calls "logical empiricism"),[2] because of its emphasis on logic and epistemology, was, according to Kourany, too focused on the prescriptive. The new program of philosophy of science (what she calls "historicism"),[3] on the other hand, because of its emphasis on the great historical moments and figures in science, was too focused on the descriptive. Kourany claims to offer, instead, a new "new"/"old" program for the philosophy of science that combines the two.

Despite the fact that this philosophical porridge is no longer too hot or too cold for Kourany, it is still not quite yet "just right." That is, not until she adds to the "complicated mix of these sources . . . moral and political philosophy, and especially feminist philosophy."[4] Therefore, even for Kourany, feminist philosophy must be something other than the simple combination of new and old that Kourany herself has cooked up.

What is this special ingredient Kourany calls feminist philosophy? How does feminist philosophy contribute to this new concoction for science and the philosophy of science? And, finally, why is Kourany so keen on adding it to her recipe for the world's best philosophy of science?

THE SPECIAL INGREDIENT

Simply stated, feminism's main goal, according to Kourany, is the achievement of "gender equality."[5] How she plans to actually manifest this political goal, however, is unclear. Though the concept of "equity" is not in need of interpretation, the notion of "gender" is. As I have argued elsewhere, gender is at best a meaningless construct and, at worst, a purely political term that confuses most equity issues and ultimately, ironically, enables sexism.[6]

Kourany's use of the term is a case in point. On the one hand she uses the term gender to mean nothing more than "sex," a term incidentally that, pre-feminism, did a fine job demarcating men from women. And Kourany's use of the term usually means nothing more. When, for example, she says that Western science has been shown to be a place that "is not a site of gender equality,"[7] she simply means that science has

> [denied] women access to universities and other centers of scientific learning . . . [given women] less financial assistance . . . [excluded] women from the most important scientific meetings and collaborations and information networks and tended to leave women largely invisible in its knowledge and research . . .[8]

and often "portrayed us [women] in negative terms."[9]

Now, although I have no problem with the beauty and richness of natural language, that is, no problem with synonyms per se, there is a problem when the same term is used at the same time to mean two different things. Gender is such a term.

Feminist theorizing insists that the term gender be given a meaning independent from that of sex. While sex denotes a purely biologically constructed category, gender, it is claimed, denotes some kind of socially constructed category. Now, aside from the fact that no one has ever sufficiently defined this category,[10] it must at least be admitted that it is odd that the class of all those beings which one genders feminine is precisely identical with the class of all those beings which one sexes as female. Nonetheless, feminists insist that the two terms mean fundamentally different things.

Odder still is the possibility that some feminists, in a desperate desire to save their precious gender construct, might want to claim that the two classes do not have identical denotation. After all, one could allow for a biological male who is gendered female or a biological female who is gendered male. But even if there are such cross-gendered beings, whom is it that Western science has, in fact, discriminated against? Men gendered female? Women gendered male? Or just plain ole biological women—regardless of their gender?

Despite the fact that gender seems to be a distinction without a difference, the myth of its power must be kept alive, if feminism—specifically the feminism, feminisms, and/or feminists that Kourany cites—are to have any teeth. It is no trivial claim that without gender, there would be no evidence of gender bias in Western science.

This is not to say that the history of science (and philosophy) is not riddled with sexist men. But it does not follow from the words, theories, or deeds of a few men, that Western science and/or philosophy is itself sexist. I have argued elsewhere[11] that there is a flaw with every level of the argument for the essential gender-bias nature of Western science (and philosophy.) Despite numerous and well-supported claims showing that essential gender bias is a myth created by gender-obsessed feminists, Kourany still maintains that Western science has either ignored the "science done by women"[12] and/or "portrayed women in negative terms."[13] Is it unfair at this juncture to ask who, exactly, was ignored or is now being ignored? Is it unfair to ask those making such charges to offer actual cases of inherently sexist commitments against specific women?

The few supposed examples cited in the literature—even by Kourany's own hand—have been, as far as I can tell, thoroughly debunked in "Sorry Virginia, There is No Feminist Science."[14] If there are other cases, they should be offered. And they should be offered not as some kind of vague general comment of male conspiracy, but specifically. Who are these "women scientists, past and present"[15] that represent such obvious examples of gender bias in Western science that evidencing them by name isn't even necessary?

Since the concept of gender qua something "more" than sex is so ambiguous, anything and everything can be blamed on it. When a woman does not become a scientist, it is because of gender bias; when a woman scientist does not succeed in her field, it must be gender bias; when a woman does succeed but not as much as a man, it must be gender bias; and even when she does succeed in every sense that men do, it is, according to feminists, in spite of gender bias. What could be more scientifically suspect, more unfalsifiable, than this thesis of gender bias? Feminists, I'm afraid, have done more than "sketch gender into philosophy of science's picture of science,"[16] they have misguidedly carved it in with a vengeance.

THE SPECIAL CONTRIBUTIONS

Feminism's unfair attacks on science aside, what positive contribution has feminism made to the same science and/or the philosophy of science? According to Kourany, feminism has:

(1) Added women scientists to science and the philosophy of science, (2) Added a gender aspect to the already present epistemic aspect of the philosophy of science, (3) Added a social/epistemic critique of science to the traditional critiques, (4) Made suggestions for reforming science and making headways into greater social accountability, and (5) Aimed at making better knowledge and a better world.[17]

Has feminism really achieved any of these goals? Clearly it has accomplished the second goal. My suggestion above, however, is that this is more of a detriment than an achievement.

Goal three, however, is problematic. Should feminism be given credit for something done first by men? If anyone in the philosophy of science should be given credit for adding a social dimension to the philosophy of science it is, as Kourany herself points out, Kuhn[18] and Feyerabend.[19] The fourth goal must go to Feyerabend as well. Five sounds great, but "aiming at" and actually succeeding are two different things. The question of actual achievements is on the table at this time.

This leaves us with only the first goal as a serious consideration, and it too is on shaky ground. Although adding women to the fields of science and philosophy may be an admirable goal, I see no reason to believe that gender feminists sincerely have this goal, or if they do, that they should be given credit for making any real contributions in this way. At the very least, Kourany and her feminist colleagues should have to cite some statistics evidencing their success. (Personally, I have found that my feminist colleagues in academia have, and have admitted publicly to having, an interest not in the success of women in general, but in their own success and the success of their cronies.)[20]

What really would make science better for women? Equal opportunity. Equal consideration. Equal treatment. Equal acknowledgment. Equal pay. Does gender feminism—the ingredient so desired by Kourany—offer this? No.

Gender feminism, in its attempts to distinguish itself as something special, something different from classical Western science, is not only incapable of distinguishing itself, but ends up being inconsistent with its only legitimate goal: equity. Feminism cannot merely be about equity, for then its theoretical constructs would no longer be special. Indeed, they would no longer be necessary. After all, equity constructs are as old as Plato, and most contemporary accounts have been developed almost exclusively by men. In other words, since Western philosophy, with respect to equity, has "been there and done that," gender feminism must be about something else if it is about anything at all.

On the other hand—and this is the surprise—to distinguish themselves from the traditional corpus, gender feminists have gone so far as to give up equity completely. This is evidenced most obviously in their accounts of philosophy of science and epistemology where classical concepts such as "objectivity," "evidence," and "truth" are reappropriated to mean something fundamentally biased. Kourany acknowledges and accepts the fact that what is special about feminism is that all of the above universal concepts are relativized by starting all such investigation "from women's lives."[21]

In the final analysis, it seems that what is special about the contributions of gender feminism are esoteric theoretical claims that are, at best, irrelevant, and may be even inimical, to the achievement of the most important political goal of women: equity.

KOURANY'S MISCONCEPTIONS

What does Kourany really want? A better world? A world in which "justice prevails"?[22] A world in which women have equal opportunity in the sciences and the philosophy of science? If she answers with a simple "yes," then she and I have no quarrel.

Although she herself was trained in the classical tradition of Western science and philosophy, since her seduction by gender feminism Kourany argues that medicine, sociology, and psychology have harmed women[23]—"sciences" whose methodologies too often play fast and loose with objectivity—while, ironically, in the same breath, she cites feminists who argue that physics (which takes objectivity more seriously than any other science) should not set the standard for science's methodological commitments.[24] Instead of simply affirming classical science and its commitment to objectivity and impartiality (which she knows are important tools for ferreting out sexism),[25] Kourany cites gender feminists who tag such methodological desiderata (including objectivity, simplicity, and consistency) as "male" simply to denigrate them.[26] Kourany claims that she wants a socially responsible model for the philosophy of science, but cites feminists who state that impartiality can only be gained if we bias science from a feminist standpoint that sees scientists as "fast guns for hire."[27]

Finally, the gender feminists Kourany cites to support her belief in the need for a feminist science and philosophy of science misguidedly claim that women's survival depends on their being "sensitive to the moods and dispositions of those for whom they care and those they serve . . . [and developing] perceptual capacities, communication skills, a facility for emotional management, conflict resolution . . . skills that give women a special ability to engage in, and contribute to collaborative enterprises. . . ."[28] (Interestingly, Schopenhauer[29] makes similar claims about the character of women, only he uses evidence of these traits to defend his sexist belief that no woman should be taken seriously in any realm outside the home, let alone science.)

Unfortunately, Kourany's desire to change science and the philosophy of science means changing the nature of scientific observation and experiment and their roles in research; changing the nature of the claims scientists make (factual statements, empirical laws, theories, and so forth), their explanatory and other functions in science, and the ways they are assessed; the way science, its aims, methods, and subject matter develops over time; [changing] the nature of the results of scientific inquiry, whether science provides truth about the world, or only useful information, and the like.[30]

But change for the sake of change alone is not always the best policy. And in the case of classical science and philosophy of science, I suggest that such changes are not only an unwarranted overreaction, but they will prove to be ultimately harmful to women.

I also hope to usher in a new era of opportunity for women, but I believe that the future needs to look to the past. "Better knowledge and a better world" will come only when women resist gender feminism and realize that what science and philosophy of science need is a megadose of classical objectivity, not gyno-bias.

NOTES

1. Janet Kourany, "What Does Feminism Contribute to Philosophy of Science?" in this volume, 126.

2. Kourany, 119.

3. Kourany, 120–21.

4. Kourany, 126.

5. Kourany, 113.

6. E. R. Klein, *Feminism Under Fire*, (Amherst, Mass.: Prometheus Books, 1996) and "Gender Constructs for Feminism: Voice or Vice?" *Zietschrift Fur Philosophie* (April–June 1999): 26–35.

7. Kourany, 113.

8. Kourany, 113–14.

9. Kourany, 115.

10. Klein 1996.

11. E. R. Klein, "Sorry, Virginia, There is No Feminist Science," in this volume, 131–53.

12. Kourany, 116.

13. Kourany, 117.

14. Klein, in this volume.

15. Kourany, 116.

16. Kourany, 125.

17. Kourany, 126.

18. Thomas Kuhn, *The Structure of Scientific Revolutions* (Chicago: University of Chicago Press, 1970).

19. Paul K. Feyerabend, *Against Method* (New York: Verso, 1975) and *Farewell to Reason* (New York: Verso, 1987).

20. Klein 1996.

21. Kourany, 125.

22. Kourany, 124.

23. Kourany, 114–15.

24. Kourany, 118.

25. Kourany, 115.

26. Kourany, 122.

27. Kourany, 126.

28. Kourany, 117.

29. Arthur Schopenhauer, "On Women," in *Schopenhauer Selections*, ed. DeWitt H. Parker (New York: Charles Scribner and Sons, 1956), 434–47.

30. Kourany, 113.

12

No Need to Be Sorry, Virginia

Janet A. Kourany

Ellen Klein's essay "Sorry, Virginia, There is No Feminist Science"[1] is nothing if not bold. She takes on major feminists such as Genevieve Lloyd, Evelyn Fox Keller, and Sandra Harding, and finds their work utterly deficient. She delivers sweeping indictments of feminism and feminists—feminism "simply goes about ignoring her critics while continuing to repeat the same old false stories to her followers until they become, like religious lore, unquestioned dogmatism,"[2] "feminists, in their hearts, are relativists at best, sexists at worse,"[3] "any commitment to objective criteria, including the hard facts provided by empirical investigations, is viewed by feminists . . . to be yet another male trick to oppress women,"[4] and so on. And she concludes that we should "throw feminism to the wind and reappropriate the classical tools of logic, reason and evidence."[5] Quite a bit for twenty-three pages. How does she do it?

Shortcuts. Klein takes plenty of shortcuts. For example, Klein suggests that the views of Genevieve Lloyd, as developed in her book *The Man of Reason*, are "false,"[6] a "myth,"[7] and she takes feminists to task for endlessly citing them. But Klein does not take the time to set out Lloyd's views: indeed, she does little more than quote feminists citing Lloyd—a sentence from Charlotte Witt, two sentences from Lorraine Code, a sentence from Elizabeth Grosz, a sentence from Moira Gatens, a sentence from Virginia Held.[8] Nor does Klein take the time to set out the historical evidence Lloyd adduces in support of her views, or any reasons she (Klein) has for thinking that Lloyd's evidence is insufficient, or for thinking that Lloyd's views are problematic in other ways. Klein, in fact, merely *asserts* that Lloyd's (unspecified) views are false, and then chides feminists for citing them. But since when is it a sin to cite someone else's research results, especially when no reason has been given to impugn them?

Similar problems beset Klein's treatment of Evelyn Fox Keller. Klein takes up two issues concerning Keller: Keller's "McClintock story" and Keller's "metaphor mongering." But here again, Klein does not take the time to set out and evaluate Keller's views and their rationale. Generally, feminists have charged that Western science has been "male-biased"[9]—masculine or masculinist—in at least four ways: (1) Western science has sought to dominate a nature conceived of as feminine, with a method characterized by disinterestedness and emotional detachment, and (at least in recent times) aggression and competitiveness; (2) men have controlled this science right from the start; (3) this science has tended to leave women largely invisible in its knowledge and research; and (4) this science has often portrayed women, and things feminine, in negative terms when it *has* considered us.[10] Regarding the "McClintock story," although Keller, in her writings about the life and work of Nobel Prize-winning biologist Barbara McClintock, has included such details as McClintock's early difficulties finding a position commensurate with her abilities and the "dual theme of success and marginality"[11] that characterized her professional life, Keller's McClintock story relates to 1 rather than 2. "If we want to think about the ways in which science might be different," Keller's "A World of Difference" begins, "we could hardly find a more appropriate guide than Barbara McClintock." And Keller devotes that chapter of *Reflections on Gender and Science* as well as most of her *A Feeling for the Organism: The Life and Work of Barbara McClintock* to exploring McClintock's "different" approach to science—"different" as compared with the dominant masculine approach referred to in 1. Keller tells us, for example, that McClintock did not aim, in her conceptualizations of the objects of her research, to reduce nature to simplicity in an effort to *master* it, to predict and control its behavior; she aimed, rather, to "listen to" it, to know its living forms in minute detail so as to understand and appreciate their complexity and diversity. All this "listening to" nature, this concern with complexity and diversity, this desire to know in detail and firsthand, of course, took time. No thought of competition here, no race to a common goal, no rush to publish, to "scoop" opponents, to convince others. And far from taking a detached, unemotional, disinterested stance toward the objects of her research, McClintock identified with them, merged with them; "her vocabulary is consistently a vocabulary of affection, of kinship, of empathy."[12] Indeed, it was McClintock's intimate personal relationship with the objects of her research, Keller tells us, that enabled her to make her revolutionary scientific discoveries, discoveries that were different in kind from those made using more traditional methods.

How does Klein respond to this "McClintock story"? First, she points out that "McClintock got plenty of recognition and honors for her work on maize during her lifetime as well as posthumously."[13] But Keller herself has pointed this out, explaining, remember, that a complex combination of success and marginality described McClintock's career. And in any case, the point has more relevance to 2 than 1 and its associated McClintock story. Second, Klein points out that "there is no reason to think that [McClintock's] ideas either sprang from her being a woman or were in any way especially feminist."[14] But no one has said otherwise. What *has* been said, remember, is that McClintock's approach was *nonmasculine*—not feminine, or "gynocentric," or feminist, but simply *human*.[15] What has also been said is that this approach may have been more possible for McClintock to develop because she was a woman responding to a masculine science, but in any case it is an approach thought possible and helpful for *everyone*, men as well as women, an approach that has already been used by some men and certainly not all women.[16] Third, Klein points out that McClintock's main theoretical contribution to science

> is not scientifically remarkable. For one thing, Barbara McClintock's self-organizing and strongly interactive "models of transposition and gene action can, in the end, be understood in traditional reductionistic (i.e., male) terminology"; for another, in the long run her account may not have the predictive success of its more linear sister or some other, future, account.[17]

But everyone agrees that McClintock's theoretical contribution *is* scientifically remarkable (e.g., worthy of the Nobel Prize) even if the rest of what Klein says is true. What's more, *every* scientific theory, however "remarkable," may in the long run prove predictively inferior to some other theory. And Klein has no reason to say that McClintock's models of transposition and gene action can be understood in traditional reductionistic terminology. Alas, she misquotes her source, Helen Longino, who *actually* says: "*As [Keller] herself notes* about Barbara McClintock's models of transposition and gene action, *reductionistically inclined biologists claim* that, in the end, the self-organizing and strongly interactive aspects of McClintock's models can be eliminated or understood in reductionist terms" (emphasis mine).[18] Most importantly, however, the McClintock story, like 1, has to do with scientific aims and methods—with McClintock's scientific *approach*—not with her particular results. So, all of Klein's points here are actually irrelevant.

What is the upshot? In the end Keller's McClintock story receives the same treatment from Klein as Lloyd's views: it is called a "myth" throughout her discussion, and feminists are criticized for making use of it, all with no justification. Also, as should be obvious from the above, the McClintock story is not "the leading argument for sexism in science (and the philosophy of science)."[19] Indeed, the McClintock story is not an argument for any of theses 1–4, but rather a model of an alternative to 1, that is, a model of a nonmasculine way of doing science. And the McClintock story is certainly not an argument for sexism in *philosophy of science*, though it is an interesting contribution, I think, to philosophy of science. Finally, the McClintock story is obviously not "the foundation for all feminist philosophy of science to date,"[20] dealing as it does only with 1.

What about Klein's stance with regard to Keller's "metaphor mongering"? Here Klein runs together claims concerning the masculinity of the aims of science (1 above), the negative portrayal of women and things feminine within science

(4 above), and the masculine kinds of concepts (concepts of dominance, hierarchy, competition, etc.) favored in scientific theorizing. To counter the first kind of claim, Klein provides just one of Keller's quotations from Bacon and then exclaims that "one must wonder whether any single quotation citing a metaphorical use of the 16th Century conception of marriage can possibly be charged with the serious crime of having made all of contemporary science—its methodological commitments to objectivity, evidence, reason and logic—inherently sexist."[21] Klein conveniently forgets here all the other quotations from Bacon as well as all the quotations from other historical figures that Keller provides, and the complex discussions and carefully qualified conclusions in which these quotations are situated—Keller, please note, devotes *three chapters* of *Reflections on Gender and Science* to the aims of science, and related issues, in three historical periods. To counter the second kind of claim—concerning women's (and the feminine's) negative portrayal within science—Klein provides a single quotation from Darwin, about a "wonderfully intelligent" and loyal female terrier whose behavior leads Darwin to conclude that "with most of our domesticated quadrupeds, strong individual antipathies and preferences are frequently exhibited, and much more commonly by the female than by the male."[22] At the same time, Klein leaves out Keller's and other feminists' numerous case studies documenting Darwin's and other scientists' portrayal of women as inferior to men in intelligence, moral, sexual and social development, and the like. Finally, to counter the third kind of claim—concerning the masculine kinds of concepts favored in scientific theorizing—Klein seems to suggest that such concepts (or, perhaps, scientific concepts in general) will be interpreted as masculine or not depending on who is doing the interpreting ("when the interpretation of the text is performed by a feminist, it seems the male-biased boogeyman can be found everywhere").[23] But Klein gives nothing to support her view: the example of Bacon (already discussed) she then trots out does not relate to alternative interpretations of scientific concepts, now as masculine and now as not, but rather to the aims of science. Klein also seems to suggest (and this conflicts with the other claim) that for every scientific concept that can be viewed as masculine, one can "just as easily" find a concept that can be viewed as feminine.[24] But no support is provided for this claim either: the fact that "in his famous astronomical piece entitled the *Harmonies of the World*, Kepler actually composes pages of music to accompany the different voices of the planets and their moons to help him understand, explain, and predict the motions of the celestial bodies in our solar system"[25] does not show that Kepler is using "feminine" concepts to describe nature. Klein must *show* that using Kepler's musical concepts to describe nature exemplifies what is stereotypically associated with femininity (nurturance, emotionality, physical weakness, passivity, etc.).

Nevertheless, there *is* something to be said against this third kind of claim. Indeed, I tried to say it in a paper published back in 1989.[26] I referred there to Keller's *Reflections on Gender and Science,* just as Klein is doing, to the concepts of dominance that Keller finds and reports on in the physical and natural sciences. More specifically, I referred to Keller's claimed predisposition in biology to kinds of theory that posit a single central governor rather than global interaction—instanced by the view of pacemaker cells in slime mold aggregation, and by the view of genes, and later of DNA, as the central actor in a cell, governing all other cellular processes. I referred, as well, to Keller's perception of dominance in classical physics:

> Newton's laws, for example, depict a universe unfolding in strict causal sequence; once the forces are specified, its state at any future moment is completely determined by its configuration at an initial moment in time. Control, in this model, is located in the original Creation, the winding and setting of the cosmic clockwork; subsequent order is maintained by Newton's laws of motion.[27]

In reply I pointed out that the original creation, that which makes Newtonian mechanics a case of a theory involving (male) dominance for Keller, is not part of Newtonian mechanics, at least not in the form in which it is currently accepted and taught by the scientific community; so that the element of dominance that Keller finds in Newtonian mechanics is not there after all. And I pointed out that it is not clear, in the case of Keller's two biological examples, that the elements of control that *are* present in them—genes or DNA governing cellular processes, and pacemaker cells doing their thing in slime mold—can plausibly be called cases of portraying reality in terms of masculine traits. At least, an important element of male dominance is the subjugation of another *person's* (e.g., a woman's) *will* (we do not, for example, tend to speak of "dominating" a table even if it is always up to us where the table is). And this element is absent from the biological examples. To be sure, we probably have as much right to call Keller's biological examples cases of portraying reality in terms of masculine traits as we have for calling, say, the principle of universal gravitational attraction in Newtonian mechanics a case of portraying reality in terms of feminine traits (such as the disposition to interact with, to merge with, others).

I said other things relevant to this discussion back in 1989 as well—for example, that even if masculine concepts *were* favored in scientific theorizing, it would not be especially damaging to the scientific enterprise, since the theories in which these concepts occur might be empirically adequate nonetheless. The important point now, however, is that this was all said back in 1989. In the meantime, Keller has ceased to focus on the masculinity of scientific concepts, choosing instead to concentrate on the scientific, technological, and social impact of such concepts—a fascinating and productive venture pursued in such works as *Secrets of Life, Secrets of Death: Essays on Language, Gender and Science* (1992), *Keywords in Evolutionary Biology* (1992), and *Refiguring Life: Metaphors of Twentieth-Century Biology* (1995). Klein takes into account none of this, however, choosing to respond only to Keller's 1985 *Reflections on Gender and Science*.

From Keller, Klein moves to feminists in general, and then to Sandra Harding, and then me, in particular. Regarding feminists in general, Klein claims that "there is a great deal of evidence, in the literature, of the feminist commitment to relativism, specifically the brand made popular by Thomas Kuhn."[28] None of this "great deal of evidence" is cited, however, nor are any names named, and one is left to wonder how any feminist at all *could* be a relativist and still be a feminist—that is to say, and still be committed to the ideal of gender equality, still be cognizant of the inequalities that women confront in our society, and still be determined to move society closer to that ideal using analyses and strategies grounded in the best information, including the best scientific information, available. Ironically enough, Klein quotes a feminist, Claudia Murphy, who says just this—"relativism is unacceptable because feminism is not only an epistemology but also a political ideology . . . relativism is politically and morally repugnant" etc., etc.[29] One is then left to wonder how even Klein herself could believe that feminists are relativists. Needless to say, Klein never takes the time to explain.

"Some feminists," we are next told,[30] have moved from Kuhnian relativism to feminist standpoint theory but, again, no names are mentioned nor is any documentation provided: the sole citation given (footnote 87) is for the phrase "invisible and intact" that Klein has plucked from an essay of my own that says nothing remotely like what she is saying. "With standpoint, however, feminism has jumped out of the relativism pan, and into the fire of sexism."[31] How so? "This . . . becomes obvious when one examines more closely Harding's standpoint theory," and Klein now quotes from Harding: "It is because women have struggled against male supremacy that research starting from their lives can be made to yield up clearer and more nearly complete visions of social reality than are available only from the perspective of men's side of these struggles."[32] Klein continues:

> In other words, feminists must fight so-called 'male-bias' by inventing female-bias.
> . . . Harding and all other feminist standpoint theorists have simply replaced the so-called 'male' objective perspective with the victimized female perspective. Hierarchy remains, the master/slave dynamic remains, and bias remains, all that changes is who is on top.[33]

But is this as "obvious" as Klein suggests? To begin with, Harding has urged that research *start* from women's lives, not end there, suggesting that this can be made to yield a better understanding of social reality than is available *only* from the perspective of men's side of these struggles. In short, she is urging that we *add* women's perspectives to those of men (which is all we were given in the past), but also that we privilege the women's perspectives, at least at the *start*, the reason being that women have been the oppressed, and hence, in a better position to see what is going on than the oppressors, who have a vested interest in the status quo. Of course, at this point many questions remain—for example, exactly how the addition of women's perspectives to men's perspectives, and the initial privileging of them, "can be made to yield" the better results, how feminism is involved (it is, after all, *femi-*

nist standpoint theory), and so forth—and Harding, in her various lectures and publications, has tried to answer these questions. If Klein takes a dim view of the answers, she needs to sketch them out and show the problems, not simply ignore them. As it is, Klein simply begs the question against Harding.

Klein finally moves to me. Alas, the misunderstandings are rampant. My "early feminist commitments" are *not* "consistent with the Kuhnian relativism" she has described. I do *not* "claim Kuhn offered theorists a way to shift the program of science from one committed to pure prescription with respect to the establishment of the desiderata for science to one that incorporates the descriptive accounts of the socially situated lives of scientists themselves—their fears, needs, and desires." I do *not* "argue that a feminist change that could 'deeply' affect science would be to make the primary aim of science to be something that concentrates on both the 'descriptive and prescriptive,' equally."[34] And so on. Indeed, I do not even know what these statements *mean*! But then, what *am* I saying in the paper to which Klein is referring?[35] I argue, to begin with, that modern Western science has been masculine right from the start—in the way it has aimed to dominate a nature conceived of as feminine, with a method characterized by disinterestedness and emotional detachment, aggression, and competitiveness; in the way men have controlled it right from the start; in the way it has tended to leave women largely invisible in its knowledge and research; and in the way it has often portrayed women, and things feminine, in negative terms when it *has* considered us—just the theses 1–4 noted previously. I argue, as well, that this masculinity of science has had damaging effects on all of us, but especially on women ("modern Western science . . . is afflicted with serious ills related to its masculinity"), and thus deserves careful diagnosis and treatment. (My epigraph, which structures my paper, is taken from Virginia Woolf's *Three Guineas*: "Science, it would seem, is not sexless; she is a man, a father, and infected too." Klein takes over this epigraph in her paper.) The question I then raise is: What role ought philosophy of science to play in this venture? I argue that the prescriptive program of logical empiricism and the descriptive program ushered in by Thomas Kuhn and others in the early 1960s did much to keep the masculinity of science and its damaging effects invisible and intact—some of these points are summarized in my paper in this volume. I then show how newer work—by David Hull, Evelyn Fox Keller, Ann Oakley, Helen Longino, and feminist standpoint theorists—not only helps to make the masculinity of science visible, but also helps us to deal with it. I end by detailing how these ideas change the basic issues of philosophy of science—indeed, how they move us toward a new program for philosophy of science.

What emerges from Klein's extended diatribe on feminist philosophy of science? What is her conclusion? She does not deny that there are problems for women in science, but she does not affirm it either; she does not deny that change is needed, but she does not affirm it either. Indeed, she leaves us with but one positive recommendation: that we "reappropriate the classical tools of logic, reason and evidence."[36] Would that Klein had followed her own advice.

NOTES

1. E. R. Klein, "Sorry, Virginia, There is no Feminist Science," in this volume, 131–53.
2. Klein, 132.
3. Klein, 143.
4. Klein, 141.
5. Klein, 147.
6. Klein, 132.
7. Klein, 132.
8. Klein, 132.
9. Klein says "inherently male-biased" (see, for example, Klein, 133), though no feminist I know has used this locution. Indeed, if feminists thought science were *inherently* male-biased, they would think it impossible to reform it, to make it more female-friendly. But this is just what feminists critiquing science (most of whom are scientists) are engaged in doing!
10. For more details and justification, see Janet A. Kourany, "A New Program for Philosophy of Science, in Many Voices," in *Philosophy in a Feminist Voice: Critiques and Reconstructions*, ed. Janet A. Kourany (Princeton, N.J.: Princeton University Press, 1998).
11. Evelyn Fox Keller, *Reflections on Gender and Studies* (New Haven, Conn.: Yale University Press, 1985), 159.
12. Keller, 164.
13. Klein, 135.
14. Klein, 136.
15. See, for example, Keller, 174–75.
16. For more details, see Kourany, 248–50.
17. Klein, 136.
18. Helen Longino, *Science as Social Knowledge* (Princeton, N.J.: Princeton University Press, 1990), 208.
19. Klein, 133.
20. Klein, 133.
21. Klein, 139. Also, on pages 139–40, Klein talks about how Kepler composed pages of music in his *Harmonies of the World* to accompany the different voices of the planets and their moons. But this seems to have nothing to do with the aims of science, Kepler's or anyone else's, and so cannot help her case.
22. Klein, 140.
23. Klein, 139.
24. Klein, 139.
25. Klein, 139–40.
26. Janet A. Kourany, "Science Sexist?" in *Freedom, Equality, and Social Change*, eds. Creighton Peden and James P. Sterba (Lewiston, N.Y.: Edwin Mellen Press, 1989), 147–57.
27. Keller, 132, quoted in Kourany, 148.
28. Klein, 143.
29. Klein, 143.
30. Klein, 144.

31. Klein, 144.
32. Klein, 144.
33. Klein, 144.
34. Klein, 145.
35. Kourany, "A New Program for Philosophy of Science, in Many Voices."
36. Klein, 147.

Section IV

Feminism and Social Theory

13

A Millennial Feminist Vision

Rosemarie Tong

Because feminism is both a sociopolitical and cultural movement, its meaning changes depending on where, when, how, why, and in what forms it manifests itself. Since this is so, I plan to focus on feminism in the United States. I will examine U.S. feminism both as a sociopolitical movement and as a cultural movement, proceeding on the commonly held assumption that U.S. women have ridden through two waves of feminism and are now in the process of riding through a third one. The first wave of U.S. feminism began in the mid-nineteenth century and ended in approximately 1920. The second wave began in the 1960s and ended very early in the 1990s. The third wave emerged later in the 1990s. At present there is uncertainty as to whether the third wave will increase or decrease in size. In the course of describing each of these waves of U.S. feminism, I will note the differences as well as the similarities between them. My intent is to determine the degree to which U.S. feminism is progressing beyond its borders, and whether this movement signals the further development of feminism or the replacement of feminism with a perspective yet to be named.

THE FIRST WAVE OF U.S. FEMINISM

The first wave of U.S. feminism is rooted in eighteenth- and nineteenth-century liberal thought as articulated by Mary Wollstonecraft, John Stuart Mill, and Harriet Taylor Mill, in particular. According to Wollstonecraft, since men and women have the *same* capacities for rationality and morality, the key to developing these capacities equally in both sexes is to provide all individuals with the same education in the sciences and humanities. Wollstonecraft believed that if women were educated like men, women would stop acting like children—or, worse, like caged birds, hothouse plants, or decorative ornaments—and start acting like autonomous and responsible persons with meaningful life projects.[1] Although Wollstonecraft realized that women's access to men's education might depend to some degree on women's economic and political independence from men, she did not advise women to work in the public world. Nor did she urge women to fight for suffrage. Instead, Wollstonecraft envisioned properly educated women exercising their mature personhood primarily in the domestic realm—as "observant daughters," "affectionate sisters," "faithful wives," and "reasonable mothers."[2]

Interestingly, as much as John Stuart Mill and Harriet Taylor agreed with Wollstonecraft that men and women are each other's equals morally and intellectually, they did not agree with her that women's economic, but especially political, participation in the public world was entirely optional. Both of these nineteenth-century thinkers claimed that society should change its political, legal, and economic institutions to permit women as well as men sufficient latitude to make genuine choices about their life trajectories. Mill and Taylor claimed that unless women are able to enter and leave the domestic realm (especially the institution of marriage) on the same terms as men typically do, women cannot *really* choose between being wives and mothers only, working women only, or full participants in both the public and private spheres.[3] Their choice of lifestyle will—absent major social reform— remain constrained by the wishes of the men in their lives. Therefore, Mill and Taylor declared that to overcome their dependence on men, women needed the vote, a direct voice in shaping a society in which all systems, structures, and attitudes of oppression would be eliminated beginning with those based on sex and race, and progressing to those based on class.[4]

According to social philosopher and activist Angela Davis (who has fought for improvements in the conditions of oppressed people, particularly U.S. African Americans), Mill's and Taylor's optimistic beliefs about the consequences of enfranchising women help explain the connections between the nineteenth-century U.S. women's rights and abolition movements.[5] Familiar with English liberal thought, many educated U.S. women promptly took a stand against sex discrimination. Sarah Grimké and her sister, Angelina, for example, wrote several passionate essays and letters on behalf of women's rights. Both claimed that women's inferiority is a product not of nature but of nurture; that traditional family structures and marriage contracts keep women in a subordinate position; that male-dominated institutional religions like Christianity make men into leaders and women into followers; and that men monopolize all the lucrative professions, leaving for women mostly low-paying occupations.[6]

As they became cognizant of the relationship between sex discrimination and race discrimination, first-wave U.S. feminists began to defend slaves' rights as well as women's rights. So eloquent were they that male abolitionists eagerly enlisted them in the cause of slaves' liberation. However, because the general public seemed reluctant to view women as an oppressed group, male abolitionists asked first-wave U.S.

feminists like Lucy Stone to downplay the women's rights cause until the slaves were free. Acceding to this request, she agreed to speak on slaves' rights on weekends, relegating her more controversial pleas for women's rights to sparsely attended mid-week meetings.[7]

Believing that male abolitionists wanted men and women to be equal participants in the abolition movement, the first-wave U.S. feminists who attended the 1840 World Anti-Slavery Conference in London were sorely disappointed. No woman, not even Lucretia Mott or Elizabeth Cady Stanton, two of the most prominent leaders of the U.S. women's rights movement, was allowed to speak at the meeting. Angered by men's silencing of women, Mott and Stanton vowed to hold a women's rights convention on their return to the United States. Eight years later, in 1848, 300 women and men met in Seneca Falls, New York, and produced a Declaration of Sentiments and twelve resolutions.

Modeled on the Declaration of Independence, the Declaration of Sentiments stressed the issues that Mill and Taylor had emphasized in England, particularly the need for reforms in marriage, divorce, property, and child custody laws. The twelve resolutions emphasized women's rights to express themselves in public, to speak out on the burning issues of the day, especially "in regard to the great subjects of morals and religion,"[8] which women were thought to be more qualified to address than men. The Seneca Falls convention endorsed all the resolutions brought before it, with the notable exception of Susan B. Anthony's Woman's Suffrage Resolution, which read: "Resolved, that it is the duty of the women of this country to secure to themselves their sacred right to the elective franchise."[9] Apparently, the majority of the convention viewed Anthony's resolution as an extremely radical request that would alienate mainstream U.S. citizens otherwise sympathetic to the cause of women's rights. This same majority also expressed the wish that Anthony's friend, Stanton, would stop wearing unfeminine bloomers and making disparaging comments about men (for example, "we have all seen a man making a jackass of himself").[10]

Conceding that they needed to present the cause of women's rights to the general public in a less-threatening way, Anthony and Stanton agreed to moderate their more inflammatory words and actions. As they learned how to speak the public's mainstream language, Anthony, Stanton, and other first-wave U.S. feminists began to win over middle America to the cause of women's rights; but just when it seemed that women would finally obtain suffrage, the Civil War erupted. Seeing in this tragic war their best opportunity to free the slaves, male abolitionists once again secured first-wave U.S. feminists' agreement to put the women's rights cause on the back burner temporarily.

When the end of the Civil War brought new rights to black men but not to women, embittered first-wave U.S. feminists found themselves at odds with recently emancipated black men. Concerned that women's rights would be lost in the ongoing struggle to secure full legal rights for black males, the male as well as female delegates to an 1866 national women's rights convention decided to establish an

Equal Rights Association. Co-chaired by Frederick Douglass and Elizabeth Cady Stanton, the association had as its *announced* purpose the unification of the black (that is, black men's) and women's (that is, white women's) suffrage struggles. There is considerable evidence, however, that Stanton and some of her coworkers actually viewed the organization "as a means to ensure that Black men would not receive the franchise unless and until white women were also its recipients."[11] Unmoved by Frederick Douglass's and Sojourner Truth's observation that because of their extreme vulnerability black men needed the vote even more than women did, Anthony and Stanton were among those who engineered the eventual dissolution of the Equal Rights Association, largely because of its increasing support for the Fifteenth Amendment, which aimed to enfranchise blacks (that is, black men) but not women.

On leaving the Equal Rights Association, Anthony and Stanton established the National Woman Suffrage Association in 1869.[12] Six months later, Lucy Stone, who had some serious philosophical disagreements with Stanton and especially Anthony about the role of organized religion in women's oppression, founded the American Woman Suffrage Association. From that point forward, the U.S. women's rights movement was split in two. In a variety of ways, the National Woman Suffrage Association put forth a revolutionary and radical feminist agenda for women, whereas the American Woman Suffrage Association pushed a reformist and liberal feminist agenda. Predictably, most U.S. women gravitated toward the more moderate American Woman Suffrage Association, and by the time these two associations merged in 1890 to form the National American Woman Suffrage Association, the wide-ranging, vociferous women's rights movement of the early nineteenth century had been transformed into the single-issue, relatively tame woman's suffrage movement of the late nineteenth century.[13]

From 1890 until 1920, when the Nineteenth Amendment to the U.S. Constitution was passed, the National American Woman Suffrage Association confined almost all of its activities to gaining the vote for women. Victorious after years of concerted struggle, most of the exhausted suffragists chose to believe that simply by gaining the vote women had indeed become men's equals. Following a brief "flapper" fling in the 1920s, most women (but particularly white middle- and upper-class women) retreated to the supposed safety and security of the private realm. Not until the Great Depression of the 1930s and World War II did large numbers of mainstream wives and mothers leave their homes to enter the public world as full economic participants. Because the majority of men were involved in military activities, the likes of "Rosie the Riveter"[14] became the mainstay of the U.S. economy.

Despite the fact that many U.S. women established their competence in the public world in the 1940s, the bulk of them seemed willing to recede into the private realm when "Johnnie" and the other soldiers came marching home. After World War II, the general public embraced an ideology that idealized the suburban, nuclear family consisting in a wage-earning father, a stay-at-home mother, and two children. The relative affluence of the U.S. population, coupled with increasing parental permissiveness and a sense of boundless possibilities for self-development, gave children the opportunity to relax more and to work less. With time on their hands for reflection on the state of society as well as their psyche, the Baby Boomer generation began to find fault with motherhood, apple pie, and even the stars and stripes of the flag. Young U.S. citizens began to reject the conformist world of their parents, a world in which the gap between the "haves" and the "have-nots" was all too obvious.[15]

As the ideological distance between the generations widened, intergenerational tensions deepened. Soon there was open rebellion: against the conservatism of suburban living with its heavy emphasis on securing material goods, keeping up with the neighbors, and looking respectable; against the poor treatment of U.S. blacks and other minorities; against a foreign war that seemed in no one's best interests, including the people on behalf of whom it was being waged; against an ethos that preferred to make "War" rather than "Love" and that resisted (or hid) all sexual relations except those between married couples intent on having children and creating the traditional nuclear family.[16] The time was ripe for people to rethink and reevaluate all their social roles, including their gender roles. The dormant seeds of first-wave feminism erupted and, during the mid-1960s, second-wave feminism was born.

THE SECOND WAVE OF U.S. FEMINISM

As second-wave feminists saw it, suffrage had not and would never make women equal to men. Women, they said, needed the same educational, occupational, and professional opportunities men had, the same chance to succeed in a competitive public realm. These feminists, usually referred to as "liberal feminists," also stressed that women needed to control their sexual and reproductive lives to avoid being treated merely as "sex objects" or as dutiful wives and indulgent mothers confined to the domestic world of children, church, and kitchen. Already sensitized to the myriad ways in which U.S. systems, structures, and laws oppressed blacks, liberal feminists active in the Civil Rights Movement pointed to the similarities between race-based oppression and gender-based oppression.

In response to this growing interest in women's rights, President John F. Kennedy established the Commission on the Status of Women in 1961. This group produced much new data about women and resulted in the formation of the Citizens' Advisory Council, various state commissions on the status of women, and the passage of the Equal Pay Act. When Congress passed the 1964 Civil Rights Act—amended with the Title VII provision to prohibit discrimination on the basis of sex as well as race, color, religion, or national origin by private employers, employment agencies, and unions—a woman shouted from the congressional gallery: "We made it! God bless America!"[17] Unfortunately, this woman's jubilation and that of women in general was short-lived; the courts were reluctant to enforce Title VII's so-called sex amendment. Feeling betrayed by the powers that be, women's joy turned to anger, an anger that feminist activists used to energize the so-called women's liberation movement.[18]

Among these feminist activists was Betty Friedan. Reflecting on how she and some of her associates had reacted to the courts' refusal to take Title VII's sex amendment seriously, she wrote: "The absolute necessity for a civil rights movement for women had reached such a point of subterranean explosive urgency by 1966, that it only took a few of us to get together to ignite the spark—and it spread like a nuclear chain reaction."[19] The result was the founding of the National Organization for Women (NOW). It put forth an agenda that seemed both less and more demanding than the nineteenth-century Seneca Falls Convention agenda, which had been bold enough to portray "Man" as "Woman's" *chief* oppressor, and yet too timid to demand suffrage for women.[20]

Although first-wave *liberal* U.S. feminists viewed NOW's feminist agenda as *revolutionary*, second-wave *radical* U.S. feminists dismissed its proposals as overly *moderate* ones that, with the exception of abortion, paid little attention to women's need for sexual and reproductive freedom.[21] As second-wave radical feminists saw it, women would never be men's equals unless women had total control over their reproductive powers and sexual pleasures. However, in retrospect, one wonders whether NOW could have demanded much more from 1960s U.S. society than it did. After all, with the year 2000 upon us, the Equal Rights Amendment still has not passed, the average female worker in America still earns just 76 cents for every dollar a man earns, only two female workers have achieved chief executive officer status in the Fortune 500 companies, and "day care, a top priority for both middle-class women and less fortunate mothers maneuvering through welfare reform, still seems a marginal issue to feminist leaders."[22]

For those who remember neither the "reformist" nature of second-wave liberal feminism or the "revolutionary" nature of second-wave radical feminism, it helps to note that most second-wave liberal feminists came to the women's movement from groups such as NWPC (National Women's Political Caucus) and WEAL (Women's Equity Action League), the general purpose of which was to improve the "system." In contrast, most second-wave radical feminists came to the women's movement from leftist groups, the purpose of which was to destroy the system.[23] Whereas the spirit of 1960s and 1970s liberal feminists was largely the integrationist spirit that activated the Civil Rights Movement, the spirit of 1960s and 1970s radical feminists was largely the separatist spirit that energized the anti-Vietnam war protest. The goal of women in groups such as the Women's International Terrorist Conspiracy from Hell (WITCH), the Redstockings, the Feminists, and the New York Radical Feminists was to replace what they regarded as America's elitist, capitalistic, competitive, individualistic way of life with an egalitarian, socialistic, cooperative, communitarian, "sisterhood is powerful" way of life.

To be sure, the differences between second-wave radical and liberal feminists can be overstated. At root, all second-wave feminists shared some very basic assumptions about women's oppression. At that time, as historians Judith Hole and Ellen Levine observe, the ideas and issues explored in almost all feminist writings, political initiatives, and consciousness-raising groups fell into two major areas of concern: (1) a study of the "differences" argument according to which there are inherent, biological, or otherwise natural emotional, intellectual, and psychological differences between men and women; and (2) an attempt to show that these male-female differences are not really natural and biological, but instead the cultural and social product of a socially rigid system of sex-role stereotyping.[24] Yet, despite the fact that 1960s and 1970s liberal and radical feminists both focused on the sex-gender system, second-wave liberal feminists were not prepared to embrace all the views of second-wave radical feminists, especially the most controversial ones.

Initially, second-wave radical feminists, sometimes referred to as "radical libertarian feminists,"[25] aimed to explore what they saw as the pleasures of sex: consensual sex between men and women, lesbian sex, sex with both men and women, autoeroticism, sadomasochistic sex, and even intergenerational sex. They sought to free women from the beliefs that "good" sex could be experienced only in a "love relationship," and that sex for sex's sake was somehow "bad" or promiscuous. In addition, second-wave radical libertarian feminists wished to help women avoid the burdens of human reproduction, going so far as to recommend that natural reproduction be replaced by technological reproduction. They agreed with thinkers such as Shulamith Firestone that no matter how much educational, political, and economic equality women achieve, nothing fundamental will change for women so long as their reproductive role remains the same. Natural reproduction, said Firestone, is definitely not in women's best interests. Pregnancy is "barbaric," and natural childbirth is "at best necessary and tolerable" and at worst "like shitting a pumpkin."[26] What is more, insisted Firestone, natural reproduction is not in men's or children's interests either. On the contrary. It is the root of the vice of possessiveness—the favoring of one child over another on account of the child's being the product of one's own ovum or sperm—and unless people can eliminate this vice from their hearts and minds, they will never be able to overcome the hierarchies that divide the races, classes, and genders.

As might be expected, the views of second-wave radical libertarian feminists troubled not only some second-wave liberal feminists but also most mainstream Americans. Although most 1960s and 1970s Americans were more sexually permissive than their parents had been, they were not ready to abandon all of their so-called sexual hang-ups. Nor were they prepared to forsake old-fashioned procreation for in vitro fertilization and ex utero gestation. But what really caused mainstream Americans, as well as some second-wave liberal feminists, the most problems with second-wave radical libertarian feminist thought was its conception of so-called androgyny. For example, Firestone claimed that as soon as men and women were truly free to engage in polymorphous, perverse sex, it would no longer be necessary for men to display only masculine identities and behaviors and for women to display only feminine ones. Freed from their gender roles at the level of biology (that is, reproduction), women would no longer have to be passive, receptive, and vulnerable, sending out "signals" to men to dominate, possess, and penetrate them to keep the wheels of human procreation spinning. Instead, men and women would be encouraged to become either equally masculine and feminine (monoandrogynous) or as differently masculine and/or feminine as they wished (polyandrogynous). As a result, not only would men and women become androgynous persons; all of culture would become androgynous. Furthermore, in this newly evolved androgynous culture, the categories of the technological and the aesthetic, together with the categories of the masculine and the feminine, would disappear through what Firestone termed "a mutual cancellation—a matter-antimatter explosion, ending with a poof!"[27]

Not only did Firestone's "poof" trouble most nonfeminists and some second-wave liberal feminists, it also concerned some second-wave radical feminists, particularly those who wondered whether women would really gain true liberty by engaging in permissive sex, refusing to bear children, and becoming androgynous individuals. By the time the 1960s and 1970s had given way to the 1980s and the 1990s, these second-wave radical feminists—sometimes called "radical cultural feminists"[28] or "essentialists"[29]—began to caution that sex, usually understood as heterosexual sex, is more dangerous than pleasurable for most women. They urged women to extricate themselves from the institution of so-called compulsory heterosexuality,[30] which they viewed as "characterized by an ideology of sexual objectification (men as subjects/masters; women as objects/slaves) that supports male sexual violence against women."[31] Second-wave radical cultural feminists insisted that, as it has been experienced so far, heterosexuality is men's sexuality. It is about men seeking to control women's sexuality: representatively in pornography, and actually through the use of prostitutes and the selective harassment, rape, and physical abuse of women in their power. Only if women can free themselves from sex as men understand it, can women discover what sex as women understand it might be. Freed from feeding men's sexual appetites, said radical cultural feminists, women would be able at last to nurture each other's sexual needs, embracing each other in joyous, gynocentric holds.

In addition to stressing the dangers of heterosexual relations and the pleasures of lesbian relations, second-wave radical cultural feminists emphasized that artificial reproduction would more likely disempower than empower women. They urged women to see artificial insemination by donor, in vitro fertilization, and plans for an artificial womb not as new procreative options for women but as means for men to exercise complete control over women's procreative powers. Unless women realize this, said second-wave radical cultural feminists, women might unwittingly forsake the ultimate source of their real power—namely, the ability to bring new life into the world through their bodies.[32] It is women who determine whether the human species continues, whether there is human life or no human life on this planet. Women must guard and celebrate this life-giving power, for without it men will have even less respect and use for women than they have now.[33]

Finally, second-wave radical cultural feminists rejected the idea of androgyny as a desirable goal for feminists, replacing pleas for it with proposals to affirm women's essential "femaleness."[34] Far from believing the liberated woman must exhibit both masculine and feminine traits and behaviors, second-wave radical cultural feminists expressed the view that it is better to be female/feminine than it is to be male/masculine. Women should not try to be like men, they said. On the contrary, they should try to be more like women, emphasizing the values and virtues culturally associated with women including "interdependence, community, connection, sharing, emotion, body, trust, absence of hierarchy, nature, immanence, process, joy, peace and life" and de-emphasizing the values and virtues culturally associated with men including "independence, autonomy, intellect, will, wariness, hierarchy, domination, culture, transcendence, product, ascetism, war and death."[35]

In proposing that women should try to be more like women, second-wave radical cultural feminists aimed to establish that all women are oppressed by men simply because they are women who think and act like females.[36] When some women protested that they did not experience themselves as being oppressed by men, and when other women insisted that they were anything but dependent, emotional, and overly compliant persons, second-wave radical cultural feminists accused these women either of "false consciousness"[37] or "male identification."[38] If a woman claimed that all the men in her life treated her well, second-wave radical cultural feminists condemned her for living in a state of denial, ignoring the many ways in which men did, in fact, oppress her. Likewise, if a woman adopted traits traditionally associated with men, radical cultural feminists chided her for purchasing patriarchy's value system, according to which "male" ways of being, thinking, and acting are *better* than "female" ways of being, thinking, and acting, so much so that any woman who wants to be a full human person must somehow become a man.

Not surprisingly, women accused of false consciousness and/or male identification did not welcome such harsh criticism from their supposed "sisters." They claimed that the radical-cultural-feminist construct, Woman, did not represent all women, but only a certain kind of woman—namely, Woman in the image and likeness of the women (radical cultural feminists) who had created her. U.S. women, they claimed, were not about to trade in Patriarchy for Matriarchy, nor were they about to deny their many differences in pursuit of a sameness they did not feel.

THE THIRD WAVE OF U.S. FEMINISM

The construct Woman proved to be the creation that signaled the end of second-wave feminism, for it mandated ways of doing, thinking, and being that an increasing number of American women were not ready, willing, or able to embrace. This led to the birth of a new form of feminism alert to women's differences, including ones of race, class, and national origin. This form of feminism, referred to as third-wave feminism, is a form of feminism that is still in the process of developing. Third-wave feminists want to understand the relationship between gender oppression and other kinds of human oppression, and they are willing to admit the ways in which they have sometimes oppressed others. In other words, they are self-critical feminists who aim to combine the best of second-wave liberal feminism and radical feminism with the best of black feminism, women-of-color feminism, working-class feminism, pro-sex feminism, and so on. Third-wave feminists Leslie Heywood and Jennifer Drake comment:

> A third-wave goal that comes directly out of learning from these histories and work-ing among these traditions is the development of modes of thinking that can come to terms with the multiple, constantly shifting bases of oppression in relation to the mul-tiple, interpenetrating axes of identity, and the creation of a coalition politics based on these understandings—understandings that acknowledge the existence of oppres-sion, even though it is not fashionable to say so. We know that what oppresses me may not oppress you, that what oppresses you may be something I participate in, and that what oppresses me may be something you participate in. Even as different strains of feminism and activism sometimes directly contradict each other, they are all part of our third-wave lives, our thinking, and our praxes: we are products of all the contra-dictory definitions of and differences within feminism, beasts of such a hybrid kind that perhaps we need a different name altogether.[39]

Sounding through the words of Heywood and Drake are the voices of so-called dif-ference feminists, numbered among those early third-wave feminists who most force-fully rejected the construct Woman. Third-wave difference feminists, sometimes referred to as postmodern feminists,[40] are not to be confused with second-wave radi-cal cultural feminists. Whereas second-wave radical cultural feminists spoke of women's differences from men as women's departure from the culturally imposed norm Man, third-wave postmodern difference feminists spoke of women's difference "not as difference from a pre-given norm but as pure difference, difference itself, differences with no identity."[41] Unlike those second-wave radical cultural feminists who had trouble "holding apart the poles of sex and gender"[42] and distinguishing between "(1) women as biological and social entities and (2) the 'female,' 'feminine' or 'other,' where 'female' stands metaphorically for the genuinely other in a relation of difference (as in the system consciousness/unconsciousness) rather than opposi-tion,"[43] third-wave postmodern feminists easily distinguished between real women and the construct Woman. In other words, as Teresa de Lauretis comments, whereas second-wave radical cultural feminists conceived women's "Nature" as some sort of biological or ontological given, third-wave postmodern difference feminists conceived it as:

. . . the specific properties of (e.g., a female-sexed body), qualities (a disposition to nurturance, a certain relation to the body, etc.), or necessary attributes (e.g., the experience of femaleness, of living in the world as female) that women have developed or have been bound to historically, in their differently patriarchal socio-cultural contexts, which makes them women, and not men. One may prefer one triangle, one definition of women and/or feminism, to another and, within her particular conditions and possibilities of existence, struggle to define the triangle's existence, struggle to define the triangle she wants or wants to be—feminists do want differently.[44]

Just as we have no access to the triangle as it exists in itself, but only to the enormous variety of triangles we are able to construct, comments de Lauretis, third-wave postmodern difference feminists maintained we have no access to Woman as she is in Herself, but only to the enormous variety of women as they appear to us, to each other, and to themselves. Yet despite women's differences, in the same way we can recognize a triangle when we see one—be it scalene, isosceles, or equilateral—we can recognize a woman when we see one.

Choosing to resolve the perennial problem of the One and Many in feminist thought with an emphasis on women's differences, however, third-wave postmodern difference feminists lost their grip on women's sameness. Wondering what, if anything beyond two 'X' chromosomes women shared, some third-wave postmodern difference feminists worried, that in their stress on women's differences, they had lost feminism's rationale for collective political action on behalf of women's common interests. In an attempt to remedy this growing problem in feminist thought, de Lauretis suggested that when a woman (or man) becomes a feminist, she (or he) deliberately assumes a position or perspective[45] termed "gender" from which first "to interpret or (re)construct values and meanings"[46] and then to forge alliances aimed at increasing all women's freedom and well-being. For de Lauretis, gender (being feminine) is not the automatic result of sex (being female).[47] Rather it is an interpretive grid pointing to a conception of women neither as unproblematically unified nor as inseparably divided, but rather as multiple and therefore capable of unifying and dividing *at will*.

Admitting that gender is not the only position or perspective from which feminists should coalesce for political action, de Lauretis nonetheless pressed Christine de Stephano's view that, in their desire to assume other positions or perspectives such as these of race and class, feminists might "lose" women.[48] According to de Stephano, even if gender is not the only perspective or position that matters in feminism, it remains basic to feminism, a difference that makes a difference. We must, said de Stephano, "repeatedly return . . . to the [figure of the shrinking woman] . . . because to ignore her altogether is to risk forgetting and thereby losing what is left of her."[49]

de Stephano's insistence that feminists require the position or perspective of gender is affirmed by third-wave multicultural and global feminists. Like third-wave postmodern difference feminists, third-wave multicultural and global feminists reject the second-wave radical-cultural feminist emphasis on women's *sameness*. As noted above, second-wave radical cultural feminists assumed that women had to be the same if they were to unite on behalf of women's liberation; and so they used the pronoun "we" and the construct Woman in an attempt to be inclusive. Although third-wave multicultural and global feminists do not doubt the good intentions of second-wave radical-cultural feminists, they nonetheless claim that their assertions of women's "sameness" worked against the best interests of women. Assertions of "sameness," like assertions of "difference" can serve to oppress people.

In an attempt to clarify how assertions of "sameness" can serve to oppress people, multicultural and global feminist Elizabeth Spelman observes:

> The assertion of difference among women can operate oppressively if one marks the differences and then suggests that one of the groups so differentiated is more impor-tant or more human or in some sense better than the others. But on the other hand, to stress the unity of women is no guarantee against hierarchical ranking, if what one says is true or characteristic of women as a class is only true or characteristic of some women: for then women who cannot be so characterized are in effect not counted as women. When Stanton said that women should get the vote before Africans, Chinese, Germans, and Irish, she obviously was relying on a concept of 'woman' that blinded her to the 'womanness' of many women.[50]

Spelman urges feminists not to make the mistake made by historian Kenneth Stampp when he asserted "that innately Negroes are, after all, only white men with black skins, nothing more, nothing else."[51] Challenging white and "First-World" feminists in particular to ponder Stampp's words, Spelman asks why Stampp chose to describe *Negroes* as white men with black skins instead of choosing to describe *Caucasians* as black men with white skins. Could it be, probes Spelman, that Stampp was uncon-sciously committed to the view that "white" is the way all people really want to be? Moreover, could it also be that, like Stampp, white and First-World feminists unreflectively view "white" and "First World" as the preferred mode for all women's existence?

Speaking herself as a white, First-World feminist, Spelman comments that:

> If, like Stampp, I believe that the woman in every woman is a woman just like me, and if I also assume that there is no difference between being white and being a woman, then seeing another woman 'as a woman' will involve seeing her as fundamentally like the woman I am. In other words, the womanness underneath the Black woman's skin is a white woman's, and deep down inside the Latino woman is an Anglo woman wait-ing to burst through an obscuring cultural shroud.[52]

No wonder, concludes Spelman, that so many women of color and Third-World women rejected second-wave feminist thought; it was too "white" and "First World" for them. A truly inclusive feminist theory cannot claim all women are just like me, anymore than it can claim that I am just like all other women; nor can it operate on the assumption that those who are different from me want to become like me, particularly if I do not want to become like them, but to remain myself.

In their desire to affirm their differences from each other as basic to their self-identity, third-wave multicultural and global feminists initially rejected approaches such as Robin Morgan's attempt to reaffirm women's "universal sisterhood." Among others, third-wave multicultural and global feminist Chandra Talpade Mohanty criticized Morgan for claiming that women share "a common condition" best described "as the suffering inflicted by a universal 'patriarchal mentality,' women's opposition to male power and androcentrism, and the experience of rape, battery, labor, and childbirth."[53] Mohanty took particular exception to Morgan's claim that were women to ask themselves "sincere questions"[54] about their differences, they would discover that their ultimate goal is the same: namely, to constitute themselves as selves. For Morgan, white women and women of color, First-World women and Third-World women, are united in their quest for "self-identity," "self-hood," "self-realization," and "the right to be oneself."[55] But, as Mohanty saw it, Morgan's "middle-class, psychologized notion"[56] of women's supposed search for self-hood glosses over the uncomfortable fact that most women of color and Third-World women have little if any time to think about their "selves," let alone to develop them. They are, stressed Mohanty, usually too focused on surviving, on getting enough food, clothing, and shelter for themselves and their families, to worry about self-completion.

Although most third-wave multicultural and global feminists continue to doubt that "sisterhood" is a state of being all women can or should achieve, an increasing number of them are nonetheless optimistic that women who come from different "worlds" can come first to understand each other and then to work together on behalf of each other's specific interests. Among these more optimistic third-wave multicultural and global feminists is Spelman. She suggests that minimally, a way to get to know women different from one's self is to "read books, take classes, open your eyes and ears or whatever instrument of awareness you might be blessed with, go to conferences planned and produced by the people about whom you wish to learn and manage not to be intrusive."[57] A better, but also more demanding way to get to know such women, adds Spelman, is to imagine their lives and to be tolerant of their differences from one's self no matter how threatening they might seem. Finally, concludes Spelman, the best and most demanding way to get to know such women is not simply to imagine their lives and to tolerate them but to perceive and welcome them.

Spelman explains the distinction between imagining and perceiving a woman different from one's self as follows:

> When I am perceiving someone, I must be prepared to receive new information all the time, to adopt my actions accordingly, and to have my feelings develop in response to what the person is doing, whether I like what she is doing or not. When simply imagining her, I can escape from the demands her reality puts on me and instead construct her in my mind in such a way that I can possess her, make her into someone or

something who never talks back, who poses no difficulties for me, who conforms to my desires much more than the real person does.[58]

In equally clear fashion, Spelman elucidates the distinction between tolerating and welcoming a woman different from one's self by noting that if someone merely tolerates a new viewpoint, she is not ready to actively seek it out as a serious critique of her own viewpoint. She is not, in other words, open to changing herself in any substantial way. Instead, she is simply prepared to "live and let live." In contrast, if someone truly welcomes a new viewpoint, she will be prepared to change her ways. She may even try to become friends with a woman who was little more than a stranger to her before.

Stressing just how difficult it is for women from different worlds to perceive and welcome each other, third-wave multicultural and global feminists such as bell hooks caution white women and First-World women not to be disappointed if they are unable to achieve personal friendships with women of color and Third-World women. The kind of "friendship" or "sisterhood" third-wave multicultural and global feminists should seek is first and foremost political—not personal. There is, insists hooks, a major difference between "bourgeois-women's liberation,"[59] sisterhood, and third-wave multicultural and global feminist sisterhood. The former focuses on women supporting each other, where support serves "as a prop or a foundation for a weak structure,"[60] and where women, emphasizing their "shared victimization," give each other "unqualified approval."[61] The latter rejects this sentimentalized support system and offers in its stead a type of sisterhood that begins with women honestly acknowledging each others' differences, and ends with women using these very same differences to "accelerate their positive advance"[62] toward the goals they share in common. As hooks explains:

> Women do not need to eradicate difference to feel solidarity. We do not need to share common oppression to fight equally to end oppression . . .We can be sisters united by shared interests and beliefs, united in our appreciation for diversity, united in our struggle to end sexist oppression, united in political solidarity.[63]

Using their differences as a source of the feminist strength, hooks affirms that third-wave multicultural and global feminists like Alison Jaggar advise contemporary U.S. feminists to "cross borders."[64] As they move toward the new millennium, Jaggar and other feminists with her perspective increasingly offer a *both/and* approach to resolving the tension between unity and diversity in feminist thought. As they see it, women from all over the world need to realize that despite all their differences, they also have some samenesses, and that they can become political allies even when they can't become personal friends.

Reconsidering Morgan's calls for "sisterhood," third-wave multicultural and global feminist Susan Moller Okin advises third-wave feminists not to make the same mistakes first-wave and second-wave feminists made; namely, the mistake of trying to impose their understanding of feminism on all women. Okin faults Mohanty in particular for being too focused on women's differences, as if each woman was entirely separate from every other woman. Okin comments that:

> During the 1980s and early 1990s, there was a striking divergence between, on the one hand, the activities, the discourse, and the preoccupations of many Western feminist theorists (including some feminists of Third World origins working in Western academic contexts) and, on the other hand, the activities and perceptions of feminist activists in the Third World (including some First World scholar activists like Charlotte Bunch, and other activists, like Fran Hashen, who were most in contact with Third World activists).[65]

As Okin sees it, in their attempt not to falsely universalize or "essentialize" women, many First-World feminist theoreticians failed to listen to those Third-World feminist activists who were "finding that women had a lot in common."[66] Okin stresses that at several global meetings women from all over the world came to recognize "that women are greatly affected by laws and customs having to do with sexuality, marriages, divorce, child custody, and family life as a whole" ; that they "are much more likely to be rendered sexually vulnerable than men and boys" ; and that their "work tend to be valued considerably less highly than men and men's work."[67] First-World women, insists Okin, should work with Third-World women to achieve for all women the kind of freedom and well-being some women already have. To do so is not an exercise in cultural imperialism, but a simple response to a call for assistance.

Okin's case for cooperation between First-World women and Third-World women is a cogent one. But First-World women who are sincere about eliminating all forms of human oppression, beginning with gender oppression, will need to do more than talk about the need to help Third-World women achieve all that is *rightfully* theirs as women. First-World women must, as Vandana Shiva and Maria Mies have suggested, be prepared to give up some of their luxuries so that Third-World women can attain most of their necessities.[68] Stressing that there is only so much of any one material good to be distributed among the world's population, Shiva and Mies claim that third-wave feminists must take the lead in living more simply so that life on earth can continue through the next millennium and more. Bluntly put, Shiva and Mies maintain that if third-wave feminists from the First World are really serious about ending all oppression, beginning with gender oppression, they must stop being oppressors.

That Mies and Shiva should call First-World women to task is not surprising, for, as they see it, what creates the greatest divide between people is some people having too much and other people having too little. In their estimation, one wrong way to resolve this undesirable state of affairs is for the "have-nots" to wage war against the "haves." Little will be achieved by such violence except counterproductively reversing the membership of the "have" and "have not" classes.

Another wrong way to overcome the have/have not divide is for the haves to try to help the have nots join the class of haves. As Mies and Shiva see it, this strategy is destined for failure since there is no way that everyone can have everything in equal measure. Mies faults First-World economists for telling Third-World people that they can attain the same standard of living First-World people enjoy without First-World people making any sacrifices. Nothing, insists Mies, could be further from the truth. Observing that the world's population will swell to 11 billion after the year 2050, she states: "If of these eleven billion people the per capita energy consumption was similar to that of Americans in the mid-1970s, conventional oil resources would be exhausted in 34–74 years."[69] And, of course, this is but one example of why it is wrong to promise all people a lifestyle that is unsustainable except for the privileged few who continue to lead it to the detriment of others.

A third way to overcome the gap between the haves and the have nots is, then, for First-World people to honestly confront the fact that their luxurious life style is partially subsidized by a host of Third-World people who lead a Spartan life style. Mies, Shiva, and other multicultural and global feminists urge privileged feminists, most of whom live in the First World, but some of whom live in the Third World, to voluntarily give up at least some of their excesses so that the basic needs of underprivileged women can be met. For example, says Mies, the wages of Third-World women in the garment industry will be raised significantly only when First-World women are willing to pay more for imported garments.[70] The closets of many First-World women are bulging not only with clothes imported from the Third World but also with the "skeletons" of many Third-World women, most of whom have bare cupboards as well as bare closets. This type of scenario suggests that a person ought not call herself or himself a feminist—someone committed to eliminating all forms of oppression, particularly those forms that harm women—until he or she is willing to stop participating either explicitly or implicitly in oppressive systems, structures, and practices. Third-wave feminism is a most demanding form of feminism.

CONCLUSION

The message of third-wave U.S. feminism resonates in many ways with the messages of both first-wave and second-wave U.S. feminism. Nevertheless, when we compare such third-wave feminist documents as the 1995 Beijing Declaration with such second-wave feminist documents as NOW's 1967 Bill of Rights for Women and such first-wave feminist documents as the 1848 Declaration of Sentiments, we cannot fail to notice just how much feminism has changed since the late nineteenth century. The Declaration of Sentiments was, as its title implies, the expression of women's *feelings* of frustration, of their desire to break out in some measure from the narrow confines of the private realm into the broader purview of the public realm. It was written as a series of accusations against "He," the first and foremost accusation being that "he has never permitted her to achieve her inalienable right to the elective franchise."[71]

The central complaint of the Declaration is that Man has deprived Woman not only of her political and legal rights but also of her dignity. Indeed, the authors of the Declaration specifically bemoaned the fact that "He has endeavored, in every way that he could, to destroy her confidence in her own powers, to lessen her self-respect, and to make her willing to lead a dependent and abject life."[72] Of interest is the fact that the Declaration's authors viewed the Church as well as the State as playing a large role in subordinating Woman to Man, and they saw Academia as the quickest route to women's liberation. Also of interest is the fact that although the Declaration's authors faulted the so-called sexual double standard, they faulted it not because it restricted women's sexuality but because it failed to restrict men's sexuality. No plea was made to increase women's reproductive freedom, and it was simply assumed that the care of children was both woman's duty and first love. Predictably, for the times, no mention was made of women's racial, class, or religious differences, as if all women were white, married or related to well-to-do men, and Christian. The dominant messages of the Declaration of Sentiments were: (1) that men and women are created equal; (2) that it is the role of Government to help women as well as men secure their inalienable rights as human beings; and (3) that it is the responsibility of an oppressed group—in this case women—to refuse allegiance to any Government which denies them what it grants to the non-oppressed group—in this case men.

Over a century after the Declaration was proclaimed, NOW passed its 1967 Bill of Rights. Although women's suffrage was well established in law and practice by then, women continued to have far less opportunities than men to pursue their interests in the so-called public world. Unlike the authors of the Declaration of Sentiments, the authors of NOW's Bill of Rights identified women's childbearing ability and child-rearing role as the primary cause of women's inability to compete equally with men in the political forum, the academic arena, and the marketplace. Thus, NOW's authors pressed for more permissive contraception and abortion legislation, publicly subsidized child-care facilities, and maternity leave policies.

Expanding the limits of the Declaration even more, NOW's Bill of Rights mentioned race in its demand that "equal employment opportunity be guaranteed to all women, as well as men, by insisting that the EEOC enforces the prohibitions against racial discrimination."[73] And it made mention of class in its demand that "poor women be given the right" to secure job training, housing, and family allowances on equal terms with men, but without prejudice to a parent's right to remain at home to care for his or her children.[74] Like the authors of the Declaration of Sentiments, the authors of NOW's Bill of Rights stressed that women had a right "to be educated to their full potential equally with men,"[75] but unlike the Declaration of Sentiments' authors, the Bill of Rights' authors ignored topics such as morals, religion, and women's self-images. The dominant messages of NOW's Bill of Rights were:

(1) that legislation can prevent the subordination of U.S. women to U.S. men; and (2) that what U.S. women want, more than anything, is equal opportunity to compete against men in the so-called public world.

Clearly, NOW's 1967 Bill of Rights forwarded a second-wave liberal feminist agenda focused on educational, economic, and political gender disparities. Thus, second-wave radical feminists were correct to challenge its authors for failing to highlight the ways in which women's sexual roles as well as women's reproductive roles contribute to the subordination of women to men. With reference to the issue of violence against women in pornography, prostitution, sexual harassment, rape, and domestic battery as well as the issue of women's sexual preference (heterosexual or lesbian), NOW's authors were silent. Like some of their first-wave predecessors, these second-wave feminists chose to downplay such issues on the grounds that they would unnecessarily alienate many men and non-feminist women.

NOW's aim was, it seemed, to produce a Bill of Rights that most mainstream Americans could accept. Therefore, only the most public of problems, such as education and employment, were addressed; more personal or private issues were avoided in this attempt to make the Bill of Rights acceptable to the mainstream. As a result, this Bill of Rights and second-wave liberal feminists managed to make few substantial changes in women's personal and private roles. They won for women the right to work a double day, to be the Superwoman who works as hard as a man during the day in the business world, and then works just as hard at night in her home cooking, cleaning, and caring for her loved ones.

In contrast to both the 1848 Declaration of Sentiments and the 1967 Bill of Rights, the 1995 Beijing Declaration was written with the realization that women are not the same, but very different from each other.[76] The authors of the Beijing Declaration admitted that women's overall estate was far better in the year 2000 than it had been in the year 1900, but that progress had been uneven. Mention was made of *men's* roles as well as women's roles in ending all forms of oppression, particular gender oppression. Women's rights were repeatedly mentioned, but they were spoken of as women's "*human rights.*"[77]

Moreover, reminiscent of the 1848 Declaration of Sentiments, mention was made of "the right to freedom of thought, conscience, religion and belief, thus contributing to the moral, ethical, spiritual and intellectual needs of women and men."[78] Unlike the authors of NOW's Bill of Rights, the authors of the Beijing Declaration used language that goes beyond "equal rights opportunities,"[79] and focuses on the implementation and realization of the goals set forth in the document. Although the Beijing Declaration's authors made it clear that women's political and personal freedom depends on women's economic well-being, they also made it clear that a free woman is a woman who is in charge of her procreative freedom and who does not live in fear of what pain men can inflict on her body and suffering on her spirit.

Clearly, the Beijing Declaration is sensitive to issues of race, class, national origin, and religion. Its message is not an individualistic assertion of rights, but a collective expression of people's basic needs. Its theme concerns women from all over the world working with each other and men to achieve equality in opportunity and access. This goal is akin to what Mies, Shiva, and other third-wave or global and multicultural feminists have termed a "subsistence life-style,"[80] the only lifestyle these feminists believe is compatible with gender equity. This kind of lifestyle demands much from First-World and Third-World people, but particularly from First- World people. It requires that everyone take as many of the following steps as possible.

1. People should produce only enough to satisfy fundamental human needs, re-sisting the urge to produce "an ever-growing mountain of commodities and money (wages or profit)"[81] in a futile attempt to still people's endless and insatiable wants.

2. People should use only as much of nature as they need to, treating it as a reality with "her own subjectivity;"[82] and people should use each other not to make money but to create communities capable of meeting people's fundamental needs, especially their need for intimacy.

3. People should replace representative democracy with participatory democracy so that each man and woman has the opportunity to express his or her concerns to everyone else.

4. People should develop "multidimensional or synergic"[83] problem-solving approaches, since the problems of contemporary society are interrelated.

5. People should combine contemporary science, technologies, and knowledge with ancient wisdom, traditions, and even magic.

6. People should break down the boundaries between work and play, the sciences and the arts, spirit and matter.

7. People should view water, air, earth, and all natural resources as community goods rather than as private possessions.

8. Men as well as women should adopt the socialist-transformative ecofeminist view, the subsistence perspective. Mies explains this eighth point in more detail, stating:

> Ecofeminism does not mean, as some argue, that women will clean up the ecological mess which capitalist-patriarchal men have caused; women will not eternally be the *Trummerfrauen* (the women who clear up the ruins after the patriarchal wars). Therefore, a subsistence perspective necessarily means men begin to share, *in practice*, the responsibility for the creation and preservation of life on this planet. Therefore, men must start a movement to redefine their identity. They must give up their involvement in destructive commodity production for the sake of accumulation and begin to share women's work for the preservation of life. In practical terms this means they have to share unpaid subsistence work: in the household, with children, with the old and sick, in ecological work to heal the earth, in new forms of subsistence production.[84]

9. Men as well as women should cultivate traditional feminine virtues (caring, compassion, nurturance) and engage in subsistence productions, for "only a society based on a subsistence perspective can afford to live in peace with nature, and uphold peace between nations, generations and men and women. . . . "[85]

10. Most importantly, people should realize that in order for each person to have enough, no person can "have it all." Mies claimed that Kamla Bhasin, an Indian feminist, expressed this thought in a particularly forceful manner when she stated that

> sustainable development . . . is not compatible with the existing profit-
> and growth-oriented development paradigm. And this means that the
> standard of living of the North's affluent societies cannot be general-
> ized. This was already clear to Mahatma Gandhi 60 years ago, who,
> when asked by a British journalist whether he would like India to have
> the same standard of living as Britain, replied: 'To have its standard
> of living a tiny country like Britain had to exploit half the globe. How
> many globes will India need to exploit to have the same standard of
> living?' From an ecological and feminist perspective, moreover, even
> if there were more globes to be exploited, it is not even desirable that
> this development paradigm and standard of living was generalized,
> because it has failed to fulfill its promises of happiness, freedom, dig-
> nity and peace, even for those who have profited from it.[86]

Emerging between the lines of Mies's recommendations is the profile of the ideal third-wave feminist, a feminist for a truly new millennium.

The kind of third-wave feminist projected by the authors of the Beijing Declaration is very different from the kind of "feminist" that Naomi Wolf, Katie Roiphe, Camille Paglia, and René Denfield celebrate in their writings.[87] Terming themselves "power" as opposed to "victim" feminists,[88] these so-called postfeminists tend to focus on the sexual arena as the locus of women's empowerment. They want women to "have it all." For example, Wolf announces in her book that she wants "to be a serious thinker and not hide the fact that I have breasts; I want female sexuality to accompany, rather than undermine, female political power."[89]

Repeatedly, each of these postfeminists stresses that, at least in the United States, women are free to seize the day (carpe diem), to be whoever they want to be, and do whatever they want to do. Their only "enemy" is themselves. Forgetting that so much of the "power" they feel has to do with their advantaged socioeconomic position, these postfeminist celebrations of women's power are realized in selfishness, as portrayed by television characters such as Ally McBeal. Despite the fact that she works in a high-powered legal firm, McBeal does not act like a grown woman—let alone a feminist. Rather she behaves like a little girl who confuses being narcissistic, and having the means to do what she wants to do, with being "liberated." Writer Gina Bellafante points out that McBeal is so self-preoccupied that she answers the question, "'Why are your problems so much bigger than everyone else's?' with the earnest response 'Because they're mine,'"[90] and so oblivious to the situation of women less privileged than herself that "she thinks it's O.K. to ask her secretary why she didn't give her a birthday present."[91] Therefore, one may assume that if she even were to read the document, McBeal would have a hard time understanding why she should respond to the Beijing Declaration and change her lifestyle so that women on the other side of the globe may benefit. Bellafante, continuing in her article concerning contemporary Hollywood role models for women, notes that when asked if McBeal is meant to be perceived as a feminist, her creator David Kelly commented: "She's not a hard, strident feminist out of the '60s and '70s. She's all for women's rights, but she doesn't want to lead the charge at her own emotional expense."[92] To which comment I might add that she is not a feminist for the new millennium either, precisely because she is living in her own epicurean garden of delights, blissfully unaware of how really bad life is for a whole lot of women.

Contemporary, third-wave, new-millennium feminism is difficult to describe succinctly and accurately. In fact, feminism has always been difficult to analyze. Even in 1913, a woman wrote: "I myself have never been able to find out precisely what feminism is. . . . I only know that people call me a feminist whenever I express sentiments that differentiate me from a doormat, or a prostitute."[93] The reason why it is not yet time to bid adieu to feminism is precisely the fact that so many pseudo-feminists like Ally McBeal have emerged on the scene. Admittedly, part of eliminating gender oppression is breaking into the "boy's club," as well as being as sexual as one desires, but this is only part of it. The other part is asking one's self some troubling questions about women who struggle to support their families on paltry wages, about shy girls who get pawed by predatory men, and about wondering how one's high salary and liberated sexuality might be contributing to the pain and suffering these women experience. Feminism is about justice, but it is also about caring—caring enough to make some sacrifices in one's own life so that women across the United States and around the globe, particularly women who may not be of one's own race or class, may experience more of life's opportunities.

NOTES

1. Mary Wollstonecraft, *A Vindication of the Rights of Woman*, ed. Carol H. Poston (New York: W. W. Norton, 1975), 34.

2. Wollstonecraft, 61.

3. Richard Krouse, "Mill and Marx on Marriage, Divorce and the Family," *Social Concept* 1, no. 2 (September 1983): 48.

4. John Stuart Mill, "Periodical Literature 'Edinburgh Review'," *Westminister Review* 1, no. 2 (April 1824): 526.

5. Angela Y. Davis, *Women, Race and Class* (New York: Random House, 1981), 42.

6. Sarah M. Grimké, *Letters on the Equality of the Sexes and the Conditions of Woman*

(Boston: Isaac Knapp, 1838, reprinted by Source Book Press, New York, 1970), 9–10; 51; 85–86.

7. Judith Hole and Ellen Levine, *Rebirth of Feminism* (New York: Quadrangle Books, 1971), 3.

8. Hole and Levine, 434.

9. Hole and Levine, 434.

10. Hole and Levine, 8–9.

11. Davis, *Women, Race and Class*, 75.

12. Hole and Levine, 10.

13. Hole and Levine, 12.

14. Elisabeth Egan, "The Other Declaration of Independence," *Self* (July 1998): 107.

15. Nicholas Davidson, *The Failure of Feminism* (New York: Prometheus Books, 1988), 6–7.

16. Davidson, 10–11.

17. Caroline Bird, *Born Female* (New York: David McKay Company, 1968), 1.

18. Hole and Levine, 90.

19. Betty Friedan, "NOW—How It Began," *Women Speaking* (April 1967), 4.

20. "Declaration of Sentiments," *Self* (July 1998): 106–7.

21. "NOW (National Organization for Women) Bill of Rights" (Adopted at NOW's first national conference, Washington, D.C., 1967), in *Sisterhood is Powerful*, ed. Robin Morgan (New York: Random House, 1970), 513–14.

22. Gina Bellafante, "Feminism: It's All About Me!" *TIME* (June 29, 1998): 58.

23. Hole and Levine, 110–22.

24. Hole and Levine, 170.

25. See Rosemarie Putnam Tong, *Feminist Thought: A More Comprehensive Introduction*, 2nd ed. (Boulder, Colo.: Westview Press, 1998), 47–48, for distinction between radical-libertarian and radical-cultural feminists.

26. Shulamith Firestone, *The Dialectic of Sex* (New York: Bantam Books, 1970), 198–99.

27. Firestone, 190.

28. Tong, *Feminist Thought*, 47.

29. Linda Alcoff, "Cultural Feminism Versus Poststructuralism: The Identity Crisis in Feminist Theory," *Signs: Journal of Women in Culture and Society* 13, no. 3 (1988): 488.

30. Adrienne Rich, "Compulsory Heterosexuality and Lesbian Existence," in *Living with Contradictions: Controversies in Feminist Social Ethics*, ed. Alison M. Jaggar (Boulder, Colo: Westview Press, 1994), 487–88.

31. Ann Ferguson, "Sex Wars: The Debate Between Radical and Liberation Feminists," *Signs: Journal of Women in Culture and Society* 10, no. 1 (Autumn 1984): 109.

32. Adrienne Rich, *Of Woman Born* (New York: W. W. Norton, 1976); Sara Ruddick, "Maternal Thinking," in *Mothering: Essays in Feminist Theory*, ed. Joyce Trebilcot (Totowa, N. J.: Rowman and Allanheld, 1984).

33. See, for example, Genea Corea, *The Mother Machine: Reproduction Technologies from Artificial Insemination to Artificial Wombs* (New York: Harper & Row, 1985), 213–49.

34. Alice Echols, "The New Feminism of Yin and Yang," in *Powers of Desire: The Politics of Sexuality*, ed. Ann Snitow, Christine Stansell, and Sharon Thompson (New York: Monthly Review Press, 1983), 445.

35. Alison M. Jaggar, "Feminist Ethics," in *Encyclopedia of Ethics*, eds. Lawrence Becker and Charlotte Becker (New York: Garland, 1992), 364.

36. Judith Grant, *Fundamental Feminism: Contesting the Care Concepts of Feminist Theory* (New York: Routledge, 1993), 25–26.

37. Grant, 31–33.

38. Grant, 32–33.

39. Leslie Heywood and Jennifer Drake, "Introduction," in *Third-Wave Agenda: Being Feminist, Doing Feminism*, eds. Heywood and Drake (Minneapolis: University of Minnesota Press, 1997), 3.

40. Tong, *Feminist Thought*, 6–7; 278.

41. Elizabeth Grosz, "Sexual Difference and the Problem of Essentialism," in *The Essential Difference*, eds. Naomi Schor and Elizabeth Weed (Bloomington, Ind.: Indiana University Press, 1994), 91.

42. Margaret Whitford, "Luce Irigaray and the Female Imaginary: Speaking as a Woman," *Radical Philosophy* 43 (Summer 1986): 7.

43. Whitford, 7.

44. Teresa de Lauretis, "The Essence of the Triangle or, Taking Risks of Essentialism Seriously," in *The Essential Difference*, ed. Schor and Weed (Bloomington: Indiana University Press, 1994), 3.

45. Linda Alcoff, "Cultural Feminism versus Post-Structuralism: The Identity Crisis in Feminist Theory," *Signs: A Journal of Women in Culture and Society* 13, no. 3 (1998): 434–35.

46. de Lauretis, "The Essence of The Triangle," 10.

47. Teresa de Lauretis, *Technologies of Gender* (Bloomington, Ind.: Indiana University Press, 1987), p. x.

48. Christine de Stephano, "Dilemmas of Difference," in *Feminism/Postmodernism*, ed. Linda J. Nicholson (New York: Routledge, 1990), 75.

49. de Stephano, 63.

50. Elizabeth V. Spelman, *Inessential Woman: Problems of Exclusion in Feminist Thought* (Boston: Beacon Press, 1988), 11–12.

51. Spelman, 12.

52. Spelman, 13.

53. Chandra Talpate Mohanty, "Feminist Encounters: Locating the Politics of Experience," in *Destabilizing Theory: Contemporary Feminist Debates*, ed. Michelle Barrett and Anne Philips (Stanford: Stanford University Press, 1992), 78–79.

54. Robin Morgan, *Sisterhood is Global* (Garden City, N.Y.: Crossing Press, 1984), 1.

55. Morgan, 1.

56. Mohanty, "Feminist Encounters: Locating the Politics of Experience," 83.

57. Spelman, 178.

58. Spelman, 178.

59. bell hooks, *Feminist Theory: From Margin to Center* (Boston: South End Press, 1984), 404.

60. hooks, 404.

61. hooks, 404.

62. hooks, 404.

63. hooks, 404.

64. Alison Jaggar, "Globalizing Feminist Ethics," *Hypatia* 13, no. 2 (Spring 1998): 27.

65. Susan Moller Okin, "Feminism, Women's Human Rights, and Cultural Differences," *Hypatia* 13, no. 2 (Spring 1998): 42.

66. Moller Okin, 44.

67. Moller Okin, 45.

68. Maria Mies, "The Myths of Catching-Up Development," in *Ecofeminism*, ed. Maria Mies and Vandana Shiva (London: Zed, 1993), 60.

69. Mies, "The Myths of Catching-Up Development," 67.

70. Mies, "The Myths of Catching-Up Development," 67.

71. "Declaration of Sentiments," 107.

72. "Declaration of Sentiments," 107.

73. "NOW Bill of Rights," in *Sisterhood is Powerful*, ed. Robin Morgan, 513–14.

74. *Sisterhood is Powerful*, 513–14.

75. *Sisterhood is Powerful*, 513–14.

76. "The Beijing Declaration," in *Women in the Third World: An Encyclopedia of Contemporary Issues*, ed. Nelly P. Stromquist (New York: Garland Publishing, Inc., 1998), 673–75.

77. "The Beijing Declaration," 673.

78. "The Beijing Declaration," 673.

79. "The Beijing Declaration," 673.

80. Tong, *Feminist Thought*, 271.

81. Maria Mies, "The Need for a New Vision: The Subsistence Perspective," in *Ecofeminism*, ed. Maria Mies and Vandana Shiva (London: Zed, 1993), 319.

82. Mies, "The Need for a New Vision," 319.

83. Mies, "The Need for a New Vision," 320.

84. Mies, "The Need for a New Vision," 321.

85. Mies, "The Need for a New Vision," 322.

86. Mies, "The Need for a New Vision," 322.

87. Naomi Wolf, *Fire With Fire: The New Female Power and How It Will Change the Twenty-First Century* (New York: Random House, 1993); Katie Roiphe, *The Morning After: Sex, Fear, and Feminism on Campus* (New York: Little, Brown, 1993); Camille Paglia, *Sex, Art, and American Culture: Essays* (New York: Random House, 1992); René Denfield, *The New Victorians: A Young Woman's Challenges to the Old Feminist Order* (New York: Warner Books, 1995).

88. Leslie Heywood and Jennifer Drake, "Introduction," in *Third-Wave Agenda: Being Feminist, Doing Feminism*, ed. Leslie Heywood and Jennifer Drake (Minneapolis: University of Minnesota Press, 1997), 3.

89. Wolf, *Fire With Fire*, 185.

90. Bellafante, "Feminism: It's All About Me!" 58.

91. Bellafante, 58.

92. Bellafante, 58.

93. Nancy Gibbs, "The War Against Feminism," *TIME* (March 9, 1992): 51.

14

Maritime Policy for a Flat Earth

Michael Levin

In the spirit of experiment (or adventure), utter the following at a social gathering: "It's shocking how teenagers still smoke. Especially girls. Appearance matters so much to them; don't they care that they're harming their looks?" There will be an awkward silence, above all in well-educated company, followed by someone with a nervous grin calling your remark "sexist." Since no one present will actually doubt that adolescent girls care more about being attractive than their male counterparts—it just shouldn't be said—someone else may chime in that, yes, girls do fret about their appearance, but quickly add that this is because they have been taught to do so.

Assuming events go more or less as described, they exemplify feminism's main contribution to culture. It is now taboo to acknowledge any sex difference, doubly taboo to suggest that they are natural.

This taboo carries a corollary, illustrated by another incident, this time real (and typical). When, while discussing the problem of illegitimacy with a female scientist, I mentioned contraceptives, she replied, tartly, "That's no solution. Contraception is controlled by men." The corollary: insofar as men are involved in a thing, little good can come of it.

Most doctrines get something right: the facts, or an aperçu or two. But feminism's continuing denial of biological reality puts it on the wrong side of every issue. It misdescribes relations between the sexes, hence all of society; its account of these (misdescribed) relations is intuitively absurd and at odds with science; as a result it chooses unsuitable means to misconceived ends. Secretaries drawing maps, plotting courses, and negotiating naval treaties on the assumption that the Earth is flat would be no more likely to go astray.

I

As its adherents often seem reluctant to state precisely what they believe, feminism is best defined very broadly, as a demand for justice for women plus the claim that many (perhaps all) aspects of all human society, certainly its basic institutions as presently constituted, deny them this. The demand per se is not in dispute. Adopting Polemarchus' common-sense definition of justice in the *Republic* as "giving each [wo]man his due," the assertion that women deserve justice says only that they deserve their deserts. The hard part is determining what that is, and whether women are denied it.

The charge that they are is usually based on the statistical excess of men in positions of power, authority, and extrafamilial status (Congress, corporate boards), along with the currency of disparate norms for the sexes, particularly the sexual double standard and the expectation that children will be reared primarily by women. Feminists seldom specify explicitly what proportions would be proper in important activities, but any departure from 50:50 reliably prompts complaints of discrimination. Thus, the slight 54 to 46 percent male advantage in National Merit Scholarships (NMS) is regularly cited as proof of bias in the NMS qualifying test (which its designers have obediently adjusted to raise female scores, by weighting the verbal section twice as heavily as the mathematical). Federal law mandating "equitable" allocation of money in college sports is consistently interpreted to mean equal money for male and female teams, despite the manifest athletic superiority of males and their greater interest in sports. The news that a woman earns n cents for every $1 made by a man is never more than a move in the right direction so long as $n < 100$. When complaining of male failures to assume child-care duty, feminists leave the impression that, ideally, there would be no presumption at all that this is women's work. (That is why the men's rooms of compliant facilities now have diaper-changing tables, seldom used.) Equality of outcome is the asymptote to which feminist justice always converges. Hence the unrelieved negativity toward men, for when one group has far more than it should while another has far less, with no third party involved, whom to blame is clear (although sometimes a shadowy entity called "society" is accused of limiting both men and women). Here too is the rationale for discriminating against men in favor of women in employment and elsewhere ("affirmative action"), as rectifying the damage done to women in the past—still somehow borne by women today—that gives men their unfair competitive advantage.

The trouble with the feminist indictment is that statistical disparities and divergent expectations by themselves prove nothing, certainly not "oppression." After all, there are no five-year-olds in Congress—they lack even the legal right to run—yet they are not oppressed, since five-year-olds are incapable of drafting legislation and have no wish to anyway. The simple lesson: whether a discrepancy in goods, power, or status between individuals or groups is wrongful depends on why it exists. To support a finding of injustice, it must be known to have resulted from force or fraud, or else the contestants must be known to be so similar in ability and motivation that covert force or fraud is the only reasonable inference. In particular, if innate sex differences rather than oppression explain the relative positions of men and women, should it turn out that women are "held back" not by external impediments but their own nature, male pre-eminence is not unjust. There might be other reasons to seek to undo it, but unfairness would not be among them.

To be sure, a discrepancy between unequally able and motivated groups can also be unjust, to the extent that their endogenous differences cannot fully explain it. But since (see below) feminists characteristically deny *any* relevant differences between men and women, we may ignore this refinement. One must also acknowledge the many conceptions of justice to which coercion and chicanery are irrelevant, for instance (Plato's) that everyone occupy his proper place, that everyone have enough to live on, that the gap between the best and worst off not exceed some maximum, or that the interests of the worst off come first (Rawls' difference principle). However, feminists do not complain of unfairness in any of these "structural" senses; their claim is simply that men hold center stage by shoving women aside. Even the difference principle, cited favorably by some feminists,[1] is subordinate in Rawls' system to the demand for the greatest like liberty for all,[2] met so long as force is in abeyance. So structural theories of justice too are irrelevant to present purposes.

Given the importance of the "why disparity?" issue, one would expect the first order of feminist business to be to assess the antecedent of the italicized conditional— to ask whether such innate sex differences as may in fact exist can explain social reality. But it is just here that feminists leave the rails. Instead of looking at the evidence, they reject it out of hand. They assume from the outset that biological sex differences are nonexistent or trivial, then conclude straightaway that society is oppressive, patriarchal, and on through their litany of pejoratives. Indeed, the oppressiveness of society easily becomes a premise from which politically correct science is deduced, causing any mention of innate differences to be construed as right-wing propaganda.[3] And by that point emotion has taken over. Thus we find the philosopher and self-professed scientific realist Hilary Putnam calling psychologist Steven Pinker's recent review of sex differences "reactionary, dangerous crap."[4] The Holocaust is often cited in this context as cautionary precedent.[5]

Liberationists, then, rightly sense that appraisal of extant institutions turns on the reality of psychobiological sex differences, but they approach the issue in exactly the wrong way. The right way is to start with the facts insofar as they are known and then judge institutions by their light.

II

Do feminists really reject all innate sex differences in cognition and temperament? It is not news that the founding mothers, circa 1970, did. "The sexes are inherently in everything alike, save reproductive systems, secondary sexual characteristics, orgasmic capacity, and genetic and morphological structure," wrote Kate Millett. "Biology is not enough to answer the question: Why is woman the Other?" declared Simone de Beauvoir. Elizabeth Janeway found "little need to believe that men and women are born with psychological differences built into their brains because the workings of society and culture, by themselves, are perfectly capable of producing all the differences we know so well."[6] It was, indeed, these contrarian proclamations, angrily expressed, that first made feminists so mediagenic.

Since the 1980s there has been much talk of different kinds and stages of feminism. Where Polonius had only the tragical-pastoral-historical to sort out, commentators on feminism must contend with liberal, socialist, Marxist, radical, eco-, lesbian, French, postmodern, French postmodern, lesbian eco-, black lesbian, radical lesbian, and lesbian separatist feminism—allowing feminists to disown any attribution to them as too narrow, simple, or fringe. But these -isms all agree in ignoring biology. According to avant-gardist Catherine MacKinnon,

> Explaining the subordination of women to men, a political condition, has nothing to do with difference in any fundamental sense . . . power/powerlessness is the sex difference. . . . The molding, direction, and expression of sexuality organize society into the two sexes, men and women. [Sexuality] is taken for a natural essence or presocial impetus but is actually created by the social relations, the hierarchical relations. Another way to say that is, there would be no such thing as what we know as the sex difference—much less would it be the social issue it is or have the social meaning it has—were it not for male dominance.[7]

Note the circularity here—sex determines society, and society determines sex.

Many recent feminists, instead of responding directly to the question of innate gender dimorphism, call the question ill-formed—which amounts in the present context to answering it negatively, since an explanation that makes no sense cannot account for social reality. One version of this expedient as popular as it is desperate is to label sex a "construct," or, more desperately still, to quote someone French who does. Often, social constructivism about sex is part of a generalized skepticism about the possibility of objective scientific knowledge of any sort, on the grounds that science like everything else is political: "Objectivity is the epistemological stance . . . of which male dominance is the politics."[8] Invited by the *American Psychologist* to reply to an article[9] arguing that feminists are hostile to research on sex differences, psychologist Jeanne Marecek wrote:

> I have resisted the view . . . that the categories "man" and "woman" are natural, self-evident, and unequivocal . . . Some [feminist] theorists view gender as a recurring personal and cultural accomplishment produced by a complex of social process. . . . The history of psychology is replete with episodes in which what was deemed scientific fact was served up to justify the status quo. Witness, for example, early psychology's an-

swers to the "Woman Question": scientific evidence that women were less highly evolved than men [no reference is given]. [T]he agenda of preserving the status quo is as political and at least as formidable as the agenda of changing it. [What is needed] are close readings of the texts of research reports, with attention to incongruities, discordances, and conceptual slippages in the narrative. In the hands of a canny critic, they can uncover the framework of assumptions, language practices, and interpretive schemas on which scientific inquiry rests and help to reconstruct psychological theory that incorporates its own situatedness in culture and history.[10]

For the record, any equivocacy about sexual identity can be resolved by identifying men as human beings with an XY chromosome, and women as human beings with an XX chromosome. (Individuals with different arrangements are too few to blur the distinction.) On a deeper level, the "male" of any species is the morph carrying relatively small, numerous, motile gametes and the "female" the morph carrying fewer, larger, less motile ones; species for which the distinction cannot be made are asexual.[11] As for an inherent bias in science, that claim, like all skepticism, self-destructs. Is it a fact that canny critics can uncover frameworks, or a historically situated perception imposed by Professor Macerek's own interpretive schema? If a fact, one wants to know how Macerek has achieved an objectivity that eludes others. If an interpretation, one wants to know why it should be taken more seriously ("privileged" or "valorized") than any other.[12] If the concept of objective truth rationalizes male dominance, "The concept of objective truth rationalizes male dominance" is not objectively true.

Finally there are "gender" feminists, supposedly distinguished by a sometimes overardent embrace of female traits, yet for all their gynophilia conspicuously mum about where these traits come from. For instance the best-known of these, Carol Gilligan,[13] contrasts a female morality of empathy, "relationships" and "human connection" to the male morality of rules, but is emphatic that "No claims are being made" about the origin of this cognitive-affective contrast: "Clearly these differences arise in a social context in which factors of socialization and power combine with reproductive biology." Her very reference to "reproductive biology" tacitly rejects any neuroanatomical basis for the female outlook in favor of social learning—an impression strengthened by her stress on girls' cooperative games as a factor in female moral development. Likewise Sara Ruddick,[14] an apostle of "maternal thinking" as a "distinctive way of conceptualizing, ordering, and valuing,"[15] nonetheless insists that "'maternal' is a social category" and terms "false, and pernicious" the idea that it is "biological."[16] Likewise again, Chesire Calhoun[17] asks for "more knowledgeable discussions of particular differences tied to gender, race, class and power" and complains that "much of the affirmative action literature takes it for granted that women ought to want traditionally male jobs with no consideration of the possibility that women might prefer retailoring those jobs so that they are less competitive, less hierarchical." Yet she never asks where these variant preferences come from, being content to criticize male moral philosophers for not registering them.

Now one thing the reader is bound to notice is that female ways of thinking did not exactly go unrecognized until feminists brought them to the world's attention, but were, to the contrary, part of common sense until feminist rage at "stereotypes" made their acknowledgement socially unacceptable. In themselves the vaunted insights of the newer feminists are trite, indistinguishable in content from traditionalist conventional wisdom. Compare Carol Gilligan's description of female judgment as "marked by an overriding concern with relationships and responsibilities . . . a world composed of relations rather than of people standing alone, a world that coheres through human connection rather than through systems of rules" to that offered by the eponymous Victorian patriarch of Clarence Day's *Life with Father*: "Women—they get stirred up and then they try to get you stirred up too. If you can keep reason and logic in the argument a man can hold his own, of course, but if they can switch you pretty soon the argument's about whether you love them or not."

The two authors differ only in the value placed on what both are describing. Passages substantively indistinguishable from Gilligan's are also plentiful in Freud. And the comics. Gilligan talks about "The proclivity of women to reconstruct hypothetical dilemmas in terms of the real, to request or supply the information missing about the nature of the people . . . ." In *Fox Trot*, fourteen-year-old Paige is puzzling over math homework: "'Michelle wants to buy a sweater. $20 red ones are marked down 15 percent. $30 green ones are 35 percent off. Which should she buy, red or green?' "Come on," Paige complains, "I mean come on. They don't tell you what color her hair is. They don't tell you what color her eyes are." Her younger brother Jason, a math whiz, comments "This is ridiculous."[18]

Where Mr. Day and Jason Fox (and Freud) adopt a tone of affectionate superiority, Gilligan insists that female morality is as "adult" as male. Her nominal target is Lawrence Kohlberg's placement of female judgment at an intermediate stage ("Mutual Interpersonal Expectations, Relationships, and Conformity") in his well-known developmental hierarchy,[19] but instead of presenting empirical evidence against Kohlberg's classification, she simply redescribes female judgment in a flattering way: a tendency to make exceptions to rules "engages compassion and tolerance [and] reconstruct[s] hypothetical dilemmas in terms of the real;" taking things personally "tie[s] conceptions of the self and conceptions of morality," and so on. The same is true of Ruddick, Calhoun, and other recent feminists. Neither offering a fresh portrayal of familiar sex differences nor accepting a nativist account of them, they create an appearance of novelty by adopting new attitudes. (Or attitudes presented as new. It is not as if compassion or motherhood have been despised throughout history.)

Before leaving moral psychology, I would pause to urge that the male versus female morality issue be discarded as a pseudoproblem. Kant and, in this century, R. M. Hare are surely right that by definition moral thought concerns general rules. It is a matter of English usage that a person's "moral" values are those he wishes to see universalized, that the adjective "moral" as opposed to "prudential" or "aesthetic" is reserved for prescriptions meant to apply universally. Consequently, a person who doesn't care whether he treats like cases alike, who senses no inconsistency in changing his mind just because he feels like it, is not displaying a nonstandard morality at all; he is amoral. When wolves feed the young of prey species to their own young without fretting about the categorical imperative, no one talks of lupine morality. Wolves value their pups, but rightness, justice, and fairness never enter their equation. So, too, if female decision-making revolves around "connectedness," with concrete relations between people taking precedence over rules—if, as Gilligan says, women display "the willingness to 'make exceptions all the time'"—then women are simply less concerned with morality than men. This is not to criticize women, for nothing about English usage makes universalization better than its alternatives. The point is clarity. The "morality of caring" misnames what is, in fact, relative disinterest in morality.[20, 21]

The best evidence that feminists still deny innate sex differences is not their continued grumbling about the subject, striking though that is, but their silence about their immediate predecessors. If today's feminists do agree that, yes, the sexes differ for biological reasons, one would expect them to repudiate Simone de Beauvoir, Kate Millett, Germaine Greer, and all the others who proclaimed the reverse so loudly. I certainly haven't heard them do so; readers who have are encouraged to send me documentation. One might excuse feminine reticence as reluctance to throw out the baby of progressive principle with the anti-biological bathwater, but then why don't feminists hold the baby high for all to see while flushing the error away? Absent this purifying ceremony, they may be assumed to wish to retain what they still see as a fount of truth.

III

I have explained why sexual justice cannot be discussed intelligently without reference to the empirical data. I will now summarize these data under four heads: anthropological/sociological, neurological, hormonal, and evolutionary.

Anthropological/Sociological

It should go without saying—and would, but for feminism—that in point of fact, without any hidden rankings, men and women, and boys and girls, do differ. The greater aggressiveness of males both in seeking status in hierarchies and in readiness for violence is universal. Men have virtually monopolized positions of authority in all known societies.[22] In the United States, the murder rate and rates for various kinds of assault by males are ten to twenty times those by females, again a pattern observed in every society.[23] By contrast, women are always, in every society, expected to have direct charge of children.[24] Men and women have unlike but complementary sexual emotions that draw them together in lifelong bonds; marriage (in which the husband is expected to be somewhat older than the wife) is another anthropological universal.[25] Yet patterns of jealousy differ: men are moved to rage, sometimes homicidal, by sexual infidelity, while women are more troubled by alienation of affection.[26] Observable cues such as large breasts arouse men, who desire many sexual partners, while women have a less intense desire for variety and respond (more slowly) to personality traits like masterfulness. In one experiment, an attractive woman inquired of men who did not know her whether they would like to have sex with her, and an attractive man queried women who did not know him in the same manner. Seventy-five percent of the men responded positively, but not one woman.[27] The tendency of women to let feelings influence decisions about the treatment of others, as opposed to the male's stricter adherence to abstract rules, has already been discussed.

There are familiar, quantifiable cognitive differences as well. Women are more verbally fluent than men, while men are better at such spatial tasks as accurate throwing and rotating imaginary objects in three dimensions, differences present by the fourth year of life.[28] Women orient themselves in space by landmarks while men tend to use distances and angles; women manipulate small items more dexterously and notice small displacements of objects more readily than men.[29] These group differences, generally running from 0.3 to 0.5 standard deviations, are evidently universals.[30] Incidentally, homosexual males do no better than heterosexual females at overhand dart-throwing and underhand throwing,[31] an indication that the male advantage does not originate in skeleton or musculature. Men excel at abstract mathematical reasoning, dominating the high end of the distribution of this trait. In a large study of precocious seventh-grade girls and boys who had done equally well on age-appropriate mathematics aptitude tests (the girls indicating no belief that "mathematics is for boys"), thirteen times as many boys scored above seven hundred on the mathematical portion of the Scholastic Aptitude Test, a test normed on high school seniors.[32] There is controversy about general intelligence, with some authorities maintaining that the mean male IQ somewhat exceeds the female, while others dissent. Arthur Jensen infers equality of male and female means on factorial g—pure intelligence—from null correlation between the g-loadings on various IQ tests and the size of the sex differences thereon;[33] Richard Lynn[34] considers test equality an artifact because girls tend to be developmentally ahead of the chronologically same-age boys they are tested against, with male superiority emerging only after age sixteen. All sides appear to accept a greater IQ variance among males. It is striking that, women's fluency notwithstanding, the greatest writers—Homer, Shakespeare, Goethe, Dante—have all been male. The monopoly on genius in this as in every other area would seem to make a male advantage in phenotypic intelligence highly likely.

You don't really need science to tell you all this; your grandma knew most of it. Feminists rail at these home truths as "stereotypes," a word that can be roughly translated as "generalizations I do not like." Many a sociologist will concede that stereo-types do describe observed reality—their robustness would otherwise be puzzling—but insist that they exaggerate. In fact, sex stereotypes are literally accurate.[35] Rather than dichotomizing the sexes into polar opposites, as per the stereotype about ste-reotyping, the ordinary person sees them as they actually are, populations with some overlap but differing means on a variety of behavioral variables, with laymen's esti-mates of mean differences closely matching those established psychometrically.[36]

Feminists, as noted, attribute these differences (when they admit them) to con-ditioning, from which it is inferred that women have been "limited." Arguably, the falsity of the premise makes criticism of feminist logic otiose, but still the fallacy of the inference should be noted. So long as the reinforcement to which boys and girls are exposed is not consciously contrived to yield male dominance or inhibit women, its existence (assuming it does exist and is as effective as feminists say) constitutes no wrong. Suppose that, moments after birth, genetically identical Jack and Jill are stranded by accident on adjacent tropical islands. By sheer chance Jack's island pre-sents challenges he can in every case overcome, while Jill's more difficult environ-ment leaves her constantly hurt and shaken. When they meet as adults, Jill—natu-rally enough—is timorous and defers to the more confident Jack. Has Jill been wronged? If so, by whom? Does the adult Jack or anyone else oppress her when he runs things, given that (because of past reinforcements) she wants and expects him to? What, precisely, does Jack have to apologize for? So long as nobody placed them on their islands *so that* Jack would end up in charge, the worst one can say is that Jack was lucky.

(Or was he? For suppose Jill has also developed the nurturing personality that female conditioning supposedly creates. Jill's warmer ways will win her more friends when they both rejoin society, and the protectiveness her personality evokes may prompt Jack to take better care of her than she could of herself. Men would appear to hold women in the highest regard, considering how many men have died defend-ing their women and children.)

But in any event social learning cannot explain sex differences. For one thing the proposed explanation is circular. Those "sexist" messages bombarding boys and girls—who sent them? Why are the womenfolk always expected to care for the chil-dren? Why do girls like cooperative and boys competitive games? What associated genius with men? That the sexism of preceding generations created a self-fulfilling prophecy is no answer, for pushed back far enough it requires either a first patriar-chal generation whose prejudices are left a mystery, or, most implausibly, "sexist" in-frahuman ancestors. This logical difficulty leads to empirical trouble. If the assign-ment of sex roles is biologically arbitrary, it should show chance divergence across unconnected societies, with females taught to be more competitive, mathematically able, and violent than males fifty percent of the time. (There being few biological limits on what children can be taught to call cats, we expect, and find, the name for that species to vary across languages.) Somewhere—among the Bantus, Dravidians, Maori, Sioux, or Dutch—men should be children's primary caretakers. Yet this is not seen. Indeed, conscious attempts to socialize women away from traditional sex roles, as on the Israeli Kibbutzim, have uniformly failed. That sex differences always go one way contradicts social learning theory.

Second, much sex-differentiated behavior begins too early to be taught; for instance, boys more than girls are drawn to unusual objects by age one,[37] well before attention can be controlled by reward. The converse point, that drives cannot be channeled by reinforcement before they appear, eliminates early conditioning as a shaper of sexual emotions not experienced until puberty. Taken literally, the idea that "sex is social, not biological,"[38] "socially constructed,"[39] and "whatever a given society eroticizes,"[40] implies that people could be trained to find doorknobs as appealing as they now find the opposite sex. Apart from distorting (to say the least) the phenomenology of desire, this idea leaves unexplained how anything can be "eroticized" before erotic impulses emerge at adolescence, already object-directed. Sexual desire is patently a genetic timed-release program, needing triggering stimuli during a critical period, perhaps, but in content grossly underdetermined by them. The cliché that all behavior is the outcome of genes plus environment offers no real compromise, for feminists will continue to disagree with nativists about what the genetic contribution consists of;[41] feminist environmentalists allow only a few general, all-purpose associative mechanisms, while nativists postulate richer, more specific, and often sex-coded endowments. And, as noted, all-purpose learning does not suffice.

Neurological

The inference to innate sex-differentiated mechanisms, although compelling, nonetheless remained circumstantial until advances in instrumentation, particularly magnetic resonance neuroimaging (MRI) and positron emission tomography (PET), brought within reach the holy grail of functionally significant neuroanatomical dimorphism.

Sheer neuroanatomic dimorphism has been known since Broca found a male advantage in gross brain mass, currently estimated at 15 percent.[42] Moreover, the widespread belief that this gap vanishes when body weight is fixed[43] has been shown[44] to be an error caused by the interplay of two sex differences. The ratio of brain mass to body size decreases as body size increases, and at roughly the same rate for men and women, but (a) the intercept of the male trend line is higher than that of the female line while (b) female mean body weight is lower than male, so the brain mass/body size ratio of the average women coincides with that of the (larger) average man. Because of the intercept difference, however, male brains outweigh female brains by about 125 grams for any fixed body size. What, if anything, this excess signifies (greater intelligence? more neurons for spatial processing?) is not known, although the conjunction of a similar decrement in brain size between whites and blacks with a large racial IQ gap,[45] in light of the (near-?) zero sex difference in IQ, suggests organizational differences in male and female brains.

Cognitive functioning has long been thought to be more bilateralized in women— that is, that women more than men think with both left and right cerebral hemi- spheres—primarily because injuries to specific brain sites impair men more severely.[46] Also, boys when blindfolded are better at identifying objects in their left than right hands, while girls show no hand bias;[47] since the left hemisphere (which oversees spatial processing) is known to control the right side of the body, males are appar- ently left-brained while girls show no preference.[48] There was consequently much excitement when a female advantage in the size of the corpus callosum, the nerve bundle connecting the hemispheres, was announced in 1982.[49] Yet this finding was still somewhat inconclusive, based as it was on brains obtained for autopsy, as was a related study on postmortem tissue that found a female advantage in the size of the anterior commissure (a fiber tract connecting the two lobes) and massa intermedia.[50]

More recently, though, MRI on live subjects has replicated this anatomical find- ing.[51] A related in vivo study found a rightward asymmetry in the planum temporale, "generally accepted as a structural substrate of left hemisphere dominance for lan- guage,"[52] correlated with right-handedness in men and left-handedness in women. Several other studies have found sex differences in the hypothalamus[53] and the bed nucleus of the stria terminalus,[54] both regions associated with maternal and sexual behavior in infrahuman mammals. The bed nucleus, for instance, contains binding sites for the female hormone oxytocin.

More recently still (February 1995), the Shaywitzes and their associates have im- aged the greater bilateralization of phonological processing in women.[55] Only the left portion of a region called the inferior frontal gyrus was visibly activated when male test subjects were asked to judge whether nonsense words rhymed, while the same task for female test subjects activated both the left and right portions of this region. (There was no sex/region interaction on a task involving semantic informa- tion.) Independently, the lateralization of verbal fluency has been shown to corre- late negatively, in both sexes, with the size of the sex-differentiated region of the corpus callosum.[56] Just prior to the Shaywitz phonological processing study, PET live brain imaging revealed sex differences in base rates of cerebral glucose oxida- tion, with women showing lower metabolism in temporal-limbic regions and the cerebellum, and men showing lower metabolism in the cingulate regions.[57] This study complements those described earlier, as the limbic system is associated with emo- tion rather than cognition, and its authors permit themselves to speculate that "the results suggest neural substrates for domains of human behavior related to both cog- nitive and emotional processing. They support a neurobiologic explanation of some sex differences in these behavioral dimensions and thus may help to explain sex-re- lated differences in behavior."[58]

The attribution of these neurological dimorphisms to postnatal exposure to sex- ism[59] would be far-fetched conceptually and empirically. Systematically divergent training of the sort males and females supposedly receive might be expected to re- wire their brains differently or strengthen different pathways but not differentiate them macrostructurally, just as training in different languages presumably produces microstructural rather than gross anatomical differentiation. Likewise, just as any two speakers of the same language probably differ microneuroanatomically because of variation in particulars of learning history,[60] within-sex variation in male and female experiences (whatever their group mean differences) should leave sex unpredictive of molar features of the brain. Empirically, brain development is nearly complete by the sixth year,[61] and the sexual differentiation of the nucleus of the preoptic area begins between ages two and four.[62] Sexism would have to begin working implausibly early by currently unknown mechanisms to explain the cited brain differences.

Hormonal

A nativist explanation of neuroanatomy is at hand, though, in the prenatal action of hormones; to cite an early statement of this hypothesis, "data bearing on the organizing action of androgen on the neural tissues destined to mediate sexual behavior [imply] the view that a part or parts of the central nervous system are masculine or feminine, depending on the sex of the individual."[63] Antenatality must be stressed because, while some behavioral sex differences do reflect simultaneous hormone levels—mathematical skill correlates in males with serum testosterone slightly below the male mean, in females with serum testosterone slightly above the female mean[64]—most hormones are variable enough in immediate effect to allow feminists to dismiss their importance.[65] Male and female brains most fundamentally differ, rather, through exposure to different chemicals in utero. All human brains start female; the male XY chromosome signals the gonads to produce testosterone, which in turn virilizes the developing brain between weeks eight and twenty-four of gestation. The nativist hypothesis holds that this is the period of psychosexual differentiation. Occasional system malfunctions putting individuals' neurologic sex at variance with their appearance permit critical tests of this hypothesis against its feminist rival.

Female congenital adrenal hyperplasiacs [CAH] are exposed to high levels of androgens in utero that masculinize their brains and genitals. These individuals normally undergo corrective surgery and hormonal treatment soon after birth, and are raised as females. Feminist theory predicts that such girls will go on to display stereotypically female traits while the nativist hypothesis predicts the presence of masculine traits. Every relevant study[66] has confirmed the latter, finding that CAH females are "tomboys" who prefer boys' toys like fire engines to girls' toys like dolls, functional to feminine clothing, and strenuous outdoor play. Conceivably their parents have treated these abnormal girls as boys, but Berenbaum and Hines (see note 66) found no correlation between degree of preference for male toys and either parents' reported encouragement of their daughters to act as girls or overt disease characteristics such as closed labias.[67] Also, girls prenatally exposed to progestins[68] but born with unvirilized genitalia and unexposed to special postnatal treatment are found to exhibit tomboyism as well.[69] One might wonder how the brain can be wired for anything as specific as toy preferences, but it does not have to be: prenatal androgens can explain the behavior observed by wiring for (say) the general higher activity levels permitted by fire engines but not dolls.

Complementary studies of males who respond atypically to androgens have comparable results. Genetic males with normal gonads whose tissues are insensitive to prenatal male hormones, leaving them with feminine nervous systems, develop characteristically female habits,[70] contrary to the feminist prediction. Again the issue might be raised of control for subjects' appearance and subsequent socialization, but such controls were in place in a natural experiment[71] involving thirty-three males with a genetic deficiency that prevented differentiation of their genital tubercles despite in utero receipt of normal doses of testosterone. Their virilized brains invisible, these female-looking individuals were raised as girls until the standard secondary male characteristics emerged at puberty. After puberty, the subjects were psychosexually male, contrary to the feminist prediction that their upbringing would feminize them.

There is evidence that cognitive factors are also hormonally controlled. Male idiopathic hypogonadics, masculinized normally in utero but sexually immature because of pituitary dysfunction at puberty, have been found to do less well on tests of spatial ability than either normal control males or acquired hypogonadics (males deficient in serum testosterone through postpubertal external causes).[72] Fetal androgens evidently lay a ground plan filled in by gonadic androgens released at puberty.

Evolutionary

Evolutionary theory confirms a nativist interpretation of available data by integrating them into a coherent picture.[73] Since selection for heritable gender dimorphisms is exactly what the theory predicts, all the multitudinous evidence for the theory supports that prediction as well. Unless mind transcends nature, the odds of the sexes being psychologically identical given the different adaptive problems they have faced are, as David Buss says,[74] "essentially zero."

Here is how natural + sexual selection creates the observed dimorphisms: The right moves for a replication-minded gene (that is, the phenotypic expressions that maximize its inclusive reproductive fitness) depend on whether it is housed in a male or female body. Males can reproduce thousands of times with metabolically cheap sperm, so smart genes in a male body make it crave sexual access to as many women as possible, carefully sensitizing it to observable signs of youth, health, and fertility: taut clear skin, commodious hips, shiny hair, a nice layer of adipose tissue.[75] A male gene also knows its competitors think similarly, so prepares its body to battle them over access to females by programming low thresholds of aggression toward unrelated males.

It must also win consent to intercourse from females, whose genes urge caution. A woman can bear at most twenty resource-hungry offspring, making each act of intercourse fraught with consequences for her. Women programmed for easy arousal were left holding the baby, fatal for the latter in the environment of human evolution if less so today. Genes that survived the Pleistocene tell females: care for your offspring; prefer men both able to provision them—that is, strong, high-status men—and willing to do so. Thus, female genetic interests reinforce male competitiveness, since vanquishing rivals also impresses the ladies. But female interests also start an arms race. Cads try to fool women, who respond by evolving cad detectors like coyness and fickleness, good gauges of how much stress a man will tolerate yet still pay court, hence how apt he is to stick around later. Men in turn become better faithful-mate mimics, eventually evolving romantic love—since the best way to appear to desire eternal union is actually *to* desire it.[76]

Sadly, it is also in the male's genetic interest that this desire lapse well before eternity is up, to be replaced by a renewed roving eye. Hence fidelity problems persist. Now, if the best thing for a man, in terms of fitness, is to impregnate lots of women while someone else pays the bills, the worst thing, carrying horrendous opportunity costs, is to forego reproductive effort while supporting a genetically unrelated child. Cuckoldry is genetic death, its avoidance a top priority powered by fierce emotions.[77] Vigilance against one's mate having intercourse with another male is highly adaptive, as is readiness to kill both transgressors should it be uncovered. (Again, the most effective deterrent against betrayal is to seem willing to punish it by death, and the best way to seem willing is to be willing.) A related male adaptation is preference for permanent mating with virgins, known not to be carrying another man's baby and with a track record predicting future fidelity. For females, by contrast, the great threat to fitness is not unwitting investment in another woman's child, but loss of her mate's resources. (Women couldn't parlay college degrees into remunerative careers during the Pleistocene.) Hence female jealousy radar will be more attuned to rivals for her mate's affections, with his intercourse with other women per se less dangerous, a prediction verified in a series of studies by Buss (see notes 23, 26, and 73). The feminist idea that male jealousy and a desire for chastity are rooted in capitalism and private property[78] is evolutionary nonsense. It is more likely that the concept of property evolved as a spur to protecting resources (such as women).

Natural selection plausibly explains further sex differences not predicted by social learning. The hunt, once a function of bands of related men, may be hypothesized to have selected for spatial ability, needed to track large animals, kill them with accurately thrown spears and stones, and find one's way home afterward. Moral consciousness would also have been an adaptation to the hunt: each man had to trust the others to do their jobs and divide the spoils in a mutually agreeable way. Superior female location memory is predictable from the baby-watching responsibility of ancestral woman, and again was predicted by evolutionary psychologists before its psychometric verification.[79]

Enough. The point is made. The behaviors of men and women make the most sense when seen as evolved for different but complementary ecological niches. One might also note how evolutionary biology explains the destructiveness of feminist ideals on male/female relations. Feminist attacks on traditional sexual morality amount to urging promiscuity and rejection of premarital chastity, attitudes that discourage long-term commitment (such as marriage) from a male, no matter how enlightened he might think himself to be.

IV

Each sex's unique suite of traits, and their interplay, corresponds closely to the social arrangements of which feminists complain. Men hold disproportionate power because they work harder to get it, work harder to get it because they want it more, and want it more because wanting power enhanced their fitness in their evolutionary environment. Everyone expects women to care for the children because women do care for the children; they care for the children because they want to more than men do; they want to as much as they do because wanting to once enhanced their fitness. There is a double standard because the sexes have dissimilar but congruent sexual desires, with each experiencing somewhat different forms of betrayal as most threatening. They have such emotions because. . . . Attributing these arrangements to "sexist conditioning" is an error.

It is axiomatic that no one can be impeded by desires he does not mind having. To say I was kept from being a doctor by my having no desire to be one, or a positive aversion to being one, would be absurd, a bad joke. Desires don't push or hinder; I can be pushed only by outside agencies, and my desires are not agencies outside me. They are me. True, desires one wishes weren't there are experienced as alien; insofar as a person wishes he didn't want the dessert he then eats, he needs liberation from his own gluttony.[80] But the average woman does not regret wanting to care for her children, or being less aggressive than most men. Men and women are perfectly happy with the emotions evolution gave them. How could they not be? Chronic inner conflict would be deselected. So it is an error to think of women's basic desires or the institutions founded on them as barriers to freedom.

Since all feminists believe that the basic social institutions are shaped by sexist conditioning and impede women's freedom, feminists—no matter what their subspecies—are as deeply in error about human nature and society as it is possible to be.

V

One can resist this conclusion by insisting that the variance of traits within the sexes so exceeds the group mean difference as to overwhelm it. This, however, would be a non sequitur. The mean IQ of American Jews is roughly twelve points above the American average, a much smaller gap than the roughly 125 points separating the brightest and dullest in each population. Yet this mean difference in IQ distributions, which entails dramatic tail effects—Jews are "overrepresented" at IQ levels above 130 by a factor of five—is why Jews at 2.5 percent of the population comprise nearly twenty-five percent of the university professors, doctors, and lawyers in the United States. (Is this evidence that Gentiles are victimized by philosemitism?) Mean differences need be nowhere near the size of within-group variance to be socially highly significant.

A second way to resist the conclusion is to claim that society exaggerates biological sex differences. That most women are not strong or aggressive enough to fight against men does not mean all are; hence all-male armies cannot be explained (or justified). The general response to this area is that the line between "biological" and "social" is illusory. Social institutions are further phenotypic expressions of underlying population genotypes. Among the traits genes code for are dispositions to seek out, or create, certain social and natural environments; behavioral geneticists speak in such cases of active gene/environment correlation.[81] It is likely that males innately seek out male allies when violence is necessary, with all-male fighting forces simply the aggregated upshot of many individual males acting this way. In its turn, there was selection for a tendency to look for male allies exclusively because searching out the rare serviceable female wasted too much time. It is impossible to say where in this reconstruction biology ends and societal exaggeration begins.

A third way to resist, related to the second, is to point out that man, alone of all the animals, can try to overcome his genes. "Is is not ought," the argument goes; the latter should guide what we do about the former. Even if women are innately more child-oriented than men, why can't society so change itself that this difference no longer matters? Thus Sara Ruddick takes the main moral of her discovery of the value of maternality to be that "good day-care centers with flexible hours would be established to which parents could trust their children from infancy on . . . assimilating men into childcare both inside and outside the home [and] requir[ing] men to relinquish power and their own favorable position."[82]

This line of resistance misconceives the import of the nativist findings presented, which is not prospective, but retrospective. These findings imply that conditions that feminists believe to have arisen from and to be sustained by wrongdoing in fact arise from and are sustained innocently by innate factors for which no one is responsible. They show that the main reason feminists offer for undoing these conditions, namely that these conditions are oppressive, must be withdrawn. I would add that, when the origin of a thing is found to have involved nothing wrong, our prospective attitudes toward it change as well.

A simple example. Suppose Jones was born with a slight genetic advantage in running speed over Smith, which results in his besting Smith in a footrace. Suppose too that Smith could have won with a year's special training. Surely that latter fact is irrelevant to the propriety of Jones' victory. Had things been different, Smith would have run faster, but so long as the way things were was fair—Jones didn't cheat, both ran the same distance—there is nothing wrong with the actual outcome. Suppose even that we knew when they were born that, absent direct human intervention, Jones would end up beating Smith. (One mediating factor was going to be extra track time spent by Jones because his innate speed made running pleasurable—his extra training not being a "social exaggeration" of the biological but a further expression of it.) Would that have warranted society—in practice, usually the government—annulling the Jones-Smith genetic gap by giving Smith the special training he would need to pull even? The answer seems to me an obvious no. Now suppose, finally, that we meet Jones and Smith midway through a series of races, all won by Jones so far. At first we might suspect the fix is in, and naturally feel that the conditions of their future encounters should be changed. But our attitude would surely relax once we discovered that Jones' victories were due to a genuine genetic advantage in speed. We would still expect Jones to keep winning, but no longer think that intervention was called for. We would be content to let is coincide with ought. If we believe an outcome disparity arose in some ethically dubious way, we will likely think it should be curbed in the future. But if we are convinced that the disparity was immaculate in conception, we view its continuation more equably. The more clearly we see that female mothering is due to innate factors, the less inclined we will be to urge its dissolution through day-care centers, and less resentful will we be of males' "favorable position."

It is striking that feminists insist ever more stridently on sex differences while retaining a mind-set only appropriate toward superficial bias artifacts. Chesire Calhoun calls for more attention to the sexes' divergence in "basic interests," yet the sole reason she gives for doing so is "avoidance of sexism"—quite failing to see that should it go deep enough, into biology, this divergence that she alleges is "detrimentally shaped" by the "location" of the sexes is not shaped by any human agency at all, and, therefore, not obviously a detriment. So too of feminist complaints about sexual harassment and marital rape, and insistence on sensitivity training for male soldiers, although these seem in the main simply more expressions of anti-male animus. To demand the physical and psychological protection of women because they are too weak to deal with male soldiers as equals concedes the traditional idea that women are unsuited to violence, and have no place in the war machine to begin with. Women's need for psychological protection from men in the workplace gives the lie to the avowal that women only want to be treated by men as equals (that is, as men treat each other), and concedes that women have not gone as far as men for reasons other than failure to be so treated.

There is no need to unearth further inconsistencies and absurdities. Nothing feminists say need be taken seriously.

NOTES

1. For example, see J. Richards, *The Skeptical Feminist* (Boston, Mass.: Routledge, 1980).

2. J. Rawls, *A Theory of Justice* (Cambridge, Mass.: Harvard University Press, 1971), 302. To be sure, Rawls seems to have in mind civil liberties, with the difference principle in holdings superceding market freedoms.

3. See "The Idea of Gender Difference Helps Keep the Reality of Male Dominance in Place," C. MacKinnon, *Feminism Unmodified* (Cambridge, Mass.: Harvard University Press, 1987), 3.

4. "Confusions about Innateness," the 1998 Warstofsky Lecture, The Graduate Center (City University of New York, November 4, 1998). Ironically, in the book under attack, *How the Mind Works* (New York: Simon and Schuster, 1998), Pinker is plainly unhappy to be discomfiting feminists. A similarly apologetic note is struck in Robert Wright's "Feminists, Meet Mr. Darwin," *The New Republic* (November 28, 1994): 34–46, a summary of the evolutionary argument for innate differences, and in Wright's *The Moral Animal* (New York: Vintage, 1994).

5. In fact, Hitler never justified his anti-Semitism by calling Jews inferior. The Nazi grievance was Jewish success, the overrepresentation of Jews as compared to Germans in science, medicine, theater, music, retailing, banking, and journalism. Some passages in Hitler's speeches curiously resemble the anti-male rhetoric of feminists and the antiwhite rhetoric of racial egalitarians. These points are made in detail in George Farron's unpublished monograph, *Nazism and the Holocaust*.

6. Further examples can be found in my *Feminism and Freedom* (New Brunswick, N.J.: Transaction, 1987).

7. *Feminism and Freedom*, 51–123.

8. MacKinnon, 50.

9. A. Eagly, "The Science and Politics of Comparing Women and Men," *American Psychologist* 50, 3 (1995): 145–58.

10. Jeanne Marecek, "Gender, Politics, and Psychology's Way of Knowing," *American Psychologist* 50, 3 (1995): 162–63. Whereas the issue is sex differences, Marecek alternates between "sex" and "gender."

11. On the evolution of sex itself see A. Anderson, "The Evolution of Sex," *Science* 257, (July 17, 1992): 324–26, and W. Hamilton, R. Axelrod, and R. Tanese, "Sexual Reproduction as an Adaptation to Resist Parasites," *Proceedings of the National Academy of Science* USA 87 (May 1990): 3566–73.

12. See Margarita Levin, "Caring New World," *The American Scholar* (Winter 1988): 100–6.

13. Carol Gilligan, *In a Different Voice* (Cambridge, Mass.: Harvard University Press, 1983).

14. Sara Ruddick, "Maternal Thinking," in *Women and Values*, ed. M. Pearsall (Belmont, Calif.: Wadsworth, 1986), 340–51; also see her *Maternal Thinking* (Boston: Beach, 1989).

15. "Maternal Thinking," 348.

16. "Maternal Thinking," 349.

17. Chesire Calhoun, "Justice, Care, Gender Bias," *Journal of Philosophy* 85 (September 1988): 451–63.

18. Bill Amend, *Black Bart Says Draw* (Kansas City, Mo.: Andrews & McNeel, 1991), 12.

19. See L. Kohlberg and R. Kramer, "Continuities and Discontinuities in Children and Adult Moral Development," in *Human Development* 12 (1969): 93–120; for a summary of the stages, see L. Kohlberg, *The Philosophy of Moral Development* (New York: Harper & Row, 1981), 409–12.

20. Kohlberg (1981, 354) responds somewhat similarly to an early version of Gilligan's

criticism, calling an ethics of "agape" an alternative to an ethics of justice that would simply not consider "justice problems."

21. Anyway, there is plenty of room for feeling and connectedness in classical (male) moral philosophy. Hume bases all moral distinctions on "sentiment" rather than "reason." Utilitarianism concerns itself exclusively with the positive and negative feelings generated by actions. Kant recognized imperfect duties arising from imperatives whose generalization is self-consistent, but which no one would want to see universal. And of course relatedness counts in every classical theory: Stoics, Kantians, Aristotelians, and Utilitarians all make room for a special duty to keep a date with, for example, a man one has promised to meet.

22. D. Brown, *Human Universals* (Philadelphia: Temple University Press, 1991), 91–92, 110.

23. See Brown; M. Daly and M. Wilson, eds., *Homicide* (New York: Aldine de Gruyter, 1988); R. P. Dobash et al., "The Myth of Sexual Symmetry in Marital Violence," *Social Problems* 39, 1 (1992): 71–91; D. Buss et al., "Sex Differences in Jealousy: Not Gone, Not Forgotten, and Not Explained by Alternative Hypotheses," *Psychological Science* 7, 6 (1996): 375.

24. Brown, 137.

25. Brown, 109. Women always prefer men taller than themselves.

26. D. Buss, *The Evolution of Desire* (New York: Basic Books, 1994), 127–29.

27. R. D. Clark and E. Hatfield, "Gender Differences in Receptivity to Sexual Offers," *Journal of Psychology and Human Sexuality* 2 (1989): 39–55; also see Buss, 73–96.

28. D. Kimura, "Sex Differences in the Brain," *Scientific American* (September 1992): 119–25. For similar results concerning somewhat older children, see K. Kerns and S. Berenbaum, "Sex Differences in Spatial Ability in Children," *Behavior Genetics* 21 (1991): 383–96.

29. D. Kimura, "Sex, Sexual Orientation and Sex Hormones Influence Human Cognitive Function," *Current Opinion in Neurobiology* 6 (1996): 259–63.

30. V. A. Mann et al., "Sex Differences in Cognitive Abilities: a Cross-cultural Perspective," *Neuropsychologia* 28 (1990): 1063–77.

31. Kimura 1996, 261.

32. C. Benbow and J. Stanley, "Sex Differences in Mathematical Ability: Fact or Artifact?" *Science* 210 (1980): 1282–84.

33. Arthur Jensen, *The g Factor* (Westport, Conn.: Praeger, 1998), 536–41.

34. Richard Lynn, "Sex Differences in Brain Size and Intelligence: A Paradox Resolved," *Personality and Individual Differences* 17 (1994): 257–71, and "Sex Differences in Intelligence: Some Comments on Mackintosh and Flynn," *Journal of Biosocial Science* 30 (1998): 555–59.

35. I endorsed the exaggeration view in *Feminism and Freedom* and endorse it of racial stereotypes in *Why Race Matters* (Westport, Conn.: Praeger, 1997). I know of no study like Swim's (see note 36) exonerating racial stereotypes.

36. J. Swim, "Perceived versus Meta-analytic Effect Sizes: An Assessment of the Accuracy of Gender Stereotypes," *Journal of Personality and Social Psychology* 66 (1994): 21–36.

37. S. Goldberg and M. Lewis, "Play Behavior in the Year Old Infant: Early Sex Differences," *Child Development* 40 (1969). Goldberg and Lewis attribute the difference to parental reinforcement.

38. MacKinnon, 52.

39. MacKinnon, 54. In full: "sexual desire in women, at least in this culture, is socially constructed as that by which we come to want our own self-annihilation."

40. MacKinnon, 53.

41. On the general contrast, see D. Symons, "If We're All Darwinians, What's the Fuss About," in *Sociobiology and Psychology: Ideas, Issues and Applications*, eds. C. Crawford, M. Smith, and D. Krebs (Hillsdale, N. J.: Erlbaum, 1987), 121–46.

42. A. Gibbons, "The Brain as 'Sexual Organ,'" *Science* (October 1991): 957–59.

43. K. Ho et al., "Analysis of Brain Weight: I: Adult Brain Weight in Relation to Sex, Race and Age; II: Adult Weight in Relation to Body Height, Weight, and Surface Area," *Archives of Pathology & Laboratory Medicine* 104 (1980): 635–39; 640–45.

44. C. Ankney, "Sex Differences in Relative Brain Size: The Mismeasure of Woman, Too?" *Intelligence* 16 (1992): 329–36; also see J. Rushton and C. Ankney, "Brain Size and Cognitive Ability: Correlations with Age, Sex, Social Class, and Race," *Psychonomic Bulletin and Review* 3 (1996): 21–36.

45. See *Why Race Matters*, 105–6, for details and references.

46. Kimura 1992, 1996. The classic study is H. Landsdell, "A Sex Difference in Effect of Temporal Lobe Neurosurgery on Design Preference," *Nature* 1994 (1962): 852–54.

47. S. Witelson, "Sex and the Single Hemisphere: Specialization of the Right Hemisphere for Spatial Processing," *Science* 193 (1976): 425–27.

48. The presumable adaptive advantage of lateralization is built-in redundancy, but it is not clear what advantage is conferred by the greater lateralization of females, or male left-brain dominance.

49. C. de Lacoste-Utamsing and R. Holloway: "Sexual Dimorphism in the Human Corpus Callosum," *Science* 216 (1982): 1431–32.

50. L. Allen and R. Gorski, "Sexual Dimorphism of the Anterior Commissure and Massa Intermedia of the Human Brain," *Journal of Comparative Neurology* 312 (1991): 97–104.

51. L. Allen et al., "Sex Differences in the Corpus Callosum of the Living Human Being," *Journal of Neuroscience* 11 (April 1991): 933–42.

52. L. Jäncke et al., "Asymmetry of the Planum Parietale," *NeuroReport* 5 (1994): 1161–63.

53. L. Allen et al., "Two Sexually Dimorphic Cell Groups in the Human Brain," *Journal of Neuroscience* 9 (1989): 497–506; D. Schwaab and M. Hofman, "Sexual Differentiation of the Human Hypothalamus: Ontogeny of the Sexually Dimorphic Nucleus of the Preoptic Area," *Developments in Brain Research* 44 (1988): 314–18.

54. L. Allen and R. Gorski, "Sex Difference in the Bed Nucleus of the Stria Terminalis of the Human Brain," *Journal of Comparative Neurology* 302 (1990): 697–706.

55. B. Shaywitz et al., "Sex Differences in the Functional Organization of the Brain for Language," *Nature* 373 (February 1995): 607–9.

56. M. Hines et al., "Cognition and the Corpus Callosum: Verbal Fluency, Visuospatial Ability, and Language Lateralization Related to Midsaggital Surface Areas of the Corpus Callosum," *Behavioral Neuroscience* 106 (1992): 3–14.

57. R. Gur et al., "Sex Differences in Regional Cerebral Glucose Metabolism During a Resting State," *Science* 267 (January 1995): 528–31.

58. Gur et al., 531.

59. And race differences in brain size to postnatal racism.

60. Cf. W. V. O. Quine's metaphor of topiary animals, identically shaped but partwise heteromorphic.

61. S. Blinkov and S. Glezer, *The Human Brain in Figures and Tables*, trans. B. Haigh (New York: Basic Books, 1968).

62. Swaab and Hofman.

63. W. Young et al. in "Hormones and Sexual Behavior," *Science* (1964): 216.

64. See Kimura 1996, 261, figure 3.

65. J. Richards refers sarcastically to "The Testosterone Contingent," in *The Skeptical Feminist*, 272.

66. J. Money, *Sex Errors of the Body* (Baltimore, Md.: Johns Hopkins University Press, 1968); J. Money and A. Erhardt, *Man and Woman, Boy and Girl* (Baltimore, Md.: Johns Hopkins University Press, 1972); J. Money, "Prenatal Hormones and Postnatal Sexualization in Gender Identity Differentiation," in *Nebraska Symposium on Motivation*, eds. J. Cole and R. Diensteber (Lincoln, Neb.: University of Nebraska Press, 1973): 221–95; A. Erhardt and S. Baker, "Fetal Androgens, Human Central Nervous System Differentiation, and Behavior Sex Differences," in *Sex Differences in Behavior*, eds. R. Friedman et al. (New York: Wiley, 1974), 455–66; A. Erhardt and H. Meyer-Blauberg, "Effects of Prenatal Hormones on Gender-Related Behavior," *Science* 211 (March 1984): 1312–18; S. Berenbaum and M. Hines, "Early Androgens are Related to Childhood Sex-Typed Toy Preferences," *Psychological Science* 3 (May 1992): 203–6.

67. The difference between time spent playing with male toys by CAH and control females was 0.89 standard deviations, quite large by social scientific standards.

68. Androgens seemingly must be converted into estrogen before they can affect cell nuclei, hence exogenous progestogen and estrogen can masculinize fetal brains.

69. J. Reinisch and W. Karow, "Prenatal Exposure to Synthetic Progestins and Estrogens: Effects on Human Development," *Archives for Sexual Behavior* 6 (1977): 257–88.

70. D. Mascia, J. Money, and A. Erhardt, "Fetal Feminization and Female Gender Identity in the Testicular Feminizing Syndrome of Androgen Insensitivity," *Archives for Sexual Behavior* 1 (1971): 131–42; J. Money, A. Erhardt, and D. Mascia, "Fetal Feminization Induced by Androgen Insensitivity in the Testicular Feminizing Syndrome," *Johns Hopkins Medical Journal* 123 (1968): 105–14.

71. J. Imperato-McGinley, et al., "Steroid 5a Reductase Deficiency in Man: An Inherited Form of Male Pseudohermaphroditism," *Science* 186 (1974): 1213–15; J. Imperato and R. Peterson, "Male Pseudohermaphroditism: The Complexities of Male Phenotypic Development," *American Journal of Medicine* 61 (1976): 251–72; J. Imperato-McGinley, T. Gaultier, and E. Strula, "Androgens and the Evolution of Male Gender Identity among Pseudohermaphrodites with 5a-Reductase Deficiency," *New England Journal of Medicine* 300 (22): 1233–37.

72. D. Hier and W. Crowley, "Spatial Ability in Androgen-Deficient Men," *New England Journal of Medicine* 306 (1982): 1202–5.

73. A few standard sources are D. Barash, *The Whisperings Within* (New York: Penguin, 1981); R. Dawkins, *The Selfish Gene* (Oxford: Oxford University Press, 1989); D. Buss (see note 23), "Evolutionary Psychology: A New Paradigm for Psychological Science," *Psychological Inquiry* 6 (1995): 1–30, and "Psychological Sex Differences: Origins Through Sexual Selection," *American Psychologist* (March 1995): 164–68; D. Symons, *The Evolution of Sex* (New York: Oxford, 1979); R. Trivers, *Social Evolution* (Menlo Park, Calif.: Benjamin, 1985); "Parental Investment and Sexual Selection," in *Sexual Selection and the Descent of Man*, ed. B. Campbell (New York: Aldine de Gruyter, 1972), 136–79; R. Frank, *Passion Within Reason* (New York: Norton, 1989); the essays by Buss, Daly and Wilson, and Ellis, as well as Symons

in C. Crawford, M. Smith, and D. Krebs, eds., *Sociobiology and Psychology: Ideas, Issues, and Applications* (Hillsdale, N.J.: Erlbaum, 1987); L. Barkow, L. Cosmides and J. Tooby, eds., *The Adapted Mind* (New York: Oxford, 1992). *The Behavioural and Brain Sciences* frequently runs articles with peer commentary on sociobiological (or as it is now called, evolutionary psychological) topics.

74. Buss, "Psychological Sex Differences," 164.

75. So beauty is not something "invented by Madison Avenue"; standards are culturally universal (see the discussion in Buss 1994, 52ff). A striking finding is that facial features near the average are found the most attractive, perhaps because they signal the absence of unusual, hence potentially harmful genes.

76. See the discussion in Frank of love and other emotions as precommitment doomsday devices; also see R. Ainslie, *Picoeconomics* (New York: Cambridge University Press, 1992).

77. Men are hundreds of times likelier to assault or kill their adopted children than their natural children.

78. See A. Johnson, *Strong Mothers, Weak Wives* (Berkeley, Calif.: University of California Press, 1988).

79. I. Silverman and M. Eals, "Sex Differences in Spatial Abilities: Evolutionary Theory and Data," in Barkow, Cosmides and Tooby, 533–49; see Buss 1995 for discussion.

80. See H. Frankfort, "Freedom of the Will and the Concept of a Person," *Journal of Philosophy* 68 (1971): 5–20.

81. See J. DeFries, J. Loehlin, and R. Plomin, "Genotype-Environment Interaction and Correlation in the Analysis of Human Behavior," *Psychological Bulletin* 34 (1979): 309–22; S. Scarr and K. McCartney, "How People Make Their Own Environments: A Theory of Gene-Environment Effects," *Child Development* 54 (1983): 424–35.

82. "Maternal Thinking," 349. (If she really valued maternality, surely the last thing she would want would be mothers handing over their children to hired strangers.)

15

Has Ally McBeal Destroyed Feminism, and Other Afterthoughts

Michael Levin

Were I to rewrite my main essay in light of Professor Tong's, I would specify the central complaint of feminism to be oppression rather than "injustice." Not that this change would make much difference overall, since the kind of injustice I had feminists complaining about is oppression—the forcible prevention of women from getting what they want and can achieve. And my response to the protest thus reformulated would be as before: male dominance, extant sex roles, and sexual norms result from the biologically differentiated preferences of men and women. Since biology never oppressed anyone, women are not oppressed.

I must also thank Professor Tong for inadvertently confirming my attribution. She cites many feminist denominations, but one doctrinal tenet keeps popping up: "Liberal feminists" deplore "gender-based oppression"; "[S]econd-wave radical cultural feminists aimed to establish that all women are oppressed"; "Third-wave feminists want to understand . . . gender oppression." There are "self-critical feminists who aim to combine the best of second-wave liberal feminism and radical feminism with the best of black feminism, women-of-color feminism, working-class feminism, pro-sex feminism, and so on." And all these syncretists agree on "'the multiple, constantly shifting bases of oppression.'" We are far from done, for "Third-wave difference feminists, sometimes referred to as postmodern feminists, are not to be confused with second-wave radical cultural feminists"; for these "third-wave postmodern difference feminists" the chief issue is the struggle in "patriarchal socio-cultural contexts." Nor can one neglect the "third-wave multicultural and global feminist" who "fight[s] to end sexist oppression." To be sure these sects all sound similar, and Professor Tong lapses into nonsense seeking to distinguish them, as when she takes one third-wave postmodern difference feminist's construal of "feminine" as "an interpretive grid pointing to a conception of women neither as unproblematically unified nor as inseparably divided, but rather as multiple and therefore capable of unifying and dividing at will." (Pay attention; this will be on the final.) Perhaps the idea is that First-world second-wavers thought that all women are oppressed while Third-World third-wavers think that different women are oppressed in different ways. Whatever; it is oppression *über alles*.

Professor Tong's summary also confirms by omission that none of these sects pays the least attention to biology. She herself devotes but one sentence to it. Finally, I thank her for deploring the 76 cents to the male dollar that women make and the less than one percent representation of women among Fortune 500 chief executive officers, substantiating the claim that feminists will settle for nothing less than proportionality of outcome.

Although Professor Tong does not do so, most feminists, when proof of male oppression is demanded, wave the bloody shirt of rape. So perhaps I should say a few words on that topic.

According to the FBI's Uniform Crime Statistics, there are about 140,000 rapes per year in the United States, a figure that has fallen in the last decade along with other violent crimes, and far fewer than feminists would have one think. At the same time there are about 15,000 murders annually, the vast majority victimizing men. Likewise, mostly men are the victims of the million-plus robberies and assaults perpetrated each year. In other words, most societal violence is perpetrated by men against men, a curious circumstance if violence against women is meant to control them. Just who is controlling the men? It should also be kept in mind that the majority of rapes are committed by blacks.[1] The chief oppressors (if that is how one wishes to view the matter) are thus not males of the dominant group, but of a racial minority that the dominant group supposedly oppresses along with women. That picture of the situation cannot be considered plausible.

Neither can the statement that rape functions to intimidate women, that is, that it exists and persists because it intimidates women, and further that men commit rape with the purpose of intimidation consciously in mind. (If the statement does not mean the latter, what does it mean? By what mediating mechanism other than intent can rape persist because of this supposed effect?) And indeed feminists do subscribe to this view, as witness Susan Brownmiller, according to whom rape is "a conscious process of fear and intimidation by which all men keep all women in a state of fear."[2] It is very doubtful that the typical rapist has such thoughts in mind.

Rape is heavily penalized everywhere. In many societies it is a capital crime. Why would other men execute allies who help them stay in charge?

In any event rape has nothing to do with any of the other phenomena feminists consider oppressive, such as the assignment of child-rearing to women or male dominance in extrafamilial hierarchies. Women do not gravitate to childcare because they fear being raped.

So, has Ally McBeal destroyed feminism? I normally wouldn't discuss movies or TV I have not seen, but, through promos and reviews, I have formed a general idea of the show. Professor Tong, like others, calls Ally "postfeminist," but this means only that she leads the life feminists advocated when such advocacy was less socially endorsed. In truth, Ally is their poster girl. As a lawyer she pursues a traditionally male career, which involved, I gather, a break with the love of her life. That's what feminists call smashing stereotypes to achieve full personhood. She has, I also gather, taken control of her own sexuality and expresses it shamelessly; that is, she is promiscuous. The bathroom at her law firm is unisex; how much more devoutly egalitarian and antisexist can one be? And it ill becomes feminists to upbraid Ally for self-involvement, for they flatter themselves that social institutions exist for no other reason than to keep them down. Wasn't it feminists whose elevated consciousnesses gave them the right to lecture any male unfortunate enough to hold a door or whistle?

Ally's sin is her obsession with getting married and having children, longings that expose the ugly underside of feminism. When she entered the public world, a woman's life was supposed to blossom like a flower opening so wide that family and children would no longer circumscribe it but instead become just one good among many and perhaps foregone for their sake. And, in one way, this is what has happened. As women have pursued careers the birthrate has dropped. Fertility decreases linearly with education as do marital rates, and age of first marriage for women rises. Part of the reason, of course, is that college (postgraduate work even more so) takes time. The launch window for childbearing is much narrower for a woman who puts off thinking about marriage to her mid-twenties than for one who looks forward to marriage at eighteen. Another reason is female hypergamy, the preference for males with higher status. How many women eminent in the professions marry blue-collar workers? Feminists themselves want only very high-status mates.[3] When a woman achieves a status as high as Ally's, she has priced herself out of the reach of the great many men below her, leaving her relatively few to marry. Even the usually clear-eyed Norman Podhoretz is misled by optimism here. Seeing Ally's popularity as a sign of return to normalcy, he predicts that she "will undoubtedly settle down some day to become a faithful wife and embrace 'family values' (but of course without being so square as to call them that)."[4] Unlikely: she's too old, there's nobody on the horizon, her status is too high, and she sleeps around too much. She'll have no trouble finding men willing to have sex with her. But she can look forward to little more.

Feminists hate Ally for letting the cat out of the bag. Women whose biological clocks run too long risk a life their genes program them to find empty. The urgings of their Pleistocene-designed nervous systems that women reproduce, more than anything else, is the source of the crisis in feminism. Third-wavers are radical second-wavers approaching menopause.

Unfortunately, Professor Tong does not disclose which of the positions in her historical survey she thinks correct, or most defensible. Still, she ends with a list of ten steps that, to judge from their prominence, she would like to see taken by large numbers of people, particularly in the West. Basically, her list adumbrates the left-wing Ludditism tried but never permanently established on the communes of the 1960s. Far though these ideas take us from feminism, they still deserve rebuke.

The central demand of hippie socialism is that production be restricted to satis-faction of "needs" rather than unnecessary wants. Professor Tong does not consider that modern medicines handsomely meeting the presumable "needs" of life and health require the technology that has developed only in the West's want-serving free markets. Developing, testing, producing, and distributing antibiotics—cheap anti-biotics—takes high-tech laboratory equipment, trucks, airplanes, and computers. You cannot make lasers without the kind of wealth that unbridled capitalism produces, and without lasers you cannot have the laser surgery under development for various tumors, including breast cancer. Or perhaps they can be replaced by magic, whose acceptance is suggested in Professor Tong's fifth tenet. I've rubbed my eyes several times, but that sentence remains: "People should combine contemporary science, technologies, and knowledge with ancient wisdom, traditions, and even magic." Surely Professor Tong cannot actually believe this.

There is the predictable attack on private property. As part of "socialist-transfor-mative ecofeminism," all natural resources should be viewed "as community goods." Right; Jones spends years extracting oil from the ground, and then he just, what, gives it away? It's been tried, in the former Soviet Union and the soon to be the formerly Communist China. Those experiments, costing millions of lives, reducing two talented populations to poverty, proved that socialism fails under any name, in-cluding "transformative" or "ecofeminist." And it fails not because of the selfishness of patriarchal males, but because competitors diverting resources to genetic relatives would outreproduce any gene daft enough to program socialism.

I do agree that not everyone can have it all, and see glimmers of common sense in "Third-World third-wave" feminists who recognize this. There is simply too little energy to produce for all six billion people on the Earth the amenities that 750 million Europeans and Americans enjoy. But, to judge by her emphasis on "subsis-tence production," Professor Tong takes this to mean that Americans will have to learn to do without, an inference that assumes—as I think Professor Tong does—that America and Europe are rich because the rest of the world is poor, that the First World got rich by exploiting the Third World. This is pernicious foolishness. The First World prospered through the unmatched inventiveness of its members.

It is not surprising that Professor Tong should fall for economic nostrums the rest of the world has thankfully begun to put behind it. As I said in my main essay, femi-nists are antiexperts; they are reliably wrong about everything.

NOTES

1. About 20 percent of their victims being white females; white males virtually never rape black females.

2. Susan Brownmiller, *Against Our Will* (New York: Simon & Schuster, 1975), 15. For Brownmiller, the function of rape is to teach women that "we exist for men."

3. See B. Ellis, "The Evolution of Sexual Attraction," in C. Crawford, M. Smith, and D. Krebs, *Sociobiology and Psychology: Ideas, Issues, and Applications* (Hillsdale, N. J.: Erlbaum, 1987), 273. Female medical students, already fairly high in status, are choosier about sexual relations than they were previously. As Ellis observes, this disconfirms the feminist explanation of hypergamy as female compensation for powerlessness, which predicts that women should relax their choice criteria as they gain independent power.

4. Norman Podhoretz, "'Sexgate,' the Sisterhood, and Mr. Bumble," *Commentary*, June 1998.

16

Confessions of a Winged Woman: Flying Free from a Constricting Cage

Rosemarie Tong

Twenty-five years ago I was riding the second wave of feminism together with a group of women and, yes, men. We were convinced that all human beings, irrespective of their gender, race, or class, deserved an equal opportunity to develop themselves as they saw fit in both the private and public realm. We believed then as we do now that to be full human beings, individuals had to be relatively successful in both love and work; and we believed then as we do now that human beings have a responsibility to construct just social, economic, and political institutions.

In the 1970s I was probably someone Michael Levin would have classified as an extreme exponent of the nurture side of the perennial nature-nurture controversy although, even at that time, I did not agree with Kate Millett and Elizabeth Janeway that "the sexes are inherently in everything alike . . ."[1] or that ". . . the workings of society and culture, by themselves, are perfectly capable of producing . . ."[2] all male-female differences. I had completed enough natural science courses to know that human beings were animals, shaped to some extent by their biology; but I had also taken enough humanities and social science courses to know that human beings were more than animals—that they were capable of constructing biology-modifying social environments. As a result, I agreed with Simone de Beauvoir that "Biology is not enough to answer the question: Why is woman the *Other*?"[3] Additionally, nothing in Levin's essay has persuaded me to change my mind that woman is *other* than man for economic, psychological, and cultural reasons as well as biological ones. I also believe that if women want to be *selves* like men are *selves*, women together with men can and should use the liberating powers of education and the equalizing powers of law to help produce such a state of affairs.

I have more memories than these of the 1970s, however. I remember being profoundly disturbed by the twentieth-century sociobiologists Levin finds so impressive. I am not certain what occasioned the intensity of my reaction against them,

225

given that the doctrines of sociobiology are anything but novel. In fact, sociobiology is simply the latest theory in a series of theories that teach biological determinism; that is, "the belief that genes determine behaviors and that social relationships and cultures have evolved through the genetic transmission of behavioral traits and characteristics."[4] Sociobiologists use biology to explain why men are dominant and women subordinate in most societies. In so doing, they make claims that feminists find just as "ideological" and "political" as the claims that Levin dismisses as feminist hyperbole.

Assessing the claims of current sociobiologists, Professor Ruth Bleier, a professor in the Neurophysiology Department and the Women's Studies Program at the University of Wisconsin-Madison, comments that:

> . . . Sociobiologists reinforce ancient stereotypes of women as coy, passive, dependent, maternal, and nurturant and base these temperaments in our genes. At the same time, and despite their liberal protestations, they explain and justify the existence of women's social and physical oppression by asserting the genetic origins, and hence inevitability, of rape, the sexual double standard, the relegation of women to the private world of home and motherhood, and other forms of the exploitation of women.[5]

Bleier points to numerous conceptual and methodological flaws in the writings of sociobiologists, including the political biases that underline their extrapolations of certain nonhuman animal behaviors to the human animal population.

In particular, she focuses on the writings of David Barash (cited favorably by Levin) whose reflections on rape in the plant and animal community show that he has no hesitancy about being labeled "politically incorrect." The quotes Bleier selects for scrutiny are from Barash's *The Whisperings Within*:

> . . . plants with male flowers will 'attempt' to achieve as many fertilizations as possible. How is this done? Among other things they bombard female flowers with incredible amounts of pollen, and some even seem to have specially evolved capacities to rape female flowers, by growing a pollen tube which forces its way to the ovary within each female.[6]

The fact that Barash uses the word "rape" to describe the "activities" of plants suggests to Bleier that Barash views rape as a natural, indeed "innocent" action. Her suspicion seems warranted as Barash's further reflections on plant rape indicate; he writes:

> Plants that commit rape . . . are following evolutionary strategies that maximize their fitness . . . We human beings like to think we are different. We introspect, we are confident that we know what we are doing, and why. But we may have to open our minds and admit the possibility that our need to maximize our fitness may be whispering somewhere deep within us and that, know it or not, most of the time we are heeding these whisperings.[7]

Bleier also notes that Barash's reflections on rape extend from the plant to the bird community. She stresses that according to Barash, "mallard rape" and "bluebird adultery" may help us better understand human rape,[8] and that "in their own criminally misguided way," human rapists who can't get women to have sex with them voluntarily are not really much different from "the sexually excluded bachelor mallards."[9] These rapists are just "doing the best they can do to maximize their fitness." Perhaps, I am just an old-fashioned believer in free will as well as feminism, but I do believe that human rapists, unlike "sexually excluded bachelor mallards," can prevent themselves or be prevented by others from raping women.

In using Bleier's work *selectively* to comment on sociobiologists, I do not wish to deny biology's role in *partially* shaping human behavior. In fact, over the past twenty-five years or so I have become increasingly interested in the ways that biology and society interact to produce male and female differences. Although I do not think that biology is destiny, I am equally convinced that human beings cannot be shaped randomly by society. Moreover, it is, as Levin implies, a mistake for feminists, or anyone else for that matter, to try to change those biologically connected and socially constructed human behaviors that most men and women show little or no interest in changing, provided that these behaviors are not seriously harmful to one's self or others.

When second-wave feminists, the feminists of the 1970s, first appeared on the scene, many of them were motivated by what historians of feminism currently label "liberal feminist thought." This feminist perspective receives its classic formulation in Mary Wollstonecraft's *Vindication of the Rights of Women*,[10] John Stuart Mill's "Subjection of Women,"[11] and the nineteenth-century women's suffrage movement. Its main tenet is that female subordination is rooted in a set of customary and legal constraints that block women's entrance to and success in the so-called public world. Liberal feminists maintain that because traditional society has the *false* belief that women are by nature far less intellectually and physically capable than men, it has unfairly excluded women from the academy, the forum, and the workplace. Thus, if contemporary society wishes to be just, it should give women the same opportunities as it gives men to gain entrance to and succeed in the public domain. Reasoning that if 1970s women wanted men's power, prestige, and status, they would have to prove that women are the same as men, it made sense in second-wave liberal feminists' estimation to minimize men's and women's biological differences and to insist on the strong role socialization plays in the construction of masculine and feminine behavior.

As it so happened, second-wave liberal feminists found an impressive array of evidence to support men's and women's "sameness." Carefully analyzing the sex-role socialization research done between the early 1950s and early 1980s in the United States, Lenore Weitzman and others showed how U.S. parents, siblings, friends, acquaintances, and teachers reward children who exhibit socially approved gender behaviors and punish children who manifest socially disapproved gender behaviors.

In particular, Weitzman pointed to numerous studies that demonstrated that because *typical* U.S. parents want their daughters to be "passive, nurturing, and dependent and their sons to be aggressive and independent,"[12] they "directly or indirectly punish aggression in their daughters and passivity and dependence in their sons."[13]

Not content to study only *typical* U.S. parents, Wietzman underscored the fact that an increasing number of U.S. parents are anything but "typical" in the sense of being white, middle-class, of northern European ancestry, and oriented toward the values of a consumption-driven, materialistic culture. How forcefully parents require their children to exhibit stereotypical male-female behaviors depends on their social class and ethnic background, as well as the number, spacing, and sex ratio of their children, and finally, their children's individual temperaments.[14] In this connection, it is important to stress that Nancy Chodorow, for example, has hypothesized that families in which men and women dual parent their children will probably produce children who will exhibit both male and female behaviors in equal proportion.[15] Chodorow, and those who reason like her, speculate that if children were reared equally by both their mothers and fathers, boys and girls would grow up equally capable of merging with and separating from others, of knowing when to be dependent on others and when to be independent of others, and of valuing the rewards of the private and public realms, respectively. Children reared equally by both their parents would no longer view the home as woman's domain and the office as man's domain. On the contrary, they would grow up thinking that all human beings should divide their time equally between work in the public world and intimacy and domesticity in the private world.

The point is that although all children are, with rare exception, born as biological males or biological females, their *rearers* outside as well as inside the home will affect just *how* masculine and feminine they act. In this connection, I could not help but notice Levin's suggestion that it is not simply male biology but *Jewish* male biology that accounts for the high proportion of Jewish men in the professions.[16] Perhaps this is so, but equally plausible to me is Fred Strodbeck's suggestion that diverse socialization practices best explain this remarkable phenomenon.[17] In comparing the socialization practices of Italian and Jewish mothers in encouraging achievement motivation in their sons, Strodbeck found that although both Italian and Jewish mothers had the same success aspirations for their sons, Italian mothers were much more willing than Jewish mothers to show love for their unsuccessful as well as their successful sons. In other words, the Italian mothers typically communicated feelings of unconditional love to their sons, whereas the Jewish mothers typically made it clear to their sons that successful sons would be loved and accepted far more than unsuccessful sons. In Strodbeck's estimation, it is the fear of losing their mothers' love that motivates Jewish boys to strive harder for success than Italian boys do.[18]

According to Weitzman, Strodbeck's line of reasoning suggests that were all or most U.S. parents willing to reward masculine and feminine behaviors equally in both their sons and daughters, more girls would feel free to adopt the kind of "masculine" behaviors that lead to success in the public realm and more boys would feel free to adopt the kind of "feminine" behaviors that lead to success in the private realm. But, notes Weitzman, despite the fact that an increasing number of U.S. parents are already encouraging "masculine" behavior in their daughters (even if they aren't also encouraging "feminine" behavior in their sons), relatively few women are achieving total success in the traditionally male occupations and professions.

In the spirit of a true scientist—that is, someone who is indeed committed to objectivity—Weitzman searches current studies for possible answers to why most U.S. "power brokers" are male. Significantly, the answers Weitzman finds to her questions are not the biological answers that Levin favors. Rather than blaming women's chromosomes and hormones for existing gender gaps, Weitzman speculates that there are two possible reasons why women motivated to be high achievers by their parents and others do not in fact become high achievers. The first is that women are channeled to achieve success in a different direction than men are;[19] for example, in the direction of marrying someone who is a high achiever, having a child who is a high achiever, or working for someone who is a high achiever. Noting that relatively few young women are currently going to college for the purposes of finding a husband, however, Weitzman dismisses the "vicarious achievement" reason as a weak explanation for why there are not more high-achieving women in the United States today.[20] She offers, instead, a second reason for this phenomenon. According to Weitzman, the real reason why women aren't "making it" en masse in the public realm is that they "are denied real opportunities for advancement and are discriminated against at every stage of the process leading to a professional position. . . ."[21] Only "when women are treated equally, paid equally, and given equal opportunity for advancement,"[22] says Weitzman, will we be able to truly test the impact of socializing women to succeed in the public realm. Only then will we know whether there is something about female biology that keeps women running back to the private domain no matter how much society tries to socialize them to enter the public domain.

Interestingly, five years after she singled out so-called "structural impediments" as the primary reasons for women's relative lack of success in the public realm, Weitzman suggested that the basic cause of women's continuing subordination to men in the workplace might be something about the "subtle ways" in which women are socialized even by parents and teachers who want their daughters and female students to be lawyers, doctors, and corporate executives.[23] Weitzman claims that most U.S. women, irrespective of their race and class differences, are socialized to be care giving.[24] Although Weitzman believes that an other-directed orientation is socially valuable, she suggests that to the extent this orientation is associated nearly exclusively with women, it serves to limit women's success in the public realm. She cites sociologist Teresa Marciano's argument that women's traditional virtues work to women's disadvantage in the private realm, and particularly in the public realm. Women, claims Marciano,

. . . have had to learn first to be conscious of their needs and then to value them as strongly as they value the needs of others. This applies to salary, task sharing, work assignment, ranking in firms, area of specialization—to mention just a few—and in the absence of raised consciousness, women will compromise or give in far more than will men.[25]

To be sure, Levin could respond to Weitzman and Marciano that women can't be "socialized out" of their other-directed orientation because the source of this orientation is female biology; but I believe there is considerable evidence that women can be taught to care for themselves as well as others and to value their own interests, desires, and achievements as much as those of others. In fact, I believe that morality demands that women do this, as much as it demands that men learn how to care for others as well as themselves and to value others' interests, desires, and achievements as much as their own. To be a morally developed person is to be a person who values all persons equally—who has equal respect and consideration for all persons, including one's self. Becoming such a person requires an effort of the will. It does not come "naturally," for if it did saints and heroes would be far less rare than they are in our society and others like it. Moreover, and, precisely because it is difficult for people to become fully morally developed individuals, it is in society's best interests to provide all individuals with the benefits—equitable education, laws, occupational and professional opportunities, family support systems, and so on— that typically enable individuals to do and be the best human beings they can. Not only do women need more access to the rewards and challenges of the public world, men need more access to the rewards and challenges of the private world. To suggest, as Levin does, that anyone truly believes that diaper-changing counters in men's rooms can effect the kind of changes in men's behavior[26] our society so desperately needs is to trivialize the importance of society's ability to enable men as well as women to become better persons than they currently are.

Levin repeatedly invokes *the* facts. What he does not always acknowledge is the ideological perspective that provides the interpretation of the facts he invokes. Moreover, absent from Levin's presentation of the facts is any mention that respected scientists such as Ruth Bleier,[27] Ruth Hubbard,[28] and Anne Fausto-Sterling[29] have offered compelling, competing interpretations of the same facts. Each of these feminist scientists is very familiar with the work of their nonfeminist, sociobiological counterparts, which they aim to assess objectively even as they take it to task vigorously. Of significance is the fact that these feminist scientists, unlike their nonfeminist, sociobiological counterparts, openly confess that their feminist politics might indeed cause them to "bias" their interpretation of the facts. Anne Fausto-Sterling is particularly honest about this possibility. She comments:

> The reader is by now in a position to ask me a tough question. I have mentioned scientists who fail to maintain their objectivity, suggesting that blind spots are an inherent aspect of science and are more frequent and dangerous when one studies socially

urgent topics. In writing this book, am I guilty from a feminist standpoint of just what I accuse others of doing from a nonfeminist one? My answer, of course, must be no. In this book I examine mainstream scientific investigations of gender by looking closely at them through the eyes of a scientist who is also a feminist. Because of my different angle of vision, I see things about the research methods and interpretations that many others have missed. Once pointed out, much of what I have to say will seem acceptable, even to those whose research I criticize; but some of what I write will be controversial.[30]

Feminist scientists are not afraid of *good* scientific data about men's and women's biological differences. On the contrary, they see in these data some of the information that health-care practitioners need to address women's particular health concerns and that teachers need to help their female students compete in a world in which science, mathematics, and technology reign supreme. However, feminist scientists still insist that *context* mediates and modulates the role that biological facts play in men's and women's lives. No doubt, certain biological facts probably played a very large role in people's lives when men made "a living tracking down mammoths" and women helped out by "digging up tasty roots."[31] But these same biological facts play but a small role in our contemporary world where we do most of our hunting and gathering at grocery stores. Further minimizing the role that biology currently plays in our individual and collective destiny is the fact that our communications technologies seem to require not active people, but people who can sit in front of computers for hours on end.

Moreover, our reproduction-controlling and reproduction-assisting technologies serve to erode the traditionally privileged position of genes in our lives. Genetic parenthood loses its force in a world of sperm and egg donors, surrogate mothers, and blended families. Women and men, as Levin correctly points out, do not need each other as much as they used to, a state of affairs that seems to worry Levin overly much. To be sure, a world in which sexual dimorphism is not rigidly maintained, and in which women (thanks to cloning) may soon not need men to reproduce, and in which men (thanks to the projected artificial womb and cloning) may soon not need women to reproduce, is a world that is bound to frighten many of us. Indeed, a world in which men's and women's basic reproductive roles are fundamentally altered causes *me* some concerns. But these concerns are not great enough for me to long for the days in which women were viewed first as vehicles of human reproduction, and second as persons.

My reluctance to go back to the world that existed before the second wave of feminism hit the United States in the 1970s is, of course, shared by other feminists. However, contrary to what Levin suggests, it is also a reluctance shared by many U.S. men and women who do not identify themselves as feminists. Increasingly, college-educated men as well as college-educated women, for example, claim that they want an "egalitarian marriage"[32] in which both spouses have careers and in which both spouses share the burdens and blessings of rearing children and doing domestic chores. Of course, not all men and women share the desire for an egalitarian marriage. Some would prefer a traditional marriage distinguished by stereotypical gender roles and duties. However, the current U.S. economy, coupled with Americans' materialism, if nothing more, will propel wives into the workplace and husbands into the nursery if only to make the kind of living that Americans associate with the so-called good life. Admittedly, not all women who work want to work, and relatively few women want the kind of high-powered professional careers that keep people in the office sixteen hours a day. But the point is, most men also do not want this type of life, and I predict that it will become more apparent in the new millennium as men increasingly gain the courage to express their appreciation of life in the private as well as the public realm.

Men and women are not nearly as different as Levin would have us believe. Despite the fact that he discredits the objection that differences within the same sex are greater than differences between the sexes, the fact is that they are. A basic understanding of biological sex differences is based on acknowledging that hormones—particularly the androgens, estrogens, and progestins—are responsible for differentiation of the sexes.[33] However, even though males and females differ in the amounts of each hormone they produce, within each sex there is also a considerable range of secretions of each hormone.[34] Everyday observations tell us that we have seen men with so-called female characteristics (for example, shorter than average height, smaller body frame, higher voice) and women with so-called male characteristics (for example, taller than average height, larger body frame, deeper voice). Clearly, hormones and biological differences do not rigidly define human bodies; neither do they rigidly define personalities, mental abilities, and talents. Environmental, rearing, cultural, and educational differences contribute to differences between humans. Psychologist Virginia Valian affirms: "Biological sex differences arise through the actions of sex hormones operating in our physical and social environments."[35]

In light of the connections and interplay between biology, physical environment, and social environment, Levin's statement—" . . . if innate sex differences rather than oppression explain the relative positions of men and women, should it turn out that women are 'held back' not by external impediments but their own nature, male preeminence is not unjust"[36]—is unclear. Men and women are obviously different in terms of innate sex differences, including organs and hormones. But as pointed out above, hormone levels, for example, are not equal for all males (as a group) and all females (as a group). For a woman to be "held back" by her own nature—for example, her hormone levels, which generally differ from the male average levels—means that all women who are oppressed must be equal to each other, that they all must be equally below men in some hormonal capacity. And, by the way, this means that all men who enjoy status as pre-eminent oppressors must be equal to each other. This is not reality and, as mentioned above, is refuted by everyday observations of human beings with a mixture of abilities, talents, interests, and personality traits.

Also significant in showing that biology should not be the sole focus of why women as a group are oppressed is the fact that science and technology are currently offering numerous ways to circumvent or alter the biology given to humans genetically. The fact that it is increasingly easier for human beings to modify their biological endowment means, contrary to Levin, that the question of *ought* human beings do so is all the more important. In the future, we will have the capacity to alter human beings' basic physical, intellectual, and even moral attributes. According to LeRoy Walters and Julie Gage Palmer, genetic enhancement projects will have both health-related and non-health-related applications. Health-related applications will probably include the *physical* one of immunization against infectious diseases, the *intellectual* ones of eliminating the genes associated with mental retardation and senile dementia, and the *moral* one of eliminating the genes that contribute to sociopathic behavior.[37] Additionally, non-health-related applications will probably include the *physical* ones of reducing the need for sleep and increasing human longevity; the *intellectual* ones of increasing the efficiency of long-term memory and improving the cognitive functioning of people who already fall in normal ranges; and the *moral* one of adding the genes that stimulate friendly and cooperative behavior. Given the ambitious scope of these projects, improving women's mathematical skills and diminishing men's aggressiveness through genetic intervention is well within the realm of possibility. Therefore, the idea that biology is destiny, that biology seals the fate of humans, seems increasingly unconvincing as the human species enters the third millennium and it becomes ever more imperative for us to consider what *kind* of human beings we want to be.

I invite Michael Levin to look forward optimistically to the third millennium instead of looking backward nostalgically to the first millennium. Our physical and biological evolution is slowing down, as our mental and moral evolution is speeding up. It is time for all men and women to stop fighting old wars and start building new bridges between the sexes. I cannot understand why Levin resists feminism so ferociously, for all that feminists really want is a world in which men and women can equally strive to be whole persons, participate in and contribute to their communities in the ways they choose, and be all that they have the capacity and desire to be.

NOTES

1. Quoted by Michael Levin, "Maritime Policy for a Flat Earth," in this volume, 199–200; originally from Kate Millet.

2. Levin, "Maritime Policy," 200; originally from Elizabeth Janeway.

3. Simone de Beauvoir, *The Second Sex*, 2nd ed., trans. H. M. Parshley (New York: Vintage Books, 1974), 41.

4. Ruth Bleier, *Science and Gender: A Critique of Biology and Its Theories on Women* (New York: Pergamon Press, 1984), 46.

5. Bleier, 46.

6. David Barash, *The Whisperings Within* (New York: Harper & Row, 1979), 30.

7. Barash, 31.

8. Barash, 55.

9. Barash, 55.

10. Mary Wollstonecraft, *A Vindication of the Rights of Women*, ed. Carol H. Posten (New York: W. W. Norton, 1975).

11. John Stuart Mill, "The Subjection of Women," in John Stuart Mill and Harriet Taylor Mill, *Essays on Sex Equality*, ed. Alice S. Rossi (Chicago: University of Chicago Press, 1970), 184–85.

12. Lenore J. Weitzman, "Sex-Role Socialization: A Focus on Women," in *Women: A Feminist Perspective*, ed. Jo Freeman (Palo Alto, Calif.: Mayfield Publishers, 1975), 172.

13. Weitzman, 172.

14. Weitzman, 76–183.

15. Nancy Chodorow, *The Reproduction of Mothering: Psychoanalysis and the Sociology of Gender* (Berkeley: University of California Press, 1978), 218.

16. Levin, 211–12.

17. Fred Strodbeck, "Family Interaction, Values and Achievement," in *Talent and Society*, ed. David McClelland et al. (Princeton, N.J.: Van Nostrand, 1968), 135–94.

18. Strodbeck, 135–94.

19. Weitzman, 218.

20. Weitzman, 222.

21. Weitzman, 222.

22. Weitzman, 223.

23. Weitzman, 222.

24. Weitzman, 223.

25. Teresa Donati Marciano, "Socialization and Women at Work," *National Forum* (Fall 1981): 24.

26. Levin, 198.

27. Bleier, *Science and Gender*.

28. Ruth Hubbard, "The Theory and Practice of Genetic Reductionism—from Mendel's Laws to Genetic Engineering," in *Towards a Liberatory Biology*, ed. H. Rose (London: Allison and Bushby, 1982).

29. Anne Fausto-Sterling, *Myths of Gender: Biological Theories about Women and Men* (New York: Basic Books, Inc., 1985).

30. Fausto-Sterling, 11.

31. Barbara Ehrenreich, "Making Sense of Difference," *TIME* (January 20, 1992): 51.

32. Fausto-Sterling, 9.

33. Virginia Valian, *Why So Slow?: The Advancement of Women* (Cambridge, Mass.: The MIT Press, 1998), 68–69.

34. Valian, 69.

35. Valian, 68.

36. Levin, 199.

37. LeRoy Walters and Julie Gage Palmer, *The Ethics of Human Gene Therapy* (New York: Oxford University Press), 99–142.

About the Contributors

Claudia Card is a Fully Revolting Hag at the University of Wisconsin, with tenure in the Department of Philosophy and teaching affiliations in Women's Studies and Environmental Studies. She is the author of *Lesbian Choices* (1995) and *The Unnatural Lottery: Character and Moral Luck* (1996) and editor of *Feminist Ethics* (1991), *Adventures in Lesbian Philosophy* (1994), and *On Feminist Ethics and Politics* (1998). In 1996, she was honored as the Distinguished Woman Philosopher of the Year by the Society of Women in Philosophy. She chairs the American Philosophical Association's Committee on the Status of Lesbian, Gay, Bisexual, and Transgendered People in the Profession. She is currently at work on a book on the concept of evil, for which she has received an American Council of Learned Societies Senior Fellowship and a Resident Fellowship at the Institute for Research in the Humanities at the University of Wisconsin.

Jane Flax teaches political theory at Howard University and is a psychotherapist in private practice in Washington, D.C. She has written within and across the boundaries of philosophy, political theory, psychoanalysis, and feminist theory. Her most recent book is *The American Dream in Black and White* (Cornell, 1998). She is currently working on a new book, *Subject Stories: Vicissitudes of Postmodernity.*

Virginia Held is Distinguished Professor of philosophy at the City University of New York Graduate School and Hunter College. Among her books are *The Public Interest and Individual Interests* (1970); *Rights and Goods: Justifying Social Action* (1984); *Feminist Morality: Transforming Culture, Society, and Politics* (1993); and the edited collections *Property, Profits, and Economic Justice* (1980); and *Justice and Care: Essential Readings in Feminist Ethics* (1995). She has been a fellow at the Center for Advanced Study in the Behavioral Sciences, and has had Fulbright and Rockefeller Fellowships.

She has been on the editorial boards of many journals in the areas of philosophy and political theory. She has also taught at Yale, Dartmouth, UCLA, and Hamilton. She is currently writing a number of essays on the ethics of care and the challenge these kinds of theories present to standard moral theories.

Ellen R. Klein is an associate professor of philosophy at Flagler College in St. Augustine, Florida. She is an outspoken critic of academic feminism. Klein, via her numerous publications and public speaking engagements, argues against feminist epistemology, philosophy of science, pedagogy, and the constructs of "gender" and "date rape." She is the author of *Feminism under Fire* (1996) and *Just Problems* (2000).

Janet Kourany teaches philosophy of science and feminist theory at the University of Notre Dame, where she is also a fellow of the Reilly Center for Science, Technology, and Values. Her publications include *Scientific Knowledge* (1987, 1998), *Feminist Philosophies* (1992, 1999), and *Philosophy in a Feminist Voice* (1998). Among her forthcoming works are *The Gender of Science* (2000) and *The Multiple Dimensions of Science* (2002).

Michael Levin is a professor of philosophy at City College and the Graduate Center of the City University of New York. He is the author of several books, most recently *Why Race Matters* and (with Laurence Thomas) *Sexual Orientation and Human Rights*. He has published numerous articles on epistemology, philosophy of science, and foundations of set theory; and, in more popular outlets, on egalitarianism and the free market.

Martha Nussbaum is the Ernst Freund Distinguished Service Professor of Law and Ethics at the University of Chicago, with appointments in the Law School, the Philosophy Department, and the Divinity School. She is an associate in the Classics Department, a member of the Board of the Center for Gender Studies, and an affiliate of the Committee on Southern Asian Studies. Her most recent book is *Women and Human Development: The Capabilities Approach* (2000).

James P. Sterba teaches moral and political philosophy at the University of Notre Dame. He has written more than 150 articles and published 18 books, including *How to Make People Just; Contemporary Ethics; Feminist Philosophies,* 2nd ed.; *Earth Ethics,* 2nd ed.; *Morality in Practice,* 6th ed.; and *Three Challenges to Ethics.* His book, *Justice for Here and Now,* published with Cambridge University Press, was awarded the 1998 Book of the Year Award from the North American Society for Social Philosophy. He is past president of the International Society for Social and Legal Philosophy, American Section; past president of Concerned Philosophers for Peace; and past president of the North American Society for Social Philosophy. He has also lectured widely—in Europe, Asia, and Africa, as well as in the United States.

Rosemarie Tong is a distinguished professor in health care ethics in the Department of Philosophy at the University of North Carolina at Charlotte. An award-winning teacher and a prolific writer and lecturer, she is the author of *Women, Sex, and the Law* (1984), *Feminine and Feminist Ethics* (1993), *Feminist Approaches to Bioethics: Theoretical Reflections and Practical Applications* (1997), and *Feminist Thought: A More Comprehensive Introduction* (1998). Tong is currently the co-coordinator of the International Network on Feminist Approaches to Bioethics; and she is co-editor of an anthology entitled *Globalizing Feminist Bioethics: Crosscultural Perspectives*, which is scheduled for publication in 2000